Understanding Business

Financial Decisions

SECOND EDITION

D. R. Myddelton

 Longman

LONGMAN GROUP LIMITED
Longman House
Burnt Mill, Harlow, Essex CM20 2JE, England
and Associated Companies throughout the World

First published 1976
Second Edition 1983
Second impression 1985
ISBN 0 582 35401 3

Filmset in ten on twelve point Lasercomp Plantin
by Northumberland Press Ltd, Gateshead

Printed in Great Britain
by Spottiswoode Ballantyne Printers Ltd.,
Colchester and London

Contents

Acknowledgements

We are grateful to the following for permission to reproduce copyright material. They bear no responsibility for the interpretation of the statistics.

The Controller of Her Majesty's Stationery Office for various statistics from issues of *Financial Statistics* and the *National Income and Expenditure Blue Book*, used in Figures 3.2, 5.1, 5.4, 5.8, 6.1, 6.4, 6.10, 6.12, and 8.3; for Retail Price Index statistics from the *Department of Employment Gazette*, used in the Appendix on Inflation; and for statistics from the *Wilson Report on Financial Institutions*, used in Figures 6.3 and 6.8. The Bank of England for statistics from the *Quarterly Bulletin*, used in Figures 5.5 and 5.6. The Stock Exchange for statistics from the *Stock Exchange Fact Book*, used in Figure 6.1; and for statistics from the *Stock Exchange Shareholder Analysis at 31st December 1980*, used in Figure 6.3. Beecham Group, The General Electric Company, and Marks and Spencer for statistics from their annual accounts, used in Chapter 3. Dr. R. H. Pike for statistics from his unpublished PhD thesis at the University of Bradford, used in Figure 4.16. The Financial Times for statistics used in Figures 5.3 and 6.4. Express Newspapers for material from *The Standard* on which problem B12 in Chapter 3 is based. The British Broadcasting Corporation for material from which the Walton Bakery case (problem B13 in Chapter 3) has been adapted. The Receiver of Laker Airways for material from the company's accounts on which problem B6 in Chapter 8 is based. McGraw-Hill Inc. for material on which Chapter 10 is based, adapted from cases on the Burmah Oil Company written by Professor R. A. Brealey and Dr. Elroy Dimson. Harvard University, Graduate School of Business Administration for material on which the following cases are based: Newman Machines, Plastic Products, Telford Toys, Dragon Paint, Hastings Manufacturing, and Northern Stores; and for the discount tables in the Appendix.

Introduction to the Series

This series produces a new approach to the teaching of business. It is suitable for young managers, students and academic sixth-formers. It has been developed over the last decade to give understanding of the nature and purpose of business activity, whilst also stimulating the minds of the more academically gifted members of society.

The material provides for an analytical understanding of people's problems and behaviour within organisations. The texts discuss the nature of problems, and explore concepts and principles which may be employed to aid their solution. Test materials have been selected from industrial and commercial organisations; from the private and public sector; from non-profit-making institutions. The material is as much to provide general understanding about industrial society and the workings of organisations, as it is to help those who are already engaged in their business or professional career.

The approach of decision-making has been used to draw together ideas, and produce significant elements of reality; the approach gives purpose and challenge to the reader. Any organisation is striving towards more or less closely defined objectives by deciding how to carry out, and control, its activities within constantly changing conditions. The programme looks carefully at these processes of decision-making; it provides the student with an understanding of their overall nature. Ideas from the four functional areas of human behaviour, quantitative data, accounting and the economic environment are drawn together within a decision-making framework; the approach is then applied to different areas of business activity, particularly to those of finance, marketing and production.

This series of eight books has been designed to meet the needs of students (and their lecturers/teachers) studying the business world. The up-to-date materials within each book provide many ideas and activities from which the teacher can choose. Lecturers on management courses may use the books to introduce analytical concepts to practitioners; tertiary management courses may use them as a first text and as a source of well-tried and up-to-date cases; BEC and 'A' Level students may use the books as complete courses.

To meet these different needs, each book in the series has been designed to stand either as a part of the whole, or complete in its own right.

All books have the same chapter format:

a chapter objective and synopsis so that the purpose and pattern are clear;

a factual/explanatory text with case examples where applicable;

a participative work section to provide materials for learning, application and discussion.

The participative sections are an integral part of the whole text and allow students to gain understanding by doing. They are usually divided into three parts. Firstly, some simple revision questions to enable the students to check their own basic understanding. Secondly, a series of exercises and case problems to test their application and to increase their knowledge of the area. Thirdly, a set of essay questions.

There is a teachers' booklet accompanying each student text which introduces the topic area, clarifies possible objectives, suggests approaches to the selected materials and adds additional ideas. The teachers' booklets also provide solutions, where appropriate, to the participative work sections.

The philosophy, approach and materials have been forged in discussion with businessmen, lecturers and teachers. Trial and error has refined much of the text and most of the participative work. The whole venture has been co-ordinated by the Cambridge Business Studies Project Trust. Initial work developed from a link between the Wolfson Foundation, Marlborough College and Shell International Ltd. Trustees for the Project include Professor John Dancy, Sir Michael Clapham and Sir Nicholas Goodison; much early guidance was also given by Professor Sir Austin Robinson.

The series can be used as the basis for an 'A' Level examination run by the Cambridge Local Examinations Syndicate and established in 1967. The examination syllabus and objectives are in line with the materials in these texts.

Richard Barker
Series Editor

Preface to the Second Edition

The aim of this edition, like that of the earlier edition by Roger Davies, is to introduce the student to the logic and framework of financial decisions in business. The book is intended to be useful for people in business and studying in business schools, as well as for students in polytechnics and colleges of further education, and for sixth-formers on business studies courses. The text has been completely rewritten.

Part I of the book contains an introductory 'Overview' chapter. Part II consists of seven chapters of text and questions, covering investment in assets and their financing. Part III comprises two different kinds of 'case studies'. Chapter 9 contains a number of separate problems related to two imaginary companies (Park Products and Langley Engineering), which may form a useful basis for revision. And Chapter 10 deals with some of the fascinating financial aspects of the Burmah Oil Company's affairs over the past 20 years, together with a series of questions.

The book is intended for readers working on their own, as well as for students enrolled in courses in business schools or colleges, or on company programmes. For teachers of courses there is an extensive Teacher's Guide available from the publishers. It contains worked answers to all the B questions and case studies, as well as detailed summaries of key points in each chapter, suggestions about alternative ways of using the text, and an analysis of the B and C questions by chapter section and by 'difficulty' grading.

Much attention has been paid to the three sets of questions at the end of each chapter: the A Revision questions, the B Exercises and case studies, and the C Essay questions. Less than a third of the questions in the first edition have been dropped, while 100 A questions have been added, more than 100 B Exercises and case studies, and more than 50 new C Essay questions.

The Glossary too has been substantially extended, containing an explanation of about 250 words or phrases. The Glossary should be used extensively by readers, since failure to understand the meaning of the terms used is bound to impede mastery of the subject.

In this edition the A Revision questions have been set out, and separated, in order of the sections in each chapter. Thus they can easily be referred to, if desired, as one is reading through each chapter. The A questions taken together cover the essential content of the book, and all students are strongly advised to make extensive use of them.

The number of B Exercises and case studies has been increased substantially, especially since many single questions contain several sub-questions. This is deliberate, partly to help students tackle problems one step at a time, and partly to help the teacher, either in class or outside it, to use the exercises as flexibly as possible. Seven new case studies of one and a half pages or more, while challenging, provide the opportunity to consider financial questions within the broader business framework. The B questions have been set out, in section order, in three grades of ascending difficulty.

The C Essay questions have been divided between easier and more difficult questions, again set out in section order within each chapter. Since there are many more B and C questions than any one reader or teacher is likely to want to use, there is a need to be selective in deciding which ones are most appropriate.

I am very grateful to Professor Peter Forrester of the Cranfield School of Management for providing time, as well as financial support, for me to write this book. I must also acknowledge gratefully the extent to which this edition has built on the earlier book by Roger Davies, especially with respect to many of the questions. I also want to thank Marek Kwiatkowski, John Powell, and Ron Stevens at Marlborough College, and Richard Barker, Headmaster of Sevenoaks School, for their detailed and most helpful comments on the contents, and for continual encouragement. I have no doubt learned, and failed to learn, from my students (who used this book in draft form) nearly as much as they from me.

D. R. Myddelton

Part I   Overview

Chapter 1

Overview

1.1   Introduction
1.1.1   Introduction
1.1.2   Financial Objective of a Business
1.1.3   Owners and Managers
1.1.4   Uses and Sources of Funds

1.2   Accounting
1.2.1   Balance Sheet
1.2.2   Profit and Loss Account
1.2.3   Return on Net Assets
1.2.4   Accounting Concepts

1.3   Problems in Finance
1.3.1   Time
1.3.2   Uncertainty
1.3.3   Liquidity
1.3.4   Gearing
1.3.5   Tax
1.3.6   Inflation

Objective: To identify the basic financial goal of a business; to discuss the different roles of owners and managers; and to describe the main ways in which a business uses funds and the sources from which it gets funds.

To review the content and format of the two main accounting statements, the balance sheet and the profit and loss account; to define the key items in the balance sheet; to describe the main financial measure of operating performance, the Return on Net Assets ratio; and to explain the four fundamental accounting concepts (going concern, accrual, consistency and prudence).

To identify six significant problem areas in finance (time, uncertainty, liquidity, gearing, tax and inflation), and to explain why they are important and some of their main implications in business.

1.1 Introduction

1.1.1 Introduction

This book starts with an 'overview' of the subject of financial management, aiming to show how its various aspects are related to each other. Most readers will probably find it helpful to look at the chapter again – with greater understanding – after they have studied the later chapters.

This section discusses the financial goal of business firms, the roles of owners and managers, and the main uses and sources of funds. Section 2 deals with accounting statements, and section 3 briefly indicates some of the major problems in finance, which we shall come across throughout the book.

People with some knowledge of accounting already should find section 2 of this chapter a useful revision. Readers with no background in accounting will need to study the section carefully, and may want to refer to it from time to time.

1.1.2 Financial Objective of a Business

The main **financial objective** of a business enterprise is to maximise the wealth of its owners. This means nearly the same as 'maximising profits', except that **wealth** takes into account the *timing* of profits.

Why are profits desirable? From an owner's point of view, because larger profits will help make him 'better off', by enlarging his purchasing power. From society's point of view, because – in normal competitive markets – *both* buyer and seller can expect to benefit from a voluntary market exchange. In general, therefore, the higher total profits, the more individuals will have become better off (than they otherwise would have been) as a result of market transactions. It is an elementary fallacy to think that if the seller makes a profit, the buyer must *lose* to the same extent! (We must also remember that a high proportion of all 'business' activity is between one firm and another, not simply a firm selling to an individual or vice versa.)

Why are profits ever possible over and above a 'normal' rate of interest on capital invested? Essentially because of ignorance. If people dealing on markets *knew* everything there was to be known, the prices of products would already fully reflect consumers' valuations. On the whole, there are more profit opportunities in the factor markets, dealing in 'real' goods and services, than in the financial markets, dealing in money, where information is relatively widespread. This **arbitrage** view of profit emphasises the *information* content of price signals in the market.

1.1.3 Owners and Managers

Few large businesses are managed by their owners. The directors of the largest 100 UK companies between them own less than one-tenth of 1 per cent of the ordinary shares in their firms. They are professional managers, not owners. The possibility of profits acts as an incentive for the owners of businesses (and for their agents, the managers); and profit or loss reflects success or failure.

Owners of small businesses may not always aim to maximise their business profits as measured in accounting terms. For example, the owner of a small shop may prefer to close early, and not open on Saturdays, in order to enjoy more leisure. As a sole owner, he is perfectly entitled to do this; but he is then *combining* his function as a business owner/manager with his function as a *consumer* (of leisure).

It would hardly please the owners of a large business if its managers deliberately failed to maximise profits in order to enjoy more leisure! In a competitive market such managers would soon be replaced by others who *would* try to satisfy the owners by maximising profits.

Business firms aim to make a profit by *satisfying customers*. Thus it is a serious mistake to regard managers and workers as two 'sides' of industry. The real distinction is between the sovereign *consumers* on the one hand, and the *producers* – owners, managers and workers, – on the other.

1.1.4 Uses and Sources of Funds

There is no shortage of finance for good projects: the main problem in business is finding profitable things to do.

How firms spend money depends on the nature of the business. A major film may cost up to £10 million: this goes on writing the script, buying equipment and building the sets, hiring actors, and producing the film – all *before* the first customer pays any cash. A gold mine may take ten years to develop: surveying the land, buying it, digging the mine, equipping it, hiring miners, extracting and refining the ore – all *before* any metal is sold for cash. Such investments have to be financed.

Most businesses need financing 'in advance of sales' to some extent. (Authors, however, get rich from royalties paid on the volume of sales – or sale of volumes – so publishers may not need to finance *them*!) This applies to a firm *expanding*, as well as to a *new* business. Firms may also need short-term finance to tide them over the inevitable fluctuations which occur in business from time to time.

Thus a business *spends* money on:
1. Long-term ('fixed') assets, such as buildings and equipment.
2. Short-term ('current') assets, such as stocks of materials.
3. Wages and other operating expenses.

A firm *gets* money from:
1. Customers, in respect of goods or services sold.
2. Owners, who start the business with 'share capital'.
3. Lenders (banks and others), who provide long-term or short-term funds.

Funds deriving from sales to customers are sometimes referred to as **internal finance**, from owners or lenders as **external finance**. These major uses and sources of funds are shown in Fig. 1.1 (which also shows payments of cash dividends to shareholders, out of profits).

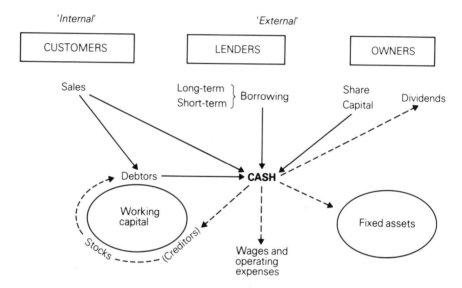

Fig. 1.1: Main flows of funds.

1.2 Accounting

Financial decisions are discussed in the business 'language' of accounting,
which it may be helpful to review briefly. (The principles of accounting are
covered in more detail in *Accounting and Decision Making* by Peter Corbett,
in this series.)

1.2.1 Balance Sheet

The **balance sheet** shows a firm's *financial position* as at the end of an
accounting period. It classifies items between:

>   Assets owned (= *uses* of funds)
> and   Liabilities (= *sources* of funds controlled by a business).

A simple example of a balance sheet is set out in Fig. 1.2, using the modern
'vertical' format. This has now generally superseded the old 'horizontal' format
(which showed liabilities on the left and assets on the right). Note that current
liabilities are usually *deducted* from current assets, to show a sub-total for
'net current assets' (also called 'working capital').

	£'000	£'000
Uses of funds		
Fixed Assets		85
Current Assets		
Stocks	45	
Debtors	40	
Cash	15	
	100	
Less: *Current liabilities*	35	
= Working capital	—	65
Net assets:		150
Sources of funds		
Shareholders' funds		
Issued ordinary £1 shares		80
Retained profits		40
		120
Long-term liabilities		30
Capital employed:		150

Fig. 1.2: Simpson Engineering Limited, Balance Sheet at 31 March, 1983.

An **asset** is a valuable resource controlled by a business. Assets are usually stated at original *cost* (less any deductions – 'depreciation' – to allow for subsequent loss of value).

Fixed assets are long-term resources of a business, used to provide goods or services, rather than to be sold in the normal course of business. They include land, buildings, machinery, vehicles and equipment. Fixed assets are normally stated at original cost less cumulative depreciation to date. Chapter 4 discusses decisions about investment in long-term assets.

Current assets are short-term resources, either already in the form of cash, or expected to be turned into cash within *twelve months* from the balance sheet date. The three main current assets are shown in reverse order of liquidity: first stocks, then debtors and cash.

A **liability** is a sum of money owed by a business to others. **Current liabilities** are due for payment within at most twelve months from the balance sheet date; the main items being trade **creditors**, taxation liabilities and bank overdrafts. They are usually deducted from total current assets, to produce a total for **working capital** (= *net* current assets). Chapter 3 discusses the various items of working capital.

The total of fixed assets plus working capital is called **net assets**: this means the net long-term uses of funds which must be financed by long-term capital sources of funds. Chapter 5 discusses types and sources of finance.

Shareholders' funds are amounts provided directly or indirectly by the owners of the business. Shareholders' funds may be regarded as ultimate liabilities of a company to its shareholders. But no amounts are legally payable as long as the company continues in business (unless the directors decide to distribute dividends out of profits).

Shareholders provide issued **share** capital directly, by paying the company cash for **ordinary shares** in the business. Shares in quoted companies can be bought and sold on the **Stock Exchange** (discussed in Chapter 6). **Retained profits** are provided indirectly: they represent profits earned by a business (and attributed to shareholders in the balance sheet) which have not been paid out in dividends.

Long-term liabilities are amounts borrowed which are repayable more than twelve months from the balance sheet date. Regular interest payments are due on the amounts owing.

The total of shareholders' funds and long-term liabilities is known as **capital employed**. The amount of capital employed (= long-term sources of funds) necessarily equals net assets (= long-term net uses of funds). Hence balance sheets always balance! This is the famous principle of 'double-entry' accounting, which Goethe called: 'The finest invention of the human mind.'

1.2.2 Profit and Loss Account

The **Profit and Loss Account** (P & L account) summarises the income and expenses of a business for an accounting period (usually a year). It shows the tax charged against profit, and the extent to which profit after tax is either paid out to shareholders in dividends, or else retained in the business. An example of a profit and loss account is shown in Fig. 1.3.

Profit may be defined as: sales revenue less total expenses for a period. A **loss** is simply a negative profit. Much of the detail in a profit and loss account consists of a classified list of the various expenses. The published profit and loss account would not normally show details of operating expenses (cost of goods sold plus overheads), which are contained in the dotted lines in Fig. 1.3. The published figures would move directly from sales revenue of £240,000 to the operating profit of £24,000 (also known as **earnings before interest and tax**).

Internal ('management') accounts, however, would show all the details needed to help run the business. They would show:

a. results for periods shorter than a year, often one month;

	£'000	£'000
Sales revenue		240

	£'000	£'000
Cost of goods sold:		
Raw materials	50	
Production labour	60	
Production overheads	60	
	—	170
Gross profit		70
Selling and administrative overheads		46
Operating profit		24
Long-term interest payable		4
Profit before tax		20
Corporation tax		7
Profit after tax		13
Ordinary dividends		6
Retained profit for the year		7

Fig. 1.3: Simpson Engineering Limited, Profit and loss account for the year ended 31 March 1983

b. expenses split into much more detail;
c. operating results analysed by product group.

Management accounts would also contain budgets for future periods, as well as actual past results.

1.2.3 Return on Net Assets

A common measure of operating efficiency is **return on net assets** (also called the primary efficiency ratio). This expresses the operating profit as a percentage of the long-term net assets employed in the business. This ratio shows how successfully a company has used its assets, and can often be used to measure the profitability of separate parts of a business. The operating efficiency with which a company's assets are employed is important because it can be judged against the returns available from alternative possible uses of scarce capital funds.

For Simpson Engineering Limited, the Return on Net Assets for the year ended 31 March 1983 is 16.0 per cent.

$$\frac{\text{Operating profit}}{\text{Net assets}} = \frac{24}{150} = 16.0\%.$$

This can also be expressed as **profit margin** times **asset turnover**:

Profit Margin 10.0% × Asset Turnover 1.6 times

$$\frac{\text{Profit}}{\text{Sales}} = \frac{24}{240} \qquad \frac{\text{Sales}}{\text{Net assets}} = \frac{240}{150}$$

Another useful way to analyse a company's rate of return earned on net assets is to set out the various items of profit and loss and of net assets in the form of a diagram, as shown in Fig. 1.4. Where appropriate, similar details can be calculated for divisions of a business, and more frequently than once a year.

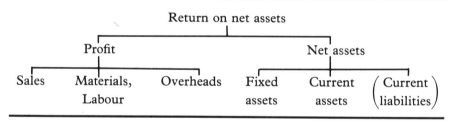

Fig. 1.4: Analysis of return on net assets.

To improve its return on net assets, a company can either increase its profit, for a given amount of net assets, or maintain its operating profit while reducing the net assets employed. Any capital thus released can be invested to earn a return (for example, with a bank); and thus increase the total profits of the business.

The three main components of operating profit (sales revenue, cost of materials, cost of labour) can each be analysed between *volume* and *price*. While the details will vary for different businesses, this general approach to analysis of operating profit will often give useful clues to possible improvements. Ultimately we are not interested in analysing past operating results for the mere sake of curiosity: we want to find ways of improving efficiency and profits.

1.2.4 Accounting Concepts

Four fundamental accounting concepts underlie the figures in any set of accounts:

1. *The going concern concept* assumes that an enterprise will continue in business in the foreseeable future. This normally means showing assets in accounts *at cost* – on the assumption that they are worth at least this much. An alternative assumption might be that the business was soon going to be wound up (liquidated): it would then be prudent to value assets at the amount they would realise on immediate sale (which might be considerably *less* than cost).

2. *The accruals concept* where possible matches expenses against revenues: it recognises revenues as they are earned and expenses as they are incurred in business transactions. An alternative approach would be to recognise transactions only when cash was received or paid: this would usually be less realistic (though some non-commercial activities, such as government operations, still use cash accounting).

3. *The consistency concept* requires the same treatment for similar items from one period to another. Otherwise comparing accounting results between periods and between businesses would be meaningless. (The same concept is applied generally to all statistical information.) For example, it would not be acceptable accounting practice to change the estimated working lives of fixed assets from one year to another, in calculating the amount of depreciation to charge as an expense.

4. *The prudence concept* means that accounts include revenues or profits only when they are 'realised' either in cash, or in the form of assets whose ultimate cash proceeds are reasonably certain. In contrast, full provision is made at once for all known losses and expenses, even where their amount has to be estimated.

The basic purpose of accounts is to show a 'true and fair view' of the business's financial position and profit or loss for the period. The balance sheet makes no attempt, however, to disclose the 'true worth' of a business (so the American expression 'net worth' to refer in balance sheets to the interests of shareholders is highly misleading). Many major assets are excluded, especially internally-generated 'intangible' assets, such as business 'know-how'.

1.3 Problems in Finance

1.3.1 Time

The difference between the near and distant future is important in finance, as in other areas of business. Long-term investments may involve expenditures not expected to show 'returns' for many years, while long-term borrowing assures a firm of funds which do not have to be repaid for a long time.

In business one may often choose to 'sacrifice' a smaller profit soon in the hope of a larger profit later: for example, pricing low with a new product in order to build up market share. Maximising the wealth of a firm's owners therefore requires some way to compare profits in different future periods. This is done by using the rate of interest, in effect, as an 'exchange rate through time' (as we discuss in Chapter 4).

In general, firms often try to 'match the maturities' of their liabilities (sources of finance) with those of their assets (uses of funds). So do financial institutions. This is not an absolute rule, but 'borrowing short and lending long' is dangerous, since a firm may have to repay borrowings at short notice without being able to demand repayment of its own long-term investments.

We shall see throughout the book that in trying to forecast cash receipts and payments in the uncertain future, we are concerned not only with the *amount* of cash flows, but also with their *timing*.

1.3.2 Uncertainty

The future is uncertain. Hence financial plans, like any other, may go wrong. Financial managers try to allow sufficient 'margin of error' to cover reasonable uncertainties, without 'playing it safe' to such an extent that there is little margin of *profit* left. The dilemma has been expressed like this: 'do you want to eat well or sleep well?' You can't expect to make profits unless you take risks; but that is *risky*! Even after the event, it is hardly ever possible to tell how much risk was involved in a particular case.

Some ways of allowing for uncertainty are discussed in Chapter 4. And in Chapter 7 we note some rules of thumb about how much 'financial risk' (gearing) a firm may take on without undue alarm. We also briefly discuss modern portfolio theory, which tries to *measure* the relationship between 'risk' and 'return'.

1.3.3 Liquidity

Liquidity means the ease with which an asset can be turned into cash. In a perfect capital market, liquidity wouldn't matter, since the owner of assets would always be able to borrow. But in the real world, with 'credit squeezes' and other difficulties, it is often true (as Jim Slater once remarked) that 'it's easier to turn cash into assets than assets into cash'.

Hence financial managers do need to be concerned with liquidity; and as with other aspects of finance, they need to seek a *balance*. Holding too little liquidity might create immediate financial problems in paying bills, while holding too much liquidity might lead to a relatively low rate of return on capital invested. Ways of measuring liquidity are discussed in section 3.5.

1.3.4 Gearing

'Financial gearing' refers to the way in which a company *finances* its business. The two main forms of finance are borrowing ('debt') and ordinary share-holders' funds ('equity'). A company is said to be 'highly geared' when borrowing forms a large proportion of its total capital structure. As explained in more detail in Chapter 7, borrowing increases the *riskiness* of a company's ordinary shares.

While financial gearing (or 'financial risk') refers to how a company *finances* its investment of funds, operating gearing (or 'business risk') refers to the nature of a firm's business operations and how it has *invested* its funds (however they are financed). How a firm invests funds is probably far more important than how it finances the business. This is because financial markets are more competitive, with better information, than many other markets. So in general they provide fewer chances of significant profit or loss.

'Operating gearing' is often used to mean the level of fixed expenses as a proportion of total expenses. Thus a school has a high proportion of fixed expenses, whereas most of the expenses of a street trader's fruit stall would be variable. Where most expenses are fixed, the amount of profit earned is very sensitive to the level of sales revenue.

There are many different aspects to business risk. It is likely to be high, for example, where:

1. A firm is heavily dependent on a single product line;
2. Market conditions make sales forecasts especially uncertain;
3. Technological changes are altering the industry's cost structure.

1.3.5 Tax

Businesses are subject to many taxes – on wages, on property, on capital. But business finance is mainly concerned with three: (a) corporation tax, on a firm's 'taxable profits'; (b) personal income tax on dividends to shareholders; and (c) capital gains tax.

A business which is concerned to 'maximise the owners' wealth' has to take account of the tax effects on individuals. But it is trying to maximise the after-tax profits, *not* to 'minimise taxes'. Unfortunately the impact of tax is much complicated by inflation. This is not properly allowed for in the tax system, hence there are some anomalies which affect the best way to finance a firm.

1.3.6 Inflation

Probably the most important aspect of business finance in the last 20 years has been inflation and its impact. In the ten years since March 1972, the pound lost nearly three-quarters of its purchasing power, representing an average rate of currency debasement of more than 12 per cent a year. The effect on the financial markets has been devastating.

One lesson to be learned about inflation is that we must be careful to distinguish between 'money' amounts and 'real' amounts. In this book we do not deal with the 'inflation accounting' argument, which has caused serious problems for businessmen and accountants for many years, and which is still not adequately resolved. (This important topic is discussed in some detail in *Accounting and Decision Making* by Peter Corbett.)

Inflation affects: (a) the appropriate extent and type of borrowing; (b) the required rates of return on new investments; (c) the management of working capital; and (d) the basis of valuing assets. So already we can see that it is crucial in finance.

In practice a critical question is whether a particular rate of inflation (whatever it amounts to) was *anticipated* or not. We must also concern ourselves with *fluctuations* in the rate of inflation. The *average* rate of inflation over the last ten years has been over 12 per cent a year, but the actual yearly rate has varied between 5.8 per cent and 26.9 per cent.

Most readers will probably find it helpful to read this **Overview** *chapter again after completing the remaining chapters of text.*

Part II   Text and Problems

Chapter 2

Managing Cash

Objective: *To identify the functions of money in the economy and of cash in a business; to distinguish between cash and profit; to analyse what comprises the rate of interest on money lent and borrowed; and to explain the process of cash forecasting within a firm.*
Synopsis: *'Cash' in business has a wider meaning than just notes and coins: it also includes bank accounts. Cash and profit are both important to business firms, but they are different. Firms hold cash to settle business transactions and to provide a margin of safety. But these benefits must be balanced against the 'opportunity cost' of holding cash – what else could be done with the money. This is normally related to the current rate of interest, which consists of three component parts: pure time preference, an inflation premium, and a risk premium. In financial planning a company may try to forecast cash receipts and cash payments month*

by month, or it may try to estimate the end-of-period balance sheet. In either case, business forecasts are likely to be subject to a wide margin of error.

2.1 Cash

2.1.1 Money

Money is any generally accepted **medium of exchange**. Its main function is to act as a means of payment. If there were no money, goods and services would have to be exchanged by **barter**. This is a cumbersome process, where A and B must each want precisely what the other has got (thus depending on a 'double coincidence of wants').

Centuries ago, gold or silver came to serve as money, being stable, durable, relatively scarce, divisible and easily recognised. The ruler's seal on a coin stated and guaranteed its weight: this avoided the need to weigh the metal at each payment, and made coins acceptable 'at face value'.

Eventually milled edges prevented coin-clipping; but rulers of nations themselves often 'debased' coins by adding base metal to the precious metal. Such swindles led to the **quantity theory of money**, which, in its simplest form, says that the larger the money supply the less the value (purchasing power) of each unit of money at any particular level of output.

Bankers held money (gold) in safe-keeping, and issued paper notes (receipts) to the owners. They represented a promise by the banker to pay the holder on demand a certain amount of gold. Soon banks saw no need to 'back' each paper note with equivalent gold in their vaults. Most people found paper notes convenient to use for payments; and in practice a bank could issue about ten times more 'paper money' than the gold it held. It could lend out the extra money at interest to borrowers.

Some bank loans would be for long periods, so if every holder of paper notes were to demand instant repayment in gold, the bank would be unable to meet its legal obligations in time. Thus bankers were always vulnerable to a 'run on the bank'; and prudent banks had to take great care to avoid any loss of public confidence in their solvency. They did this partly by matching the maturities of their assets and liabilities.

In time **central banks** evolved, to serve as banker to the government as well as to the commercial banks. They often became the sole issuer of paper notes. Eventually governments nationalised most central banks, and withdrew the right to convert paper bank notes into gold. Paper money can function well as a medium of exchange as long as people have confidence in it. But the lack of convertibility into a scarce commodity such as gold makes it easy for governments to print more notes, thus **inflating** the supply of paper currency.

As long as the purchasing power of money is reasonably stable, it can represent a **unit of account**. This allows economic calculation in terms of money as a common unit of measurement. A stable money can also represent a **store of wealth**, enabling people to buy and sell at different times. If money loses purchasing power fast, however, it becomes less useful as a unit of account; hence recent pressures for a system of **inflation accounting**. It also becomes a poor store of value over time: hence recent arguments over index-linked pensions.

In a prisoner of war camp cigarettes served quite well as money; though subject to massive inflation when new supplies arrived, and to regular deflation as people smoked part of the money supply. But the essential point was that people were prepared to trust the currency.

2.1.2 **What is 'Cash' in Accounts?**

Cash appears as a current asset in balance sheets: it may include any of four items, which together are sometimes called **liquid resources**:

1. *Cash in hand* consists literally of notes and coins. Accountants call it 'petty cash'. Most business offices hold some petty cash for small payments; but the total amount, even for a firm with many offices, would be insignificant compared with the rest of the firm's assets.

2. *Current accounts with banks* (**demand deposits**) are available whenever required to make payments by cheque, or to be drawn out in notes and coins (for example, to pay wages in cash). Their main disadvantage is that they earn no interest (though some banks are starting to pay interest on current accounts).

3. *Deposit accounts with banks* (**time deposits**) do earn interest; and can be converted into cash on short notice (often seven days).

4. *Short-term marketable securities* also bear interest. They are often included under the heading of 'cash' in balance sheets, valued at current market prices.

2.1.3 **Why Do Firms Need Cash?**

The three main reasons for holding cash are sometimes expressed as: the transactions motive, the precautionary motive, and the speculative motive.

Most people carry some cash around with them to cover various day-to-day *transactions*, such as paying for a haircut or a bus fare. In the same way, firms may need large sums of cash; for example, to pay weekly wages. In addition, cash may be required from time to time, to pay for new equipment, to settle tax bills, or to repay long-term borrowing.

Many retail shops hold large sums of cash in their tills. This is not needed for cash purchases (which would be made from other sources); nor is it merely a result of cash takings from sales (which are promptly banked). The main function of till cash is to enable shops to offer change to customers. An old

Punch joke shows a passenger apologising to a bus conductor as he offers a £50 note in payment for a 10p fare: 'I'm afraid I haven't got any change.' The conductor shovels 499 10p pieces into his lap and replies: 'Well, you have now!'.

A business may choose to hold an extra cash balance for *precautionary* reasons, so that even if things go slightly wrong it will still be able to make ends meet. In most businesses the precise pattern of weekly cash receipts and payments will fluctuate. For example, bad weather may reduce cash sales of a department store on a particular Saturday just before Christmas. The amount of the cash 'safety margin' to be held will depend on how business managers feel about the risks of running out of cash. A business, or individual, may also happen to hold cash because forecasts of the timing or amount of cash receipts or payments turned out to be wrong.

Strictly speaking what is needed is not so much cash itself as the 'ability to pay'. Thus many people now carry credit cards to let them make day-to-day purchases for which they might once have needed cash. Similarly a business which has arranged **bank overdraft** facilities (see 3.4.5.) does not need to hold any positive cash balance with its bank: it can simply continue to draw cheques up to the extent of the agreed borrowing limit.

Finally, the *speculative* motive is ever-present in business. A Stock Exchange investor may increase his cash holding by selling shares whose market price he expects to fall. To be successful (make a profit) he must guess not just the *direction* in which the market is going to move, but also the *timing*. Similar motives may underlie changes in cash holdings in many businesses; for example, where raw material price changes are expected.

A firm's cash balance can be too *large*, as well as too small. For example, to outsiders General Electric Company's bank balances of £1,070 million in March 1982 seemed rather high, amounting as they did to about 25 per cent of the company's total assets.

2.2 Cash and Profit

2.2.1 Cash and Profit are Different

Cash and profit are two of the main concerns of the financial manager. Both are important, but they are *different*. The commonest differences are classified and listed in Fig. 2.1. It may also be helpful to refer back to 1.2 in the previous chapter.

Cash is a liquid asset owned by a business, enabling it to buy goods or services (or to pay amounts due for goods or services bought earlier 'on credit').

Profit is the surplus earned in respect of a period's trading, after deducting all business expenses from sales revenue. Profit is an accounting measurement, not an asset owned by a business. Other things being equal, the larger the profit earned the better.

Profit exceeds cash

Transaction	Effect on balance sheet*
1. P & L Revenue not cash receipts	
a. Sales on credit	+ Debtors
2. Cash payments not P & L expense	
a. Purchase of long-term assets	+ Fixed assets
b. Increase in stocks	+ Stocks
c. Payments in advance	+ Prepayments
d. Dividends paid	– Equity
e. Reduction of creditors	– Creditors
f. Payment of tax	– Tax liability
g. Repayment of long-term loans	– Loans

Cash exceeds profit

Transaction	Effect on balance sheet*
3. Cash receipts not P & L revenue	
a. Issue of new share capital	+ Equity
b. Borrowing long-term loans	+ Loans
c. Sale of long-term assets	– Fixed assets
d. Prepayments by customers	– Stocks
4. P & L expense not cash payment	
a. Depreciation of fixed assets	– Fixed assets
b. Write off bad debts	– Debtors
c. Write off stock	– Stocks
d. Purchases on credit	+ Creditors
e. Tax charge not yet paid	+ Tax liability

Fig. 2.1: Why profit and cash may differ.

*The 'other side' of the balance sheet effect will be as follows:
1. Profit and Loss account (Shareholders' funds)   UP
2. Cash   DOWN
3. Cash   UP
4. Profit and Loss account (Shareholders' funds)   DOWN

If a business has sold goods for more than they cost, it will have made a *profit*. But if the customers have not yet *paid* for the goods, the business may have no *cash*.

It is often easy to tell the amount of sales revenue in a period. It includes all items which have been *sold* to customers in the period, even if they have not yet been *paid for*. Any amounts still owing to a business at the end of a period, in respect of goods sold but not yet paid for, are shown in the balance sheet as Debtors, also called Accounts Receivable.

It can be more difficult to estimate the amount of *expenses* for a period. Over time, accountants have built up conventions to ensure consistency between periods; *but most business accounts can never be absolutely accurate.* The amount of expenses in a period will usually *not* equal the amount of cash actually paid out. Any amounts still owing by a business to suppliers at the end of a period, in respect of expenses incurred but not yet paid for, are shown in the balance sheet as Creditors (Accounts Payable).

There are obvious examples of the difference between profit and cash. When a company borrows money; the immediate result is to increase the *cash* balance. But no business would dream of treating the amount as *profit*! It will have to be repaid in due course. Another example would be the accounting treatment of fixed assets, such as a new machine or an extension to a firm's factory. Where these are acquired for cash, the whole cost is not deducted from profit in the period in which payment was made. Instead the company's accounts charge only a fraction of the cost of fixed assets as an expense (**depreciation**) in each period of the asset's life.

Several British companies have recently been closing down unprofitable factories. Because they were unprofitable, these firms may have been making *losses* (negative profits). Yet by selling their factories, such firms have been converting fixed assets into liquid resources; and may have increased their cash balances as a result. For example, Courtaulds reported CCA losses of £170 million in 1980–82, but their liquid resources increased by £94 million even after repaying £38 million of long-term borrowing.

2.2.2 Funds Flow Statement

For many years, companies used to publish only two main accounting statements: the balance sheet and the profit and loss account. The balance sheet listed a company's liabilities and its assets, including cash and liquid resources, while the profit and loss account reported the profit or loss for a period.

Reflecting the increased emphasis placed on cash in times of rapid inflation, larger companies now also publish a third accounting statement: the **funds flow statement**, showing the *sources and uses of funds* during an accounting period. (In contrast, the balance sheet may be regarded as showing the *cumulative* result of all sources and uses of funds of the business ever since it was started.)

An example of a Funds Flow Statement is shown in Fig. 2.2.

Sources of funds		£'000
Internal:		
Profit before tax		20
Add back: Depreciation		10
		—
= generated from operations		30
External:		
Long-term loans borrowed		13
Share capital issued		5
		—
		48
		=
Uses of funds		
Taxation paid		7
Dividends paid		5
Fixed assets purchased		17
Long-term loans repaid		4
Working capital increased:		
Stocks	7	
Debtors	6	
Cash	4	
Less: Current liabilities*	(2)*	15
		—
		48
*() means a negative figure		=

Figure 2.2: Simpson Engineering Limited, Funds flow statement for the year ended 31 March 1983.

The precise format used for funds flow statements varies. The best practice is to disclose *gross* flows of funds: thus £4,000 repayment of loans is shown as a separate use of funds, rather than being deducted from £13,000 new loans borrowed during the year, to show only a net increase of £9,000. Similarly, taxes and dividends actually paid in cash during the period are shown as uses of funds. They may be deducted from the amount of funds generated from operations (which would produce a net figure of £30,000 − £12,000 = £18,000). Or, as above, they may be shown separately among the uses of funds.

Depreciation of fixed assets has been 'added back' to reported profit in the funds flow statement. The reason for this is explained in 2.2.3.

2.2.3 'Cash Flow' and Depreciation

The financial press often uses the term '**cash flow**' as a shorthand description meaning: 'retained profits plus depreciation' for a period. Confusion is sometimes caused by this practice of apparently including depreciation as a positive item of cash flow. Of course depreciation (of fixed assets) is *not* literally a 'source' of funds: it is merely a book-keeping entry which charges as an expense part of the original cost of fixed assets.

But depreciation does not represent a *use of funds* in the period in which it is charged as an expense. No cash is paid out in respect of depreciation: the only cash payment is for the original purchase of a fixed asset, at the start of its life. So since depreciation expense has been charged against (deducted from) sales revenue in determining net profit in accounts, it needs to be 'added back' in order to convert the figure reported for *profit* in that period into *cash flow*. (Depreciation is not the *only* item in accounts which may not represent cash, but it is often the single most important item.)

If depreciation really were a source of funds, it would be possible for a company to increase its cash balance merely by increasing its charge for depreciation expense in the profit and loss account. But if this were done, of course, the reported *profit* would then be *reduced* to exactly the same extent! Thus the net effect on cash flow (= profit + depreciation) would be precisely zero.

Example: Even if the actual £10,000 depreciation expense for Simpson Engineering were increased by 50 per cent to £15,000, the figure for 'cash flow' would remain unchanged at £17,000:

	Original accounts	Increasing depreciation by 50%
	£'000	£'000
Profit before depreciation	30	30
Depreciation expense	10	15
Profit before tax	20	15
Corporation tax	7	7
Profit after tax	13	8
Dividends paid	6	6
Retained profits	7	2
'Add back' depreciation	10	15
= 'Cash flow'	17	17

Figure 2.3: Cash flow and depreciation.

Notice that increasing the company's depreciation charge does *not* affect the company's tax bill. (If it did, it would indirectly increase the cash position.) This is because the Inland Revenue has its own rules for calculating **capital allowances** (depreciation for tax purposes), which *completely ignore* the company's own method of estimating depreciation.

2.3 Opportunity Cost

2.3.1 The Cost of Holding Cash

There are sometimes reports of mysterious Nigerians carrying £250,000 around London in used notes who stop for a cup of coffee and when they emerge find their taxi has disappeared with their cash in a bag on the back seat. Obviously bank notes – being anonymous – are subject to the risk of loss. But this does not apply to cash held on current account with a bank.

What is the main cost of holding cash on current account with a bank? It is the loss of the interest which could otherwise have been earned on it – the **opportunity cost**. For instance, suppose one could have invested money to earn an interest rate of 15 per cent a year. Then by choosing not to do so, but to hold cash instead, one is giving up that potential interest yield. *That* is the real economic cost of holding non-interest-bearing cash.

Clearly there may be a conflict here between cash and profit. A business which has too little cash may be taking too much risk of running out. On the other hand, a business which has too much cash may be sacrificing profit.

Opportunity cost is not just some vague theoretical abstraction: it is a real, often significant, economic cost. Business managers should always be asking: 'What *else* could we be doing with our resources? What *alternatives* are open to us?' This question applies not merely to cash, but to machines, land, employees, etc. In the context of finance, however, the most familiar use of the opportunity cost concept is in connection with *interest* on money lent or borrowed for a period of time.

2.3.2 Interest Rates

The **interest rate** consists of three component parts: time preference, inflation premium, and risk premium.

1. Time preference. Pure **time preference** refers to the ratio between consumers' valuations of present goods as against otherwise identical goods to be received in future. If in general consumers did not prefer present goods to future goods, they would never consume anything. The convention is to quote the ratio as an *annual* rate. In effect, a pure interest rate may be regarded as the 'price of time'.

The British government, in a major change of policy, has recently started issuing securities which are index-linked (guaranteed against inflation). Since British government securities are normally regarded as **risk free**, the yield on such index-linked securities provides a direct market measure of the rate of 'pure' time preference. In March 1982 the index-linked gilts yielded about $2\frac{1}{2}$ per cent a year.

2. Inflation premium. The second component in rates of interest on money loans is an **inflation premium**. This is needed to allow for the anticipated rate of future inflation. It explains why ordinary government securities now yield about 15 per cent a year compared with only about $2\frac{1}{2}$ per cent a year in Victorian times. There was virtually no inflation then. It also explains why money interest rates are so much higher in Brazil than in Switzerland: more inflation is expected in Brazil.

If the interest rate on a one-year loan would be 5 per cent in the absence of any inflation, and if both borrower and lender expect inflation of 8 per cent over the coming year, then the actual money rate of interest will be about 13 per cent a year. The amount of the inflation premium is the market's *estimate* of what future inflation will be. It may be wrong: in the early 1970s, it was far too low in the UK.

3. Risk premium. The third component in most business interest rates is a **risk premium**. A borrower who is regarded as a poor credit risk will be charged a high interest rate. (If the risk is too large, a bank may simply refuse to lend at all, at any interest rate.) This is the main reason why smaller businesses often have to pay higher rates of interest than large companies: they are usually riskier to lend to. (It is true there may also be certain 'economies of scale'; but differences in risk are likely to be more important.)

Modern financial theory (see 7.2.2.) suggests a linear relationship between 'risk' and required 'return', as shown by the capital market line in Fig. 2.4. Even at zero risk there is still a positive interest rate, to represent 'pure' time preference *plus* an inflation premium. (And even if we assumed zero inflation, for example for index-linked securities, there would *still* be a small positive rate of 'pure' time preference.) Thereafter as risk increases, moving to the right along the horizontal axis, so does the return required, on the vertical axis.

Thus for Project α (Fig. 2.4), the required rate of return consists of:

1. pure time preference;
2. inflation premium;
3. (medium-high) risk premium.

These are set out, starting from zero, on the vertical axis in Fig. 2.4.

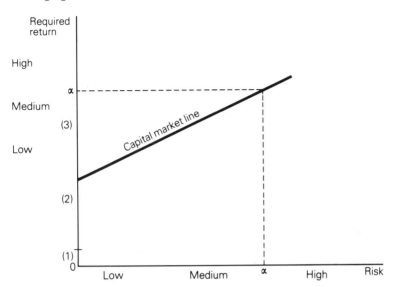

Fig. 2.4: Risk and required return.

2.4 Financial Planning

2.4.1 Forecasting Cash Receipts from Sales

A company's cash balance should ideally be high enough to protect the business against any serious chance of running out, but not so high as to tie up unnecessary funds in low-yielding uses. Financial managers of a business must decide what cash levels they are aiming at. Then they need to forecast the amount and timing of the likely sources and uses of cash in future periods.

It is obviously crucial for a company to avoid running out of cash. Otherwise it might be forced into liquidation by creditors it was unable to pay; or at least funds might have to be raised at a very high cost, and subject to conditions which might be most inconvenient. (This happens when the International Monetary Fund lends money to governments which have hopelessly mismanaged a national economy.)

Careful forecasting of the amount and timing of future cash receipts and payments has several benefits:

a. It avoids undesired accumulation of non-interest-bearing cash.

b. It reveals possible future needs to raise more capital. Especially with long-term capital, arrangements may take several months.

c. It tests the financial consequences of plans in advance of making definite commitments.

The most critical single estimate in cash flow forecasting for a business is nearly always the forecast of sales revenue. This usually represents the main source of cash receipts for the firm. (This important topic is discussed further in two other books in the series: *Marketing Decisions* by Peter Tinniswood, and *Quantitative Decision Making* by John Harris and John Powell.)

Example: Glo-lamp Limited's financial manager is preparing a six-month cash forecast beginning in January. He decides to start by estimating cash receipts from sales, with the following basic assumptions:

1. Sales revenue will be £200,000 a month for the first three months, rising to £250,000 for April and May, and to £300,000 in June.

2. 10 per cent of the sales are expected to be for cash; the rest on credit terms estimated to result in the collection of cash on average one month after the date of sale.

3. At the beginning of the period, debtors amount to £185,000.

These assumptions can be translated into a schedule of expected cash receipts from sales, month by month, as shown in Fig. 2.5.

£'000	Jan.	Feb.	March	April	May	June	Total
Underlying data							
Total sales	200	200	200	250	250	300	1,400
Credit sales (90%)	180	180	180	225	225	270	1,260
Cash receipts							
From debtors	185	180	180	180	225	225	1,175
Cash sales (10%)	20	20	20	25	25	30	140
= Total	205	200	200	205	250	255	1,315

Fig. 2.5: Cash receipts from sales.

The amount sold in the period is not immediately reflected in the same amount of cash. Over the whole six months, the totals can be reconciled as follows:

	£'000
Opening debtors	185
Add: Total sales in period	1,400
	1,585
Less: Closing debtors	270
= Cash received in period	1,315

It is worth stressing that the forecast of cash receipts from sales is often subject to a large margin of error, since it depends on three different estimates, each of which may vary unexpectedly:

1. The physical volume of sales.
2. The average selling price per unit.
3. The average delay in payment (credit period taken).

2.4.2 Forecasting Other Cash Flows

Most businesses find that cash *payments* in respect of operating expenses are often related more or less closely to anticipated sales volume. In particular, purchases of materials, which often amount to a significant proportion of total costs, will normally be **variable**; though stock levels may fluctuate for a number of reasons (see **3.2.2**).

Other expenses may be less affected by short-term fluctuations in the level of sales. The labour force, for example, is often virtually **fixed** in the short-term. And there will be a number of overhead expenses whose amount can be predicted fairly accurately, such as office rents.

It may be more difficult to forecast certain 'discretionary' expenses. They are not 'fixed': they may change from time to time. But nor are they typically 'variable': they may not vary in line with changes in the volume of sales (or of production). Hence these expenses are sometimes termed 'non-variable'. Examples might be: expenditure on research, or on advertising.

Various other cash receipts and payments need to be included in any overall cash forecast, even if they are not directly connected with day-to-day operations. Receipts other than from sales may comprise: proceeds from disposing of old equipment; receipts from issues of share capital, or from borrowing; income on investments.

Payments other than for operating expenses may include: taxation; dividend payments; purchases of investments; acquisition of fixed assets. Cash payments to acquire fixed assets will show up in operating expenses only as a result of charging 'depreciation expense' – a non-cash item – over the useful life of the asset.

2.4.3 'Pro Forma' Balance Sheets

The projected (pro forma) balance sheet method of forecasting funds requirements is based on a forecast of *all* balance sheet items (not just cash) at a *particular* future date. Four major steps are involved:
1. Forecasting the net total amount of each of the assets.
2. Listing the liabilities that can be counted on without special negotiation, such as trade creditors and taxation, and those which do have to be negotiated, such as bank overdrafts.
3. Estimating the expected profits for the period, less dividend payments. (This is needed in order to forecast the cumulative total of retained profits, as part of shareholders' funds.) Since profit is a residual between two much larger amounts (sales revenue less total expenses), this may be subject to a wide margin of error.
4. Total the expected assets, liabilities, and shareholders' funds, to reveal whether there is expected to be a surplus or a shortage of funds on the

date chosen. Further action may need to be planned, either to invest any anticipated surplus of funds or to raise money to cover any shortage.

The projected balance sheet method forecasts *all* the balance sheet items, not just cash. It can therefore be used to forecast certain financial ratios, such as return on net assets. It can be used *quickly* to make rough – yet often very helpful – forecasts where forward plans may not yet exist in sufficient detail to allow cash flow forecasting.

The method shows expected balance sheet amounts only at the *end* of the particular period selected – *not during the interim period*. Maximum needs for funds will therefore be revealed only if dates are carefully chosen to show the balance sheet at times of maximum strain. (If there is doubt about the most suitable date to choose, then several projections at different dates may be required.)

It is often a good idea to note the key assumptions underlying the forecasts *in writing*; and it can be useful to try to identify the rough *margin of error* thought to be involved in the key items. It may also be worth preparing several alternative forecasts, based on *different* assumptions. (Computers have made it possible to prepare detailed forecasts, month by month, and to test plans in advance by varying the assumptions and seeing what difference they make.)

If the same assumptions are made for the projected balance sheet method as were made for a cash flow forecast, then the two methods should, of course, produce an *identical* forecast of the end-of-period cash balance. The pro forma balance sheet method forces management to make *explicit* assumptions about fixed assets and working capital. These are surprisingly easy to overlook in a cash flow forecast; yet they can obviously be critical for many businesses. In Chapter 3 we go on to look in more detail at working capital.

We end this section, however, with a sobering definition of **forecasting**: a pretence of knowing what would have happened if what did happen hadn't!

For a description of the three different kinds of questions following this and later Chapters, all readers are referred to the Preface.

Attention is also drawn to the Glossary. In a subject like Finance there are inevitably many words and phrases which will be unfamiliar to the beginner. It is probably best to look them up straight away *when you come across them. So if you find a word or expression you do not understand, the first thing to do is look it up in the Glossary. If it is not there, the next thing to do is look it up in the Index.*

Work Section

A. Revision Questions

A1 What are the three main functions of money? Explain each fully.

A2 How does rapid inflation affect the functions of money?

A3 Why is money unsatisfactory as a unit of accounting measurement in times of rapid inflation?

A4 What is the difference between a Current Account with a bank and a Deposit Account?

A5 Name three reasons for individuals (or firms) to hold cash.

A6 How can a profitable company run out of cash?

A7 How can a company hold 'too much' cash?

A8 How can firms with 'positive cash flow' run out of funds?

A9 Define depreciation.

A10 Why does changing the way a company calculates depreciation make no difference to the amount of its corporation tax liability?

A11 Define 'opportunity cost' in the context of cash.

A12 What three constituent parts make up the rate of interest?

A13 Why are interest rates higher in Brazil than in Switzerland?

A14 Why do smaller businesses usually have to pay higher interest rates on borrowed money than larger companies?

A15 Why does even a government security which is both 'risk-free' and 'index-linked' provide a positive interest yield?

A16 Identify as many advantages as you can of regular cash forecasting.

A17 What was suggested as the single most critical estimate in cash flow forecasts?

A18 'Nearly all business deals take place on credit.' Show how this will affect the cash needs of different firms.

A19 What are the main regular payments and receipts involved in business?

A20 What is a 'discretionary expense'. Give an example.

A21 Why should depreciation of fixed assets *not* be included as part of operating expenses in a cash forecast?

A22 How will inflation affect a firm's needs for cash?

A23 What are the main difficulties in forecasting a company's cash needs?

A24 How would you forecast how much cash a company will need to provide for its working capital requirements in five years' time?

A25 Why is it often difficult to forecast retained profits for a period, by the 'pro forma' balance sheet method? Is the problem avoided by using a month-by-month cash forecast?

B. Exercises/Case Studies

B1   The owner of a small research agency is discussing the company's future with a friend. 'We're not doing badly', he says, 'we should make a profit this year, after paying our salaries, of about £5,000. We're lucky, owning our own offices; if we had to rent similar ones it would cost us another £15,000 a year.'
Discuss, using the concept of opportunity cost, whether or not the company should continue in business.

B2   An extract from the annual report of a small company runs as follows: 'We are pleased to report that the company has made an operating profit which, as a proportion of the funds invested in the business, is 10 per cent this year. It is as well we have kept up our profit, since it would cost us 16 per cent interest if we had to borrow from the bank.'
Comment on this, illustrating how using the idea of opportunity cost may give a different view of the company's problems.

B3   The longer the interval between cash payments and receipts, the larger an enterprise's financing needs in relation to sales revenue.
Comment on the cash flows (and thus the needs for finance) of:
(a) a farmer; (b) a food manufacturer; (c) a grocer; (d) a shipbuilder; (e) a school.

B4   How would a food manufacturing company's forecast of its cash needs for the next year probably be affected by each of the following unexpected events? (a) higher inflation than expected; (b) a poor crop; (c) introduction by competitors of synthetic foods: (d) rise in interest rates; (e) enforced closure of all factories for two days each week?

B5   Roughly what might be the net amount of money needed to finance the running expenses of:
a. A barrow boy who buys 250 lb of apples each morning in the wholesale market for cash?
b. A barrow boy who buys 250 lb of apples each morning in the wholesale market on one week's credit?
c. A pawnbroker who lends £500 daily, and is repaid on average after three months?
d. A supermarket chain which buys goods on one month's credit and sells them in two weeks for cash?
e. A manufacturing company with annual sales of £300,000, 20 per cent of which is profit; materials amount to half of total costs, are purchased on one month's credit, take two months to process and dispatch, and are sold on two months' credit?
f. A private house builder building 120 £20,000 houses each year?
List the six in order of the amount of money required as a percentage of sales.

B6   A company is set up with £2,000 cash, and during its first year the following take place:

12 Jan.: machinery bought for £1,000 cash
24 Feb.: goods bought for £500 cash
12 May: the same goods sold for £1,500 cash
16 June: further goods bought for £2,000 cash
12 Nov.: the goods are sold, on two months' credit, for £3,000
5 Dec.: independent valuers put the present value of the machinery at £800.

Calculate: (a) profit for the year; (b) 'cash flow' for the year. As financial director, write a short report to the managing director, explaining the significance of each of these figures.

B7 A firm buys a machine for £20,000, expecting it to last for 10 years.
  a. What depreciation would you recommend is charged each year as an expense against profits?
  b. Assuming that the annual pre-depreciation profits are £5,000, what would the annual post-depreciation profits amount to?
  c. Would your answer to (a) above change if annual pre-depreciation profits of only £1,500 were expected next year? Why or why not?
  d. Soon after buying the machine, the firm decides it would be sensible to rely on only five years' useful life from the machine. What effect would this decision have on:
  (i) the annual depreciation charge? (ii) profits? (iii) cash flow?

B8 Assuming that everyone is agreed in their expectation of the future rate of inflation, what would you expect to be the effect of introducing 'usury' laws putting a ceiling on the maximum rate of interest which could lawfully be charged to borrowers? What sort of borrowers would be affected, and what sort would not?

B9 A 20-year indexed gilt yields 2.5 per cent a year, while a 20-year ordinary (non-indexed) gilt yields 15.0 per cent a year.
  a. What is the implied annual inflation premium over the period?
  b. What conclusion can be drawn if a similar calculation in respect of five-year gilts produces a figure considerably *lower* than your answer to (a)?
  c. If people's expectations of inflation in future increase, what would you expect to happen to the yields:
  (i) on indexed gilts? (ii) on non-indexed gilts? Why?

B10 '*IT'S ENOUGH TO DRIVE YOU OFF THE RAILS FOR GOOD*'
'These costs are based on British Rail second class single tickets. And on the energy saving Sunderland Supersnarl which averages 54.3 m.p.g. at a steady 56 m.p.h., with the cost of petrol at £1.59 per gallon. 'We appreciate you have to buy an S.S. in the first place, but at least you can run it when you want, and take four more adults at no extra cost. Just try that with B.R.'

Advertisement in Sunday newspapers,
7 February 1982.

There followed a list of 45 destinations from London, with cost figures under two columns headed 'BR' and 'SS', and with mileage figures. A representative selection of four destinations is shown below:

	Mileage	BR £	SS £
Aberdeen	503	39.00	14.73
Birmingham	105	11.30	3.07
Bradford	195	19.60	5.71
Cambridge	54	5.40	1.58

Questions

a. How have the SS figures been calculated?

b. Is the comparison being made a fair one? If not, why not?

c. Roughly what would you reckon is a fair comparison for the Aberdeen to London journey? How have you calculated it?

d. What would be a fair Aberdeen–London comparison for a husband and wife with their 17-year-old son?

B11 The newly-elected government of Utopia is preparing its cash budget for the next five years. It is too late to change the plans for year 1, in which taxes are expected to total £80 billion, other receipts £8 billion, and government spending will total £96 billion. The resulting deficit will be financed by borrowing, but the Utopian government wants to reduce its borrowing (in equal stages year by year) to zero by year 5. The government also plans to reduce total taxation each year by £3 billion, compared with the previous year. (There is no inflation in Utopia.) Other receipts are expected to stay at £8 billion for years 2 and 3, then to fall to £6 billion a year. Government expenditure is split (on a somewhat arbitrary basis) between 'essential' and 'non-essential'. 'Essential' expenditure may be assumed to remain unchanged over the five years: in year 1 it totals £30 billion.

Questions

a. How much will 'non-essential' government spending have to be for each of the next four years in order for the Utopian government to achieve its plans? What proportionate fall in 'non-essential' spending (compared with the level in year 1) does this imply in each of years 2 to 5?

b. What difference would it make to your answers to (a) if taxes were to stay at the year 1 level *and* 'essential' spending in each year were £60 billion out of the total expenditure?

B12 Fenton Limited was recently formed to buy and sell wimpoles. At the end of 1981 the balance sheet simply consists of: Debtors £12,000, Stocks £27,000, and Issued Share Capital £39,000. The cash balance was zero, and there were no retained profits. The company owns no fixed assets, and has no current liabilities.

In the first quarter of 1982, the company sold 3,000 wimpoles, an increase of 1,000 on the previous quarter. These cost the company £9 each and sell for £12 each. The company expects to increase its volume of sales by 1,000 units each quarter for the next two years. Thus sales in the second quarter of 1982 are expected to be 4,000 wimpoles, in the third quarter 5,000, and so on.

Purchases are paid for in the same month as they occur, while customers (debtors) pay on average 1½ months after the date of sale. You may assume that both purchases and sales are made evenly throughout each quarter. (For example, assume sales of 1,000 wimpoles a month in each of the first three months of 1982, then 1,333 a month in each of the next three months, and so on.) The stock level held is equivalent to predicted sales volume for the next three months; so at the end of 1981 3,000 wimpoles were held in stock.

Questions

a. Forecast the quarter-by-quarter profit and loss account and balance sheet figures for the rest of 1982 and for the first half of 1983.

b. How does the expected cumulative cash balance differ from the expected cumulative balance of retained profits? (No dividend payments are planned.) Draw a graph comparing the two.

c. What is likely to be the maximum borrowing requirement? When will it be needed?

d. If the maximum amount that can be borrowed is *less* than your projections suggest will be needed, what can Fenton Limited do to reduce its need for funds?

B13 Spanner Limited, a civil engineering company, accepts a government contract to build a road bridge for £8 million. The job should take two years. Earth-moving machinery must be purchased for £1.2 million, which can be sold for £200,000 at the end of the contract. Labour costs will be £300,000 quarterly in the first year and £400,000 quarterly in the second year. After three months materials will be needed, and over the next four quarters weekly deliveries will be made at a rate of £500,000 worth per quarter. Other costs (administration, petrol, etc.) are expected to be about £200,000 each quarter over the whole contract. Assuming progress accords with an agreed plan, 'progress' payments will be made on the contract, starting from the second quarter, amounting to £700,000 per quarter. The balance of the £8 million outstanding will then be payable on completion of the contract.

Making (and stating) any further assumptions you think necessary,

a. Prepare a quarter-by-quarter table of cash receipts and payments for the two years of the contract.

b. Show what is the maximum cash 'investment' the project requires.

c. What is the expected overall profit or loss on the contract?

B14 In 1982 Newman Machines Limited wanted to replace an old turret lathe. It cost £9,000 in 1965; and had been depreciated over 15 years. The company had £9,000 (provided out of depreciation) to buy a new lathe, plus £1,000, the re-sale value of the old lathe.

But the replacement cost in 1982 was £36,000 for a lathe that would perform the same functions as the old machine, or £58,000 for a new improved model with special accessories. So Newman had only £10,000 to buy a £58,000 machine. The difference of £48,000 had to come out of profits.

To get that amount, the company needed to earn a profit of £100,000 before tax, because only £48,000 would be left after the government took corporation tax of 52 per cent. And to earn £100,000 profit, the company had to sell more than £1,000,000 worth of products to customers. Thus while £100,000 might sound like a lot of profit, in this case the owners of the business would get none of it. The government would take more than half, and the rest would go to replace a single machine.

This story explains why only a relatively small amount of profit is paid out in dividends to the shareholders. A large proportion must be retained in the business to finance expansion and replacement so that a firm can carry on and the employees continue working.

Comment on the story of the 'million pound lathe'. Is it the truth, the whole truth, and nothing but the truth?

B15 Examine a recent set of published accounts.
    a. Draw up a list of changes in each item in the balance sheet between the end of the latest year and the end of the previous year. Your list of 'balance sheet changes' should itself balance.
    b. Classify and rearrange your list of balance sheet changes into the form of a funds flow statement.
    c. Compare your version with the company's published funds flow statement. What are the main differences in presentation? Are any of the money amounts different in the two statements? If so, can you identify why?

B16 *PLASTIC PRODUCTS LIMITED*
In April 1982, Mr Charles Salford, a former marketing manager of the plastics division of a large diversified chemical company, was completing plans to start a new firm called Plastic Products Limited. He said: 'In my last job I noticed attractive opportunities to produce plastic dinnerware, but they were too small for my old company to bother with. I decided I wanted to run a company myself, to manage the full range of operations, including production and finance, not just marketing.'

After an extended search Mr Salford had found a large industrial building in which he could lease two floors adequate for his needs. He believed that his new firm could grow steadily to reach a sales volume of about £80,000 a month by the end of the first year of operations; and expected sales to remain at this level for the next two years or so.

In addition to £60,000 from his own family's resources, Mr Salford had managed to persuade friends to invest a total of £90,000 in the new firm.

He wanted to limit the total initial equity capital to £150,000. He thought the time of greatest financial strain would occur just after the company had reached the anticipated £80,000 per month level of sales volume. He therefore decided to forecast what his funds requirements would be one year after the company began operations.

Equipment

Mr Salford aimed to minimise equipment needs by buying only three new compression moulding machines, which he planned to operate on a three-shift, 24-hour basis, with labour on the second and third shifts being paid higher hourly rates. A fourth machine, to be bought second-hand. would provide standby capacity to cover peak load requirements and any breakdowns in the new machinery.

Polishing and grinding machines for the finishing operation were not expensive, so Mr Salford decided to buy enough machines to complete the finishing operation in a single shift. The operators would be women who preferred to work day-time shifts. He estimated the total cost of all the equipment would come to £120,000: on which depreciation of 10 per cent a year would be charged. After intensive negotiation, deferred payment terms were arranged on the new moulding equipment, so that after allowing for a 25 per cent down payment the rest of the £96,000 purchase price could be paid monthly over three years.

Current assets

To avoid production stoppages, Mr Salford wanted to maintain a supply of raw materials equal to one month's usage, to provide reasonable protection against both interruptions in raw material flows and sudden spurts in sales. No marked seasonal pattern in sales was anticipated, and he hoped to produce at an even rate once sales had levelled out. At the £80,000 sales level, total manufacturing costs would amount to about £60,000 a month, of which raw material costs would represent 40 per cent.

Plastic Products tableware would be sold in sets of 30 to 60 pieces. Several different designs were to be employed, each of which would use six basic colours. In order to compete successfully the company needed to have finished merchandise on hand ready for immediate delivery as orders were received from retail outlets. The original plan had been to carry one month's output of finished goods stocks; but after considering the financial burden, Mr Salford had to accept a lower target figure of three weeks' supply, costing £45,000.

It was the custom in the trade to offer retailers 30-day credit terms; but in the currently difficult economic climate some delays in payment had to be expected. Accordingly, average investment in debtors was projected at 1½ months' sales, or £120,000. Mr Salford knew from experience that there was bound to be some variation in the rate of incoming orders. To provide for such fluctuations, he wanted to maintain a bank balance of £30,000 (equal to about two weeks normal expenditure).

Sources of finance

Having estimated likely funds requirements at the end of 12 months to amount to £327,000 (see below), Mr Salford turned to the task of generating sufficient funds to finance this investment in the business. After detailed calculation, he reckoned that the company would become profitable after about six months of operations, and that profit in the second six months should be sufficient to recoup the losses of the first six months. Hence the owners' equity investment should be restored to its initial amount of £150,000 by the date of the projected balance sheet.

Creditors would consist of amounts payable for raw materials. The terms of purchase were 30 days net, so a figure of £24,000 was projected as a normal figure for creditors. After allowing for the £48,000 still outstanding on the equipment acquired on deferred terms, the projected sources of funds totalled £222,000 – leaving a gap of £105,000.

As a first step towards filling this gap, Mr Salford investigated the possibilities of bank credit. He found one bank that was prepared to allow a revolving overdraft, under which it would advance up to 50 per cent of amounts owed to Plastic Products by customers. This implied an overdraft ceiling of £60,000, so Mr Salford felt it was realistic to project an actual overdraft of £48,000 without any cash balance.

At this point, finding he was still £27,000 short, Mr Salford had to face some unpalatable choices. He was most reluctant to reduce the scale of the enterprise, since he thought a smaller operation could expect to have little impact in the market, and would not be able to carry enough advertising to support sales. Consequently he felt he would have to risk operating with only a two-week supply of finished goods, thus reducing the cost of the investment in finished goods stocks to £30,000.

Next he considered other possibilities for credit. After investigation he found a leading supplier of plastic powder (his principal raw material) who was willing to grant 45-day credit terms instead of the usual 30 days, provided that Plastic Products would concentrate its purchases with that one firm. This made possible an extra £12,000 of continuing credit, increasing the level of creditors to £36,000.

Sources and uses of funds could now be made equal, and Mr Salford appeared to have prepared a feasible financial programme. Yet he wondered whether his plans really made adequate allowance for unforeseen problems.

Questions

a. Identify the main:
   i.   policy decisions which have affected the projected financial position after 12 months;
   ii. forecasts about the uncertain future which Mr Salford made;
   iii. actions which Mr Salford has already undertaken.
b. What could 'go wrong'? Can you quantify the most important possible

developments which might cause the actual need for funds to vary from
the amounts shown in the projected balance sheet?
c. One of Mr Salford's friends withdraws his agreement to invest £15,000
in equity shares in Plastic Products Ltd (out of the £150,000 total).
You are offered the chance to take his place. Assume you have about
£100,000 available for equity investment. Would you be prepared to
invest £15,000 of it in Plastic Products? Why or why not? (A smaller
investment is *not* possible.)

Plastic Products Limited

Projected balance sheet after one year of operation

	Original projection (£'000)	Revised projection (£'000)
Current assets		
Stocks: Raw materials 24	69	54
Finished goods 45		
Debtors	120	120
Cash at bank	30	—
	219	174
Fixed assets: Equipment, net	108	108
	327	282
Current liabilities		
Creditors	24	36
Equipment – deferred liability	48	48
Bank overdraft	—	48
	72	132
Equity capital	150	150
	222	282
Shortfall:	105	—
	327	282

Note on stocks: Original projection Raw materials 24, Finished goods 45 = 69. Revised projection Raw materials 24, Finished goods 30 = 54.

C. Essay Questions

C1   Money is a means of exchange, a store of value, and a means of economic measurement. To what extent is each of these functions essential in a modern economy?

C2   In a film called *The Million Pound Note*, Gregory Peck was able to go shopping in London without ever having to spend any cash because he could show he possessed a bank note for £1 million.
Explain.

C3   'Within the next generation credit cards will almost completely replace cash.' Do you agree? Why or why not? What would the consequences be?

C4   'Even a profitable company can easily run out of cash if it doesn't plan ahead.' Discuss.

C5   A certain company, wishing to improve its profits, is considering three alternative strategies:
   a. It may raise the price of its product, thus reducing sales but increasing the profit per item.
   b. It may aim for a larger market share, increasing advertising expenditure and lowering its price.
   c. It may undertake research, aiming to produce a better product which could sell at a higher price than at present, but in the same quantities and at the same production cost.
As financial director, you are asked to write a short report setting out the impact on the company's cash position of the early stages of each policy.

C6   Is depreciation a source of funds? Why or why not?

C7   'Provided I have at least £100 in the bank, it costs me nothing to run my current account.' Comment. Do you consider such an arrangement is a good bargain? For you? For the bank?

C8   'It costs me interest to borrow money to finance the acquisition of a new machine, but if I've got enough money in the bank it doesn't cost me anything.' Discuss.

C9   Explain how you would set about forecasting your firm's cash needs for the next five years, showing the main assumptions you would need to make.

C10   'Credit squeezes tend to undermine businesses by putting pressure on the very spending essential to their long-term survival.' Discuss.

C11   Cash is essentially a short-term concept, whereas profit is a longer-term one. Do you agree? Why or why not?

C12   If there were no inflation interest rates would be zero. Discuss.

C13   'The principle of index-linking has revolutionary implications in nearly all areas of business finance.' Discuss.

C14   How is inflation likely to affect a company's cash position, if it wishes to continue at the same 'real' level of activity?

Chapter 3

Managing Working Capital

Objective: *To identify the financial importance of working capital and the stages of the working capital cycle; to examine what determines levels of investment in stocks and debtors; to describe the various kinds of current liability; and to identify the main measures of business liquidity.*

Synopsis: *Long-term funds are needed to finance investment in net working capital. The main factors affecting stocks (of raw materials, work in progress, and finished goods) are: sales volume, the relationship of production to sales, and the cost of holding stock. The amount invested in debtors depends on sales volume and average credit periods taken by customers. Current liabilities (of which trade creditors are usually the most important) can be related to current assets by two main measures of liquidity: the current ratio and the acid test ratio. But caution is needed in interpreting financial ratios.*

3.1 Working Capital

3.1.1 The Importance of Working Capital

Working capital is the name given to the excess of current assets over current liabilities. The two main items are **stocks** and **debtors**: they represent a firm's investment in goods which are unfinished, unsold, or unpaid for. Stocks and debtors, which are partly financed by trade credit from suppliers, together amount to about *half* of the total assets of UK quoted companies. In view of its size, working capital is clearly important to many firms.

A hotel may be permanently full even though no individual person is always resident. In the same way there is a *permanent* need to finance working capital, even though the individual items are continually being turned into cash.

In managing working capital a firm needs to determine a suitable *level* of investment; then it must decide how to *finance* its chosen level of working capital; and finally a firm's managers need to see that their policy on working capital is actually *carried out*. (A firm may 'decide', for example, that debtors should average one month's sales, but someone still needs to make sure that customers owe no more than that.)

In this chapter we discuss stocks, debtors, current liabilities and measures of liquidity. In Chapter 4 we then discuss investment in long-term ('Fixed') assets; and in Chapter 5 we look at the various types of long-term funds needed to finance both long-term assets *and* the permanent net balance of short-term ('current') assets over short-term liabilities.

3.1.2 The Working Capital Cycle

The working capital cycle of a manufacturing business is shown in Fig. 3.1.

The business first purchases **raw materials** on credit, then uses labour and capital equipment, in various proportions in different industries, to convert the raw materials into **finished goods**. (Often there are intermediate stages of partly-completed goods, known as **work-in-progress**.) When the finished goods are sold, legal title passes to the purchaser, who either pays cash or, if he buys on credit, owes the price to the selling company. The transaction is completed when the debtor finally pays cash to settle his account.

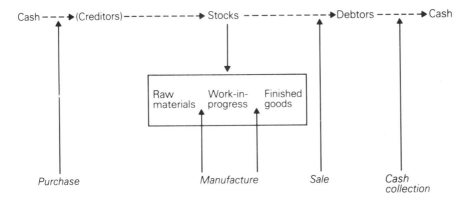

Fig. 3.1: Working capital cycle.

Thus the working capital cycle is represented by cash being used to acquire raw materials and to pay labour wages to convert the materials over time into finished goods, which are then sold to customers and finally paid for. In a business making a profit, the cash received at the end should exceed the total cash amounts paid out during the working capital cycle. This is necessary in order to pay (a) taxes on profits, (b) interest on borrowings, (c) ordinary dividends to shareholders, and (d) to acquire capital equipment.

In times of inflation, merely increasing the money amount of assets may not represent 'real' growth. This serious accounting complication affects both the financial planning of cash and the accounting measurement of 'profit' or 'loss'. Several British companies have recently been forced to issue more ordinary shares mainly in order to maintain their 'real' level of working capital. It is a worrying sign if a company can maintain its *existing* level of operations only by raising more long-term capital, by either borrowing or issuing more ordinary share capital. A business ought to be able to maintain its present size out of 'internally-generated' cash flow; though it may have to raise new long-term capital in order to expand.

3.2 Stocks

3.2.1 Types of Stock

The three main types of stock in a manufacturing company are: raw materials, work-in-progress, and finished goods. (Nearly all firms also hold stocks of supplies, such as stationery and maintenance materials, for use in the course of operations.)

Stocks are normally stated 'at cost' or, if lower, at **net realisable value**. 'Cost' comprises expenditure incurred in bringing a product to its present location and condition: it includes all related production overheads, based on the normal level of activity, even if these accrue on a time basis (such as factory rent).

For UK manufacturing industry as a whole, *each* of the three main kinds of stock at any time represents about 25 per cent of the annual output (**value added**). Thus at the end of 1980, the total book value of manufacturing industry stocks amounted to £37 billion, some 77 per cent of 1980 Value Added.

	1980 value added	End 1980 stocks	Per cent
	(£ billion)	(£ billion)	
Agriculture, Forestry, Mining and Quarrying	7.5	5.3	71
Manufacturing	48.1	37.1	77
Distribution	19.3	15.9	82
	74.9	58.3	78
★ Other (mainly services)	118.6	9.6	8
Total	193.5	67.9	35

Fig. 3.2: Value added and end-of-year stocks, by sector, 1980.

Service industries naturally tend to have low stocks, as shown in Fig. 3.2, because their product usually cannot be 'stored' in finished form. The same is true of some manufacturing companies, such as newspaper publishers or bakeries.

Value added is used as a measure of output in National Income statistics to avoid 'double counting'. Simply adding up the market value of the sales revenue of each productive unit would produce a total far higher than the value of output actually available for consumption. This is because of all the vitally important 'middle men' in a market economy (such as distributors).

For example, adding together the sales value of retail bread sales, plus bakeries' bread sales, plus flour mills' flour sales, plus farmers' wheat sales, would involve counting the value of the *same* wheat four times! So each firm's 'value added' is the sales value of its output *minus* the value of the inputs it buys from other firms.

3.2.2 Levels of Stock

1980 was an unusual year for UK industry, because the physical amount of stocks in both manufacturing and distribution actually *fell* by about 7 per cent

---

* See Question C6

of the year-end level. This represented a decline of some £2.5 billion in manufacturing stocks and £1.2 billion in distribution.

What determines stock levels? In general, the level of sales; the relationship between production and sales; the nature of the production process; and the cost of investment in stocks. (For more detailed discussion, see *Production Decisions* by John Powell in this series.) Costs of holding stocks will vary for different industries, and may include handling, storage, insurance, obsolescence and interest. Average stock-holding costs probably total as much as 25 to 35 per cent of book value a year.

Raw materials stocks depend mainly on buying considerations: the nature of the commodities (e.g. whether they are perishable, bulky, expensive); anticipated interruptions to supplies (e.g. from strikes); how quickly suppliers can deliver more goods (e.g. some Japanese car manufacturers fly in supplies of components by helicopter every two hours!) the economics of bulk purchasing; anticipated changes in future prices and in sales volume.

Work-in-progress depends largely on the method of production (e.g. batch versus flow); the length of the production process (e.g. bakeries will have lower work-in-progress than shipyards); the importance of set-up costs; and the possibility of sub-contracting.

Finished goods stock levels depend mainly on selling considerations: whether goods are being made to order; the reliability of sales forecasts; policy on risk of stock-outs; and anticipated changes in sales volume.

Forecasting whether a change in sales volume is temporary or more permanent can be crucial in deciding whether to change the rate of production. A wrong decision could mean either piling up unwanted stocks, or else running out of stock and thus losing potential sales. Either could be very expensive. *The essence of business is judging the direction, extent and timing of changes in market conditions in the uncertain future.*

In managing stocks, as in many other areas of business, a useful control

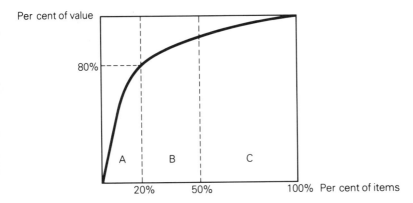

Fig. 3.3: ABC analysis.

device can be ABC analysis (Fig. 3.3.). This is based on the 'rule' that a small proportion (say 20%) of the total *number* of items will usually account for a large proportion (say 80%) of the total *value* of all items. The implication is obvious: rather than pay equal attention to all items, it makes better commercial sense to give priority to the relatively few items which account for most of the investment, starting with Class A items, then looking at Class B items, and only at the end considering the Class C items.

3.3 Debtors

3.3.1 Risk and Return on Investment in Debtors

Selling for cash avoids any need to 'invest' in debtors, but most companies want to offer credit terms as attractive as their competitors. The two main risks in extending trade credit are that the customer will either take *too long* to pay, or else *fail to pay* at all (**bad debts**). The 'return' from extending credit to customers consists of the marginal contribution to profit resulting from the extra sales made. Trade credit policy has to balance the return against the risk.

One of the main determinants of the amount invested in debtors (accounts receivable) is the *volume of sales*. Since increasing sales volume is usually desirable, the main way of trying to control total credit extended is to limit the average *period of credit taken* by customers. This depends both on the credit terms *offered* and on the efficiency of the seller's credit control and collection procedures.

Example: The gain from controlling credit can be large. The General Electric Company Limited's average credit period of 137 days in March 1970 was reduced to 92 days by March 1974. With sales of nearly £100 million a month, the 'saving' of 45 days credit amounted to nearly £150 million. At an interest rate of 14 per cent a year, the annual expense saved must have been about £20 million – more than one eighth of GEC's total 1974 profit (Fig. 3.4).

	March 1970	March 1974	'Saving'
Annual sales	£ 891m.	£1,144m.	@ £1,144m.
Debtors, end of year	£ 335m.	£ 287m.	£ 143m.
Average credit period	137.2 days	91.6 days	45.6 days

★ Fig. 3.4: General Electric Company Limited, 'saving' on debtors: 1974 v. 1970.

---

* See Question B6

Another way of viewing the cost of credit is to recognise the true cost of offering a **cash discount** to customers who pay promptly. If customers on average take 45 days after invoice date before paying, then offering a 2½ per cent cash discount for payment within 10 days would cost 2½ per cent *for 35 days*. This is an *annual rate* of over 25 per cent. (Notice that the 45 days' credit *actually taken* is what matters, not the company's official credit terms of only, say, 30 days.) An alternative approach is to *charge* interest on accounts of customers who pay *slowly*; but this is not popular.

Incurring *no* bad debts at all suggests that a firm is probably taking too *few* credit risks. In view of the likely returns forgone, it makes little sense to refrain from making sales on credit to 99 customers on the off chance that one may fail to pay the whole amount due. Even if a customer goes bankrupt, a supplier of goods and services may be able to recover some, if not all, of the amount due – though perhaps only after a long delay and some extra expense.

3.3.2 Overall Credit Control

One of the most powerful tools for controlling debtors in total is simply calculating the average number of days' sales still owing at the end of a period. Changes in payment practices are then revealed, and can be investigated.

Example: If sales for the past calendar year amounted to £180,000, and debtors at the end of December totalled £30,000, it would be easy to calculate that 61 days' sales were still outstanding:

$$\frac{30,000}{180,000} \times 365 = 61 \ days.$$

As an alternative, we could carry out the calculation in two stages:

a. Daily sales $\dfrac{£180,000}{365} = £493.$

b. Outstanding: $\dfrac{£3,000}{£493} = 61 \ days.$

But depending on the precise pattern of sales, a more accurate estimate, identifying debtors with sales in particular months, could suggest an average credit period of 41 days (or 1 1/3 months), as shown in Fig. 3.5. We have simply assumed that customers pay in chronological order. Thus if December sales were £25,000 and November sales £15,000, we assume that the total debtors of £30,000 at the end of December include all of December's sales (i.e. 31 days), plus 5/15 of November's sales (i.e. 10 days).

Good credit managers are quick to respond to changes in the overall pattern of debtors: they also tend to operate with specific *targets*, either in absolute amounts or (preferably) in terms of average days' sales outstanding.

Month	Sales in month	Still owing	=	Fraction of month	=	Days' sales in debtors
	(£'000)	(£'000)				
October	5	—		—		—
★ November	15	5	=	0.33×30	=	10
December	25	25	=	1.00×31	=	31
		30		1.33 months		41 days

Fig. 3.5: Calculation of average days' sales outstanding in debtors.

If the average credit period allowed to customers is increasing, or at an unsatisfactory level, management should find out why. Has trade credit *policy* changed? Or customers' *practices*? Are the largest debtors being given appropriate priority? Are invoices and statements being sent out promptly? Are slow payers being chased up vigorously enough?

3.3.3 Individual Customer Credit

Two decisions normally have to be made about individual credit customers: whether to extend credit at all; and, if so, up to what maximum amount. There are several ways to check the credit-worthiness of a potential new customer: trade references from other suppliers, bank references, reports from a credit bureau, past financial statements, and the impression of the firm's own salesman.

A business may refuse to supply more goods if credit terms are being ignored too blatantly, either the total *amount* of credit or the *period* of credit taken. Ultimately there is an implied threat of *legal action* against customers who do not pay amounts due according to the credit terms offered. But it is better to avoid this if possible: the supplier wants his money, but dislikes all the trouble and expense of taking formal legal proceedings against debtors.

The credit control system should include a regular review of all individual customers, to ensure that they are not exceeding their maximum credit limits. (But people will tend to ignore unrealistically low credit limits, like speed limits on roads.) One surprisingly useful way to get money from debtors is simply to telephone and ask why they haven't paid. One company even telephones large customers *during* the credit period to check that the amount involved can be expected on the due date. This enables any queries to be

---

* See Question B8

sorted out in good time, as well as reminding the customer that adherence to the credit terms is expected as a normal part of a satisfactory business relationship.

3.4 Current Liabilities

The extent to which net working capital needs to be financed by long-term capital depends both on the amount of the various current assets and on the amount of the current liabilities. These are amounts owing to suppliers, banks, the tax authorities, and others.

3.4.1 Trade Creditors

Goods transferred from one business to another are often sold 'on credit' (rather than for immediate settlement in cash). The time lag between supply and payment is usually between one and three months. In total, **trade credit** can be a very important source of finance for many businesses; and just as there is a need for a 'permanent' investment in debtors (credit extended to customers), so most firms can expect to rely on a 'permanent' source of finance from trade creditors.

An example of a typical credit transaction in manufacturing industry is set out in Fig. 3.6.

Date	Event	Payment
3 May	A delivers raw materials to B	
9–13 May	B works on the goods	
13 May		B pays wages
26 May	B delivers finished goods to C	
17 June		B pays A for materials
13 July		C pays B for goods.

Fig. 3.6: A typical credit transaction.

In Firm B's balance sheet at the end of May, the amount owing to Firm A will appear under Creditors as a current liability; while the amount owing from Firm C will appear under Debtors as a current asset. (Some British firms are now using the American expressions: 'accounts payable' for creditors, and 'accounts receivable' for debtors.) Of course, in Firm C's balance sheet at the end of May, the amount owing to Firm B will appear under creditors, as a current liability.

The average *period* of credit given to customers is often similar to the average period of credit received from suppliers. But the total *amount* of debtors, for firms which sell on credit, is usually much larger than the total amount of creditors. The difference comes not only from the profit margin, but also from certain expenses paid in cash (such as wages to employees), and other expenses not reflected in creditors (such as depreciation of fixed assets). Firms whose 'added value' is high will tend to have *low* trade creditors, since much of their cost of goods sold will consist of wages rather than raw materials or bought-in parts.

3.4.2 Bills of Exchange

A **bill of exchange** is essentially a post-dated cheque given in exchange for goods. Usually the date of ultimate payment is three months after the transaction. The *seller* of goods can obtain immediate cash by selling the bill – less a discount to cover interest for the three months – to a 'discount house'. To do so he may need to pay a fee to a bank to guarantee payment of the bill when it becomes due for payment. (This is known as 'accepting' the bill.)

Bills of exchange are widely used, especially in export transactions (where it might otherwise be difficult for a seller to enforce payment without going to much trouble and expense). On the balance sheet, bills of exchange are usually shown under creditors, rather than being shown as a separate item.

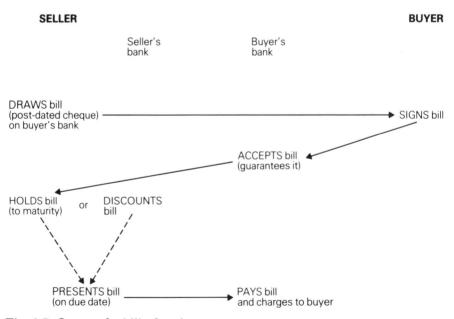

Fig. 3.7: Stages of a bill of exchange.

In this respect, Marks and Spencer Limited – whose balance sheet is summarised in Fig. 3.9. on page 51, is an exception.

3.4.3 **Taxation**

Most unpaid taxes (liabilities) are included with trade creditors (for example, local rates, National Insurance, income tax (PAYE) deducted from wages, Value Added Tax, etc.). But taxation based on *profits* is shown as a separate item, both in the profit and loss account and in the balance sheet. It is called **corporation tax** for companies, and **income tax** for sole traders and partnerships. All unpaid taxation based on profits is normally shown as a *current* liability, even if it is not legally due for more than 12 months after the balance sheet date.

There are special rules for calculating the tax liability, which mean that 'taxable profit' is not the same as the reported profit in accounts. In particular the depreciation expense charged in accounts is replaced by tax 'capital allowances', calculated according to Inland Revenue rules. Moreover, some expenses may be 'disallowed' for tax purposes, and there may be certain differences of timing for revenues or expenses.

3.4.4 **Dividends Payable**

The liability for proposed dividends on ordinary shares is shown, net of basic rate income tax, as a separate item of current liabilities on the balance sheet. Similarly the profit and loss account shows separately the total net dividends on ordinary shares for the period.

Normal UK practice is to pay an '**interim**' dividend *during* the year, and to propose a '**final**' dividend which is paid after the year-end. So the balance sheet shows only the final dividend as a current liability; while the profit and loss account shows the total of the interim and final dividends.

3.4.5 **Bank Overdrafts**

In the British banking system, customers (by agreement) may have *negative* balances ('overdrafts') on current account with banks. The amount borrowed depends on exactly how much is required at any time. Apart from a possible small 'commitment fee' (payable on the maximum limit of the agreed overdraft facility), only the actual amount overdrawn bears interest. This is calculated from day to day, at a rate which varies with money market conditions.

Bank overdrafts are legally repayable 'on demand' (i.e. without any notice), and are shown on the balance sheet as current liabilities. The overdraft system is convenient for customers; but it makes it hard for the banks to know how much of their total agreed overdraft limits with customers will actually be required at any time.

3.4.6 **Other Current Liabilities**

The four main current liabilities are: trade creditors, taxation, dividends payable, and bank overdrafts. But certain other current liabilities sometimes occur as a result of special arrangements:

a. *Special credit from suppliers.* Suppliers may be prepared to negotiate longer credit terms than usual, especially where sales are highly seasonal. These may enable hard-pressed customers to defer outstanding amounts for months. Relying on suppliers in this way, however, can have disadvantages, such as the loss of bargaining power on price, delivery and other terms.

b. *Advances from customers.* Some businesses, such as construction and ship-building, may get financial support from customers in the form either of advance payments against orders for future production and delivery or of part payments on account before the order is completed. These advances may be deducted from work in progress on the balance sheet, or shown separately as current liabilities.

3.5 Measures of Liquidity

In this section we shall look at five common measures of liquidity:
1. Current ratio.
2. Acid test ratio.
3. Working capital to sales.
4. Days' sales in debtors.
5. Days' sales in stock.

As a basis for calculating each of these measures, we shall use the working capital section of Beecham Group Limited's balance sheet at 31 March 1981 (Fig. 3.8).

	£m.	
Current assets		
Stocks	213	
Debtors and prepayments	235	
Liquid resources	129	
	——	577
Current liabilities		
Short-term borrowings	32	
Creditors and accruals	186	
Taxation	54	
Dividends	23	
	——	295
Net current assets (= working capital)		282

Fig. 3.8: Beecham Group Limited, net current assets, 31 March 1981.

3.5.1 **Current Ratio**

The **current ratio** simply divides current assets by current liabilities:

$$\text{Current ratio} = \frac{\text{Current assets}}{\text{Current liabilities}} = \frac{577}{295} = 1.96.$$

The traditional rule of thumb is that for most manufacturing companies the current ratio should ideally be about 2.00. In other words, current assets should total about twice as much as current liabilities. Ratios between 1.50 and 2.00, however, are often found in practice, and usually give no real cause for alarm.

If the current ratio fell too far, say below 1.50, it might suggest a company facing liquidity problems – since it might not be easy to find the cash to pay short-term liabilities when they became due. In most manufacturing companies one of the major current assets is stock; but since stocks are often not quickly convertible into cash a more direct measure of liquidity is the acid test ratio.

3.5.2 **Acid Test Ratio**

The **acid test ratio** divides **liquid assets** by current liabilities. 'Liquid assets' includes both liquid resources and debtors (which would normally become cash within three months). Here the traditional rule of thumb is 1.00, which Beecham Group comfortably exceeds:

$$\text{Acid test ratio} = \frac{\text{Debtors} + \text{liquid resources}}{\text{Current liabilities}} = \frac{364}{295} = 1.23$$

For *liquidity* alone, the higher the acid test ratio the better. But if it is *too* high, the 'excess' liquidity may not yield a very high rate of return, so *profitability* may be impaired. Thus such a measure of liquidity should fall within a *range*, outside which – in *either* direction – there may be a problem in balancing cash and profit.

3.5.3 **Working Capital to Sales**

Another ratio which can give a general impression of liquidity, especially if one looks at trends over time, is the proportion which net working capital bears to annual sales revenue. With annual sales of £1,195 million in the year ended 31 March 1981, Beecham Group's ratio works out at just under 24 per cent.

$$\text{Working capital to sales} = \frac{\text{Working capital}}{\text{Sales}} = \frac{282}{1195} = 23.6\%.$$

Beecham's ratio of about three months' sales in net working capital is similar to that of other large companies.

3.5.4 **Days' Sales in Debtors**

This ratio (discussed in **3.3.2**) shows how many days' sales on average are represented by outstanding debtors.

$$\text{Days' sales in debtors} = \frac{\text{Debtors}}{\text{Sales}} \times 365 = \frac{235}{1195} \times 365 = 71.8 \text{ days.}$$

With sales running at £100 million a month, Beecham has nearly 2½ months' sales in debtors; hence a total investment in debtors of just under £250 million. To judge how appropriate this amount is we would need to analyse it along the lines suggested in **3.3**.

3.5.5 **Days' Sales in Stock**

The other major current asset, stock, may be related to sales in the same way as debtors:

$$\text{Days' sales in stock} = \frac{\text{Stocks}}{\text{Sales}} \times 365 = \frac{213}{1195} \times 365 = 65.1 \text{ days.}$$

This particular ratio needs to be interpreted with care, since stocks are valued at cost while sales (of course) are shown at selling prices. It does not literally mean, therefore, that Beecham has 65 days' sales tied up in stocks. Again, however, comparisons of trends over time can be useful.

3.5.6 **The Need for Caution**

One needs to interpret accounting ratios with caution. For instance, a well-known large company (in a different industry) has liquidity ratios which at first sight may seem alarming (Fig. 3.9).

Compared with our rules of thumb of 2.0 and 1.0 respectively, Marks and Spencer's current ratio is 0.9 (269/300) and the acid test ratio is 0.5 (153/300). Thus current liabilities *exceed* current assets, and the net working capital is actually *negative*! What is going on? Is Marks and Spencer about to go bankrupt?

In all financial and accounting work, an essential rule to bear in mind is: *don't panic!* If a particular figure or ratio looks odd, even after checking your arithmetic, it is worth spending a little time thinking *why* the number works out as it does.

Since virtually all of Marks and Spencer's £1,873 million annual sales are for *cash*, the 'debtors' of £44 million probably represent mainly prepayments of various kinds, together with some advances to suppliers.

The £116 million stock at 31 March 1981 (mostly available for sale in retail stores) represents about one month's sales, so we could expect most of it to have turned into cash by the end of April. Indeed, Marks and Spencer's *stock* is a good deal more 'liquid' than many companies' *debtors*! Clearly the acid test ratio (which omits stock) gives much too gloomy a view in this case.

	£m.	
Current assets		
Stock	116	
Debtors and prepayments	44	
Certificates of tax deposit	68	
Cash and short-term deposits	41	
	——	269
Current liabilities		
Creditors and accrued charges	97	
Taxation	80	
Bills of exchange	43	
Bank loans and overdrafts	50	
Dividends	30	
	——	300
Net working capital		(31)

Fig. 3.9: Marks and Spencer Limited, working capital, 31 March 1981.

Not all the current liabilities are due within the next month or two. The proposed final dividend (£30 million) will not be paid until after the annual general meeting in July. And the £80 million taxation liability (which is largely covered by £68 million Certificates of Tax Deposit) is mostly due on 1 January 1982, just nine months beyond the year end.

So even if we assumed that all other creditors (£190 million) were due within the next 30 days, we could expect the company to have at least £157 million cash available by then. Thus the liquidity position actually seems fairly comfortable. The truth is that the balance sheet gives only a very crude idea of the real position: we need to know a good deal more about the particular business before we can begin to draw conclusions. *Accounting ratios may raise questions which need to be considered — but they do not and cannot provide the answers.*

* See Question A33

Work Section

A. Revision Questions

A1 Why is managing working capital important?

A2 Why is there a permanent need for most companies to finance working capital even though the individual items are all 'current'?

A3 What are the main types of current assets?

A4 What are the main types of current liabilities?

A5 What is the working capital cycle of a manufacturing business?

A6 What are the three main categories of stock in a manufacturing firm?

A7 Roughly what proportion of annual value added is held in stock by UK manufacturing companies on average?

A8 Why might expectations about future prices lead a business to hold *low* stocks of raw materials?

A9 Identify four different kinds of costs of holding stocks.

A10 Why may the nature of the production process affect the amount of stock held?

A11 How can one assess whether a company's levels of stock are, or are not, reasonable?

A12 What is the 'opportunity cost' of high stock levels?

A13 What is the 'opportunity cost' of low stock levels?

A14 On what basis are stocks valued in a balance sheet?

A15 What is ABC analysis? Why is it useful?

A16 What are the two main risks in extending trade credit to customers?

A17 What are the two most important factors in determining the amount of debtors (accounts receivable) outstanding at any time?

A18 How can a $2\frac{1}{2}$ per cent discount represent an annual interest rate of 25 per cent?

A19 How can one assess whether a company's level of debtors is, or is not, reasonable?

A20 Why may it be undesirable for a company which sells on credit to have no bad debts at all?

A21 Will a company whose 'added value' is low tend to have (a) a high or (b) a low level of trade creditors? Why?

A22 Why is trade credit an important source of finance for many firms?

A23 Why is the amount of trade credit received likely for most companies to be less than the amount of trade credit given?

A24 What is a bill of exchange? What are its advantages?

A25 What is the difference between (a) 'accepting' and (b) 'discounting' a bill of exchange?

A26 Why may bills of exchange be especially useful in connection with export sales?

A27 Where on a company balance sheet do liabilities for taxes other than corporation tax appear?

A28 Why does a balance sheet normally show only the final dividend as a current liability, while the profit and loss account shows both the interim and final dividends?

A29 On what basis is interest calculated on bank overdrafts?

A30 In which two ways may advance receipts from customers be shown on a balance sheet?

A31 What are the two main measures of liquidity, and how are they calculated?

A32 How would you calculate the number of days' sales in debtors?

A33 Refer to Fig. 3.9 (page 51). Which measures of liquidity would be affected, and to what extent, if the certificates of tax deposit were set off against (deducted from) taxation liability?

A34 In what circumstances may it be acceptable for working capital to be negative?

A35 What is the difference between the current ratio and the acid test?

B. Exercises/Case Studies

B1 A company with annual sales of £120,000 physically 'turns over' its stock once every three months. Its cost of goods sold percentage (to sales revenue) is 60 per cent. What average level of investment in stocks (at cost) is held?

B2 A newsagent sells £500 worth of newspapers on credit each week. He sends out bills to credit customers once a quarter; and on average they take two weeks to pay.
   a. What is his average level of debtors? (assume one month = four and one-third weeks.)
   b. What will his average level of debtors amount to if he changes to sending out bills once a month? (Assume customers still take two weeks to pay.)
   c. How much would such a change save him per year, if interest rates are 18 per cent a year?

B3 From the following 'horizontal' balance sheet, calculate:
   (a) current ratio; (b) acid test ratio; (c) amount of working capital:

	£m.		£m.
Issued ordinary shares	1.0	Land	1.0
Reserves	1.5	Machinery	1.0
Long-term loan	1.0	Stocks	2.0
Creditors	1.0	Debtors	2.0
Bank overdraft	1.5		
	6.0		6.0

B4 A company with current liabilities of £120,000 has the following current
    assets: stocks £80,000; debtors £60,000; cash £40,000.
    a. What is its current ratio?
    b. What is its acid test ratio?
    c. What is its working capital?

B5 From the following 'vertical' balance sheet, calculate:
    (a) working capital to sales; (b) current ratio; (c) return on net assets:

		£m.
Fixed assets, net		6.0
Current assets	7.5	
Less: Current liabilities	4.0	
		3.5
		9.5
Long-term debt (15%)		2.0
Shareholders' funds		7.5
		9.5

Note: Sales = £8.0 million in the last year.
Profit before tax = £1.6 million in the last year.

B6 Refer to Fig. 3.4 (page 42) showing GEC's debtors at 31 March 1970
    and 1974. For the year ended 31 March 1978, GEC's sales were £2,343
    million, and end-of-year debtors were £526 million.
    a. How many days' sales were outstanding in debtors at March 1978?
    b. Based on actual 1978 sales, how much more or less would GEC have
       needed to invest in debtors at March 1978 if the days' sales in debtors
       had been the same as:
       i. March 1970?
       ii. March 1974?

B7 It is suggested that your firm encourage prompt payment by customers
    by offering a 2 per cent cash discount off the price of any order which is

paid within one month of delivery. At present the average period of delay before settlement is two-and-a-half months after delivery.

    a. As the finance director, and bearing in mind that your bank charges 15 per cent a year on the company's overdraft, comment on this suggestion.

    b. Would it be more attractive to offer a 3 per cent cash discount for settlement within 10 days after delivery? Why or why not?

B8 Refer to Fig. 3.5 (page 44). Suppose that the £45,000 sales in the last quarter of the year represented sales of £25,000 in October, £15,000 in November, and £5,000 in December. Using the method of calculation employed in Fig. 3.5, estimate how many days' sales are still owing at the end of December, if debtors amount to £30,000 at the end of December.

B9 A company's credit sales in a year are £150,000; and end-of-year debtors amount to £40,000. Terms are settlement within one month after invoice. Sales in the last four months of the year are as follows: September £20,000; October £15,000; November £12,000; December £8,000. How many days' sales are outstanding in debtors:

    a. Using the annual sales figures?

    b. Using the monthly sales figures?

    c. Using the monthly sales figures, but assuming the pattern of sales for the last four months of the year was: September £8,000; October £12,000; November £15,000; December £20,000?

B10 Refer to B9. Assuming that nobody has paid before the due date, both for parts (b) and (c) above, what proportion of total debtors at 31 December represent amounts that are:

    a. Overdue?

    b. At least one month overdue?

    c. More than two months overdue?

B11 Centaur Limited's balance sheet contains the following items: Stocks £55,000 (raw materials £15,000, work in progress £15,000, finished goods £25,000); Debtors £48,000; Creditors (for materials) £18,000. Annual sales amount to £180,000; and cost of goods sold represent $66\frac{2}{3}$ per cent of sales (of which materials amount to $33\frac{1}{3}$ per cent of sales). Assuming that work in progress represents on average goods which are half-finished, how many days' operations does net working capital represent (ignoring liquid resources and current liabilities other than creditors)?

B12 'How will our big companies with weakened balance sheets find the cash to pull out of recession without doing themselves further damage? ... At GKN, where they have shifted a third of the work force in two years ... they reckon they have an answer. Chairman Sir Trevor Holdsworth calculates that the company can put on more business without going to the banks. An extra £100 of sales at the margin will need another £21 in working capital – but will earn £30 in extra profits. On sums like that, who needs a rights issue (of ordinary shares, to raise more equity capital)?'

The Standard, 22 March 1982.

Assume that GKN is not liable to UK corporation tax on marginal profits; and that its *average* position is the same as its *marginal* position outlined above. Assume further:
(i) Sales are £2,000 million a year; (ii) fixed expenses are £500 million a year, and all other operating expenses are variable with sales; (iii) asset turnover is 2.0.

On the above assumptions, calculate:
a. Variable expenses for a year.
b. Operating profit (before interest and tax).
c. Working capital.
d. Fixed assets.
e. Return on net assets.

B13 *WALTON BAKERY LIMITED*

Michael Downing and Ronald Black, together with members of their families, each own 50 per cent of the shares in Walton Bakery Limited, a private company operating in a northern town of 90,000 people. Downing concentrates on sales and finance, while Black is responsible for production.

The bakery's annual sales turnover last year was £450,000. It has 60 retail accounts, of which 50 are small 'corner shops' selling a wide range of foodstuffs, while the other 10 are accounts with large stores and supermarkets.

Three basic financial ratios for Walton Bakery are as follows:

	1980	1981
1. Profit/Capital employed	28 %	31 %
2. Profit/Sales	11½%	12 %
3. Sales/Capital employed	2.5 times	2.6 times

Small shop accounts

The average size of a small shop's account is £80–£100, though Michael Downing has noticed a slight increase as the demand for pastries has grown. Their percentage of Walton's turnover has been declining:

	1978	1979	1980	1981
Sales to small shops (%)	93	65	60	52

Many bakeries require daily payment of accounts. Until four years ago Walton did the same, but Michael Downing has steadily relaxed this requirement, so that almost all the small shops now pay Walton weekly. Some small retailers are even pressing for longer credit periods.

Supermarket accounts

Walton's 10 supermarket accounts were won in competition against national and local bakeries. Downing believes he still needs to be very careful in handling these accounts, to make sure he does not lose them. At the same time, he wants to increase their volume of trade with Walton. This type of outlet now accounts for nearly half the sales, up from only 7 per cent in 1978, and Downing expects the trend to continue. Supermarket accounts are roughly five times larger than the small shops, averaging about £420 per week.

The large customers are completely different from small shops when it comes to paying accounts. As part of his effort to gain the supermarkets' business, Downing agreed to relax his rules about weekly payment. Indeed, he now finds *them* tending to tell him when they'll pay! At present they pay anywhere between four and eight weeks in arrear.

Downing believes it would be difficult to insist on any of his customers paying at shorter intervals. Being too hard on the small retailers might force them out of business altogether, while if he is firm with the supermarkets he may lose their business to competitors.

Raw materials stocks

The total value of raw materials stocks amounts at its highest to £7,200: almost £3,000 of flour, and over £4,000 of other stocks. The *average* level of flour stocks is five days' supply, amounting to £1,800. The level of the other raw materials stocks, such as sugar, yeast, currants, wrappings, etc., normally amounts to 10–14 days' supply.

Downing recognises that many bakeries operate successfully with only one to two days' supply, and five days' supply of other materials; but he does not think Walton Bakery should follow suit. He considers that the bakery should never risk running out of stock, thus delaying or completely stopping production.

The problem

The company's bank manager, Mr Hobson, has asked Downing to reduce Walton's overdraft by 20 per cent over the next three months. At the moment, overdraft facilities stand at £30,000, having risen from £12,000 in 1978.

Downing doesn't think the company is in any real financial difficulty, and he thinks he could raise about £6,000 privately if necessary. However Mr Hobson's request has highlighted a worrying trend of the last four years. Overdraft facilities have risen considerably (more than the 65% level of inflation over the period); but the bakery still finds it hard to keep within the ceiling. Downing thinks this problem stems from the growth in supermarket trade, and because the paying habits of small retailers have deteriorated.

Mr Hobson has suggested another explanation. Not only is the bakery's credit control rather loose, he believes, but also the stock policies are much too conservative. In short, the bank manager thinks that Walton has excessive working capital, and could be operated far more efficiently.

Many of the possible ways of reducing the overdraft have already been ruled out. Downing and Black don't want ownership of the company to be further shared, for the time being at least. They are determined that the company should remain exclusively a family concern.

Borrowing the money from another source, even if it were possible, would not overcome the real problem. Nor would employing the services of a debt **factor** be practicable for the collection of daily accounts. Downing will not allow Walton's own debts to suppliers to remain outstanding for longer periods, for fear of delays in deliveries of raw materials.

As a result, Downing sees only three choices left:
a. he can increase the permanent capital of the business by putting up more equity capital;
b. he can cut back on credit to customers; or
c. he can cut back on stock levels.

Which alternative would you choose? Why?

B14 *TELFORD TOYS*

Telford Toys Limited made plastic toys for children, and most of its products were in a wide range of designs, colours, and sizes; including cars, guns, spaceships, musical instruments and animals. Sales of a particular item could vary by as much as one third from one year to the next. With low capital requirements and simple technology, making plastic toys was a highly competitive business, with many small companies. Any popular new toy generally commanded very high margins until competitors were able to offer a similar product. For example, Telford's introduction of flying saucers in 1979 had earned large profits; but next year several competitors had marketed a similar product and Telford's factory price for the item had dropped sharply.

Telford's sales were £3 million in 1981, and on the strength of a number of promising new products were projected at £3.6 million for 1982. Estimates of sales volume had usually been reliable in the past. Net profits had reached £86,000 in 1981 and were forecast at £108,000 in 1982 after taxes of 50 per cent. The cost of goods sold was expected to stay at about 80 per cent of sales in 1982.

Expanding operations had resulted in a strained working capital position. The company had arranged a bank overdraft, and £164,000 was outstanding at the end of 1981. The company had been assured that the bank would be willing to extend the overdraft up to £500,000 in 1982. Interest would be charged at 20 per cent a year, and any overdraft above £500,000 would be subject to further negotiations.

The company's sales were highly seasonal, over 80 per cent of annual revenue being earned during August–November. Sales were made mostly to large department store chains and toy brokers. On average customers took 60 days to pay.

The company's production processes were not complex. All runs begun were completed on the same day, so there was virtually no work-in-progress. Purchases on net 30-day terms were made weekly to cover next week's production. Telford paid trade creditors promptly.

Telford's practice was to produce in response to customer orders. Only a small proportion of capacity was needed to meet demand during the first seven months of the year. The first big orders for Christmas business arrived at the beginning of August. For the rest of the year the work force was greatly expanded and put on overtime, and all equipment was used 16 hours a day. In 1981 overtime premiums had totalled £166,000. Whenever possible deliveries were made on the same day that an order was produced; hence production and sales in each month tended to be equal.

Mr Matthews, managing director and part owner of Telford, believed the company would be able to limit capital expenditure in 1982 to an amount equal to depreciation, though 1982's projected volume would approach the full capacity of Telford's equipment. As in the past, monthly pro forma balance sheets and profit and loss accounts based on an assumption of seasonal production had been prepared for 1982. These appear in Exhibits 1 and 2.

Mr Matthews was well aware of the many problems caused by the company's method of scheduling production. Overtime premiums reduced profits. Seasonal expansion and contraction of the work force resulted in recruiting difficulties and high training and quality control costs. Machinery stood idle for half the year, then was subjected to heavy use. Accelerated production schedules during the peak season resulted in frequent set-up changes on the machinery, causing seemingly unavoidable confusion in scheduling runs and inefficiencies in assembly packaging as workers found difficulty relearning their operations.

For these reasons, Mr Matthews was seriously considering adopting a policy of level monthly production in 1982. Purchase terms would not be affected by the rescheduling of purchases. Eliminating overtime wage premiums would mean substantial savings, estimated at £180,000 in 1982. Moreover Mr Matthews expected that significant additional direct labour savings, amounting to £70,000, would result from more orderly production. A portion of the savings would be offset, however, by higher storage and handling costs, estimated at £30,000 annually. Mr Matthews speculated on the effect that level production might have on the company's funds requirements in 1982. The main changes would be to levels of stocks and creditors. To simplify the problem, Mr Matthews decided to assume that gross margin percentages would not vary significantly by months under either method of production. Operating expenses were thought likely to be incurred evenly throughout each month of 1982 under either seasonal or level production.

£000

Exhibit 1

Pro forma balance sheets 1982 (seasonal production)

	Dec.81	Jan.	Feb.	March	April	May	June	July	Aug.	Sept.	Oct.	Nov.	Dec.	Total
a. Net plant and equipment	428	428	428	428	428	428	428	428	428	428	428	428	428	428
b. Stocks	212	212	212	212	212	212	212	212	212	212	212	212	212	212
c. Debtors	1,051	383	93	108	108	100	100	108	641	1,245	1,432	1,593	1,226	
d. Cash	–	376	636	593	559	535	503	467	166	–	–	–	–	
	1,691	1,399	1,369	1,341	1,307	1,275	1,243	1,215	1,447	1,885	2,072	2,233	1,866	
Shareholders' funds	1,175	1,158	1,142	1,127	1,111	1,095	1,079	1,064	1,101	1,146	1,202	1,263	1,283	
Long-term debt	160	160	160	160	160	160	160	160	160	160	160	160	160	
d. Bank overdraft	146	–	–	–	–	–	–	–	–	324	367	390	110	
e. Trade creditors	102	13	15	17	15	15	15	17	175	199	231	247	121	
f. Tax liability	108	68	52	37	21	5	(11)	(26)	11	56	112	173	192	
	1,691	1,399	1,369	1,341	1,307	1,275	1,243	1,215	1,447	1,885	2,072	2,233	1,866	

Notes:

a. Assumes equipment purchases equal to depreciation expense (estimated at £8,000 per month).
b. Assumes stocks maintained at December 1981 level throughout 1982.
c. Assumes 60-day collection period.
d. Balancing figure (cash January to August, bank overdraft September to December).
e. Assumed equal to 30 per cent of the current month's sales. Related to material purchases of £1,080,000 for year, against sales of £3,600,000, this represents a 30-day period. Since stocks are level, purchases will follow seasonal production and sales pattern.
f. £84,000 tax on 1981 profit is due on 1 January 1983.

Exhibit 2

Pro Forma profit and loss accounts 1982 (seasonal production)

	Jan.	Feb.	March	April	May	June	July	Aug.	Sept.	Oct.	Nov.	Dec.	Total
Net sales	43	50	58	50	50	50	58	583	662	770	823	403	3,600
g. Cost of goods sold	34	40	46	40	40	40	46	467	530	616	659	322	2,880
Gross profit	9	10	12	10	10	10	12	116	132	154	164	81	720
Operating expenses	42	42	42	42	42	42	42	42	42	42	42	42	504
Profit (loss) before tax	(33)	(32)	(30)	(32)	(32)	(32)	(30)	74	90	112	122	39	216
h. Corporation tax	(16)	(16)	(15)	(16)	(16)	(16)	(15)	37	45	56	61	19	108
Profit (loss) after tax	(17)	(16)	(15)	(16)	(16)	(16)	(15)	37	45	56	61	20	108

g. Assumes cost of goods sold equal to 80 per cent of sales revenue.
h. Brackets show tax credits from operating losses, and reduce tax liability on balance sheet.

Questions

a. Prepare monthly pro forma balance sheets for 1982 assuming level production.

b. Compare the projected need for bank borrowing under level production with the need under seasonal production.

   a. How does the maximum need compare?

   b. How many months does the overdraft need exceed £500,000?

   c. What bank interest would be payable under each production method in 1982?

c. What would be the net effect on profit before tax of switching to level production in 1982?

d. Apart from the direct financial effects, what advantages and disadvantages do you see in switching from seasonal to level production in 1982? (a) In production; (b) in marketing; (c) in other areas of the business.

e. What alternatives are available concerning production in 1982? On balance, what action would you recommend? (If you need more information, say what it is and why you need it.)

B15 *DRAGON PAINT LIMITED*

On 21 April 1982, Mr Joseph Hamilton of Northern Stores, Newcastle, asked Mr William Simon, the north-east regional credit manager of Dragon Paint, to approve three-year credit terms of a £20,000 initial order for a basic inventory of the complete line of Dragon products. Mr Hamilton also wanted to know what credit terms could be arranged for 'fill-in' orders to replace goods sold. He understood that fill-in orders were usually offered on a 1/10, n/60 basis. (This means that a 1% discount was offered for payment within 10 days; otherwise net payment was due within 60 days.) He reckoned that Northern should be able to do an annual volume with Dragon of over £100,000 if such terms were offered.

Dragon Paint was operating near capacity in the spring of 1982. But with the recession dragging on, the company was preparing for increasingly keen competition, and was actively seeking new outlets through which to sell its products. Northern Stores Limited had a good reputation for being an aggressive merchandising organisation; and Dragon's weakest market coverage was in the north-east. Based on Northern's sales of paint products in past years, Mr Simon estimated that Dragon's sales should run in excess of £60,000 per year. All Northern's sales would be in more or less new territory, since only a few small hardware stores were currently handling Dragon's line in the north-east.

Dragon had often offered initial terms up to five years to enable new dealerships to purchase permanent display and back-up stock. Such arrangements were thought necessary to get adequate market coverage and to continue large volume operations, since new dealerships were often excellent market outlets but financially under-capitalised.

Dragon's credit department classified its accounts into three categories: (A) well-financed customers; (B) moderately-financed customers; and (C) financially weak customers. At 31 March 1982, category C accounts totalled just over £250,000 for accounts sold on regular terms. Mr Simon knew that Northern Stores Limited would fall in the C group, and believed that a decline in general business activity could bring substantial bad debt losses. In his view, the fact that Dragon's bad debt losses had been less than one half of one per cent of credit sales since 1975 did not measure possible losses in a bad recession.

On the other hand, about one fifth of the company's total expenses continued regardless of sales, and Dragon continually needed to get more sales volume in order to spread those fixed expenses as widely as possible.

Mr Simon reckoned there was a definite chance that Northern Stores, if allowed credit, might in the end prove unable to pay in full. Even so, he wondered if enough volume might have been achieved in the meantime to more than offset any loss.

Questions:

a. What cash flows do you estimate will result if the proposed credit terms are granted?

b. On what basis (according to what criteria) would you, as Mr Simon, make a decision?

c. Would you, as Mr Simon, offer the requested credit terms to Northern Stores Limited?

d. How, if at all, would you propose to modify the terms requested?

	£m.	
Fixed assets		11.1
Current assets		
Stock	11.9	
Debtors (net of £200,000 bad debt reserve)	7.2	
Cash and liquid resources	5.6	
Less: *Current liabilities*	(7.3)	
	——	17.4
Net assets		28.5
Shareholders' funds		23.3
Long-term borrowing		5.2
Capital employed		28.5

Fig. 1: Dragon Paint Limited, Balance Sheet, 31 December 1981.

	£m.
Sales	61.3
Cost of sales	49.5
Gross profit	11.8
Overhead expenses (including bad debts £37,000)	7.5
Profit before tax	4.3[1]
Tax	2.3
Profit after tax	2.0

[1] Total costs were composed of about 20 per cent fixed costs, with about 80 per cent variable with the volume of production.

Fig. 2: Dragon Paint Limited, Profit and Loss Account, 1981.

C. Essay Questions

C1 In what respects do the financial implications of investment in working capital differ from those relating to fixed assets?

C2 How would inflation affect a company's working capital?

C3 How would a 'credit squeeze' affect a company's working capital?

C4 'Stocks are the link between production and selling.' Discuss, with special reference to the financial implications.

C5 How can stocks (a) damp down and (b) accentuate business fluctuations?

C6 What are the main principles on which a company should aim to control the total amount of trade credit granted to customers?

C7 '*No* bad debts is too few.' Comment.

C8 What are the advantages and disadvantages of a high level of trade creditors?

C9 Should bank overdrafts be regarded as deductions from working capital, or as part of (long-term) capital employed? Was the Imperial Group Limited wrong to treat more than £300 million of short-term borrowings in 1980 as part of capital employed?

C10 'The corporation tax liability in company accounts represents, in effect, an interest-free loan from the government.' Discuss.

C11 What effect would the abolition of trade credit have on the financing of different industries?

C12 Why is caution necessary before drawing conclusions from comparing a company's current ratio with the rule of thumb of 2.0 to 1?

Chapter 4

Long-term Investment Projects

Objective: *To describe the background to capital investment decisions; to outline the two main 'traditional' appraisal methods; to discuss the concept of 'opportunity cost' and the time value of money; to outline the two main discounted cash flow methods (net present value and internal rate of return), together with ways of allowing for tax, uncertainty and inflation.*

Synopsis: *The most important thing is finding good projects. Of the traditional appraisal methods, average accounting rate of return ignores the* timing *of returns, while payback ignores* profit. *The opportunity cost of capital can be used as an 'exchange rate over time' to compare payments now with receipts in future. The two main DCF methods involve estimating both the* amount *and the* timing *of a capital project's expected future cash flows. Net present value discounts the cash flows, using a criterion discount rate, to see if the project's 'value' exceeds its costs. Internal Rate of Return compares the discount rate which produces a zero NPV (the IRR) with the criterion rate. But financial evaluation of capital projects should not be regarded as the only consideration that matters.*

4.1 Background to Capital Investment

4.1.1 Capital Projects

Capital **investment** means spending money now on capital goods in the hope of getting sufficient returns later. Commercial businesses invest money with the intention of making a *profit*. Thus investment as such is not necessarily desirable: what is desired is profitable investment.

Three main categories of capital investment are: replacement of equipment, expansion of productive capacity to meet growing demand, or provision of new facilities to make new products. The cost of education can be regarded as a form of investment in 'human capital'.

Undertaking a capital investment 'project' in a company involves a number of steps. They can be portrayed in terms of a decision framework (Fig. 4.1) similar to that set out in *Decision Making in Organisations* by Jim Clifford (in this series). In this chapter we shall be dealing mainly with the two shaded sections, on planning and decision (Fig. 4.1).

4.1.2 Identifying the Project

Easily the most important stage is the first: finding good projects. That requires imagination, creativity and alertness to spot the investment opportunity. The analytical techniques discussed in this chapter merely enable us to tell *how* good a project is, once it has been thought of. Businessmen in the past were able to make huge profits even though they had never heard of sophisticated methods of investment appraisal. It is also worth remembering that business success usually requires a certain amount of *luck*!

Army men say: 'Time spent in reconnaissance is never wasted.' The same is probably true of capital projects which are often 'irreversible', in that it may be impossible to abandon large projects except at a significant loss. Before burying oneself in the complexities of detailed analysis, it is nearly always worth ensuring that *all* practical alternatives have been considered. (If there

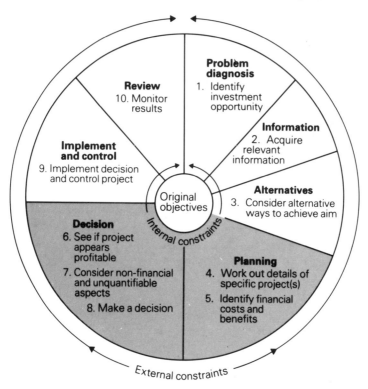

Fig. 4.1: Capital investment decision framework.

is literally 'no alternative' to a proposed course of action, then *there is no decision to be made!*)

Reaching a satisfactory answer may depend on asking the right question. For example, in capital investment proposals the alternatives may be:

a. *whether or not* to buy machine H;
b. whether to buy *machine H or machine J*;
c. whether to buy machine H *now or later*;
d. whether to *buy or lease* machine H.

For the moment we shall assume that the initial capital investment consists of a single lump sum at the start of the project. Later this simplifying assumption will be modified.

4.1.3 Estimated Benefits from a Project

It can be difficult to estimate accurately the future net benefits from a project. What consumers will want to buy in a few years' time, what competitors will be up to, how production methods may change – all are uncertain. Yet they may affect the project's life, sales volume, selling prices, costs.

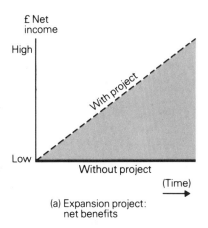
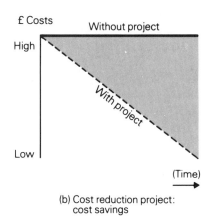

Fig. 4.2: Incremental benefits for different types of project.

We are always trying to identify the net *improvement* expected to result from a project. The forecast of sales revenue is often critical. For example, publishers may be able to calculate costs quite accurately, with a fixed selling price, but sales *volume* may be highly uncertain; or petrol companies may be fairly sure how much petrol they will sell, but not what the price will be. On the other hand, ship-building on a fixed-price contract would provide relatively certain sales revenue, but with uncertain costs and timing.

In an 'expansion' or 'new product' project, investing money will be expected to increase sales revenue by more than operating costs. The future expected *net* benefits are then compared with the initial investment (by methods we shall be discussing in the next sections).

A 'cost reduction' project, in contrast, may not affect sales revenue at all: it may simply reduce future operating costs. Such reductions are then regarded as the future 'benefits' of the project (compared to what would happen without it), and related to the initial investment. Thus in Fig. 4.2 the shaded areas represent the incremental benefit resulting from (a) an expansion project, and (b) a cost reduction project.

4.2 Simple Appraisal Methods

4.2.1 Average Rate of Return on Investment
Profitability is often expressed as an annual rate of **return on investment**. This approach can be used for particular future capital investment projects as well as for the past financial results of a whole business (see 1.2.3).

Example: Two alternative proposals for capital investment, Project A and Project B, are illustrated in Fig. 4.3. Project A requires an initial investment of £6,000, Project B of £12,000. These investment outflows are shown as negative amounts occurring at the 'end of Year 0'. Each project will last for three years. Project A will produce cash receipts of £3,000 in Year 1, £4,000 in Year 2, and £8,000 in Year 3; while Project B will produce cash inflows of £7,000 in Year 1, £8,000 in Year 2 and £9,000 in Year 3. These cash receipts are shown as positive amounts in the years concerned. The total 'net profit' is calculated by deducting the initial investment for each project from its total cash receipts.

		Project A ($£$'000)	Project B ($£$'000)
Investment	Year 0	− 6	−12
Cash Inflows	Year 1	+ 3	+ 7
	Year 2	+ 4	+ 8
	Year 3	+ 8	+ 9
1. Total cash inflows		+15	+24★
2. Total net profit		+ 9	+12★
3. Average annual profit		+ 3	+ 4★
4. $\dfrac{\text{Average annual profit}}{\text{Initial investment}}$		$\dfrac{3}{6} = 50\%$★	$\dfrac{4}{12} = 33\%$

Fig. 4.3: Project A versus Project B.

Project B produces higher total cash inflows (1) than Project A (24 versus 15). If we deduct the initial investment in each case from total cash inflows, Project B produces a higher total net profit (2) over the three years than Project A (12 versus 9). Accountants would call this charging 'depreciation': spreading the cost of the initial investment in fixed assets (probably in equal annual instalments) over the life of the project. Because the projects have the same life (three years) Project B also produces a higher average annual profit ('return') (3) than Project A (4 versus 3).

But if we divide the average annual profit by the initial amount invested, Project A produces a higher rate of return on investment (4) than Project B (50% versus 33%). Hence, using the 'rate of return on investment' approach, Project A would be preferred to Project B.

In using accounting figures to derive the average rate of return on investment, there are some tricky accounting questions to deal with. What precisely do we mean by 'return'? (Is it before or after tax? What about depreciation?) What do we mean by 'investment'? (Should we use initial or average investment? Should we include assets at original cost, or after deducting accumulated depreciation?)

Many businessmen, however, do not bother too much about the finer points of analysis. They find it relatively *simple* to calculate rates of return, and are often prepared to use the results as a guide to tell which capital projects seem financially worth investing in.

The average annual rate of return on investment (expressed as a percentage) tells us something about the profitability of a capital project. But the *averaging* process eliminates relevant information about the *timing* of returns.

Example: Suppose that Project A (details as before) is now to be compared with Project C (Fig. 4.4). The only difference between them is that while Project A's profits (rather than its cash receipts) are £1,000, £2,000 and £6,000 in Years 1, 2, and 3 respectively, Project C's profits are £6,000, £2,000 and £1,000. The order is reversed.

		Project A (£'000)	Project C (£'000)
Investment	Year 0	− 6	− 6
	Year 1	+ 1	+ 6
Net profits	Year 2	+ 2	+ 2
	Year 3	+ 6	+ 1
1. Total net profits		+ 9	+ 9
2. Average annual profit		+ 3	+ 3

Fig. 4.4: Project A versus Project C.

The average annual rate of return on investment is the same for both projects: 50 per cent a year (3/6). The only difference is that Project C gives a return £5,000 higher than Project A in Year 1, but £5,000 lower in Year 3. In total this difference 'averages out'; but it is of commercial significance.

The extra £5,000 received in Year 1 under Project C can be invested *for two years in the capital (money) markets, to yield a positive return (rate of interest). Thus taking this 'opportunity cost' into account (see 2.3), Project C is preferable to Project A.*

But this conclusion is *not* revealed by the simple method of calculating the average annual rate of return on investment – which *ignores* the *timing* of the returns.

4.2.2 Payback

The simple average rate of return on investment method of evaluating capital investment projects is widely used, despite its failure to allow for the *timing* of returns. Probably even simpler and more widely used is the **payback** method. This shows how many years it will take before the original amount invested in a capital project is 'paid back', i.e. before the cumulative returns exceed the initial investment. The shorter the payback period the better.

When calculating the payback period, it is usual to look at *cash* receipts from a project, rather than *accounting profits*. (We already know from **2.2** that they may differ.) Thus in calculating a project's net cash inflows, only *cash* expenses should be deducted from sales revenues, not depreciation.

Let us now use the figures for Project A and Project C again (Fig. 4.5).

		Project A (£'000)	Project C (£'000)
Investment	Year 0	− 6	− 6
	Year 1	+ 3	+ 8
Cash inflows	Year 2	+ 4	+ 4
	Year 3	+ 8	+ 3

Fig. 4.5: Cash flows for Project A and Project C.

Example: The 'payback period' for Project A can easily be calculated. £3,000 is 'repaid' in Year 1, and £4,000 in Year 2. Thus Project A's payback period is one-and-three-quarter years. (One year at £3,000 + three-quarters of a year at £4,000 equals the initial investment of £6,000.)

Similarly we can calculate Project C's payback period as nine months. Only three-quarters of the £8,000 cash inflow in Year 1 is needed to recover the initial investment of £6,000 (assuming that cash is received evenly throughout the year).

These results can be shown graphically, as in Fig. 4.6.

The payback method has one clear advantage over the average rate of return on investment method: it does take *timing* into account. Each project had the

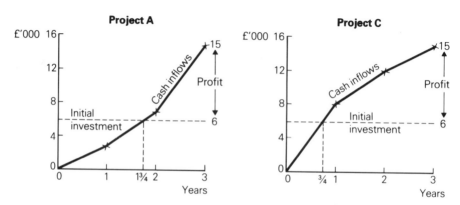

Fig. 4.6: Payback periods for Project A and Project C.

same 50 per cent rate of return; but Project C has a payback period of only nine months, compared with Project A's one-and-three-quarter years. But although a shorter payback period is preferable to a longer one, it is not clear what is the *maximum* payback period that would be acceptable. (In other words, the 'criterion' period is not easy to establish.)

Even more important, the payback method ignores cash receipts expected *after* payback. This is vital: there can be no profit unless we get back *more* than the original investment. Suppose, for example, that in Year 4 Project A produced a cash inflow of £10,000, while Project C produced only £1,000. According to the payback method, that would not change the relative attractiveness of the two projects: Project C would still be better than Project A. Indeed, even if Project A produced a cash inflow of £1 million in Year 4, that would make *no difference at all* to its calculated payback period of one-and-three-quarter years!

Thus while it may be a useful measure of *risk* (the sooner the payback the less the risk), *the payback method does not measure profitability*. In practice payback is often used – even by large companies – as a rough 'screening' device. But for more precise calculations of the profitability of capital projects, better methods are available – to which we now turn.

4.3 Measuring Profit Over Time

4.3.1 The 'Time Value' of Money

Investment means spending money now in the hope of getting returns later. To tell whether the returns are large enough to produce a *profit*, we need a way to compare returns in the *future* with investment *now*.

A given amount of money now is worth *more* than the same amount of money in future. Why? Because it can be invested today to yield a return in the meantime. This is the 'opportunity cost' concept we saw in 2.3. The rate of interest does *not* merely represent inflation: it also allows for time preference and risk (see 2.3.2).

Let us suppose that money can be invested today to yield 10 per cent a year; then £100 invested today will accumulate (compounding annually) to the amounts shown below:

In 1 year's time, to £100 × 1.10 = £100 × 1.100 = £110.00
In 2 years' time, to £100 × (1.10)² = £100 × 1.210 = £121.00
In 3 years' time, to £100 × (1.10)³ = £100 × 1.331 = £133.10.

Thus, using an interest rate of 10 per cent a year, the *future value* of '£100 now' is '£133.10 at the end of three years'. We can say the same thing the other way round: the **present value** of '£133.10 to be received at the end of three years' is '£100 (now)'.

	End of Year 0* (£)	End of Year 1 (£)	End of Year 2 (£)	End of Year 3 (£)
Future values	100.00 ⟶ 110.00 ⟶ 121.00 ⟶ 133.10			
Present values	⎧ 100.00 ⟵ 110.00			
	⎨ 100.00 ⟵—————— 121.00			
	⎩ 100.00 ⟵——————————————— 133.10			

* The 'End of Year 0' is 'the present', or simply 'now'.

Fig. 4.7: Future values of '£100 now' at 10 per cent a year.

What, then, is the present value of *£100.00* to be received at the end of three years? Clearly it must be £75.13, as shown below:

$$\frac{£100.00}{(1.10)^3} = \frac{£100.00}{1.331}\left[\text{ or } \frac{£100.00}{£133.10} \times £100.00\right] = £75.13$$

We can prove this, by showing what would happen if we invested £75.13 at 10 per cent a year. Each year the effect of compound interest is to add 10 per cent of the start-of-year cumulative amount invested:

After 1 year the amount becomes: £75.13 + £7.51 =   £82.64
After 2 years the amount becomes: £82.64 + £8.27 =   £90.91
After 3 years the amount becomes: £90.91 + £9.09 = │ £100.00 │

Thus we can show the present value of £100.00 to be received at any future date.

	End of Year 0 (£)	End of Year 1 (£)	End of Year 2 (£)	End of Year 3 (£)
Future values	75.13 ⟶ 82.64 ⟶ 90.91 ⟶ 100.00			
│ Present values │	⎧ 90.91 ⟵ 100.00			
	⎨ 82.64 ⟵—————— 100.00			
	⎩ 75.13 ⟵——————————————— 100.00			

Fig. 4.8: Present values of '£100.00 in future' at 10 per cent a year.

Assuming an interest rate of 10 per cent a year, the present value of *any* amount (call it *x*) to be received at the end of three years is £0.7513*x*. 0.7513 is the **discount factor** for three years at 10 per cent a year. It is equivalent to $1 \div (1.10)^3$.

In effect this gives us an 'exchange rate over time'. Just as compound factors tell us the future values of present money amounts, so *discount factors tell us the present values of future money amounts*. (See the Appendix for tables of discount factors on pages 224 and 225.)

In Fig. 4.9 a vertical *log-scale* shows the accumulating amounts connected by *straight lines*. Since the rate of increase is a constant 10 per cent a year, all the lines are parallel. (With an ordinary vertical scale, the chart would show *upward-curving* lines for the cumulative amounts, representing compound interest.)

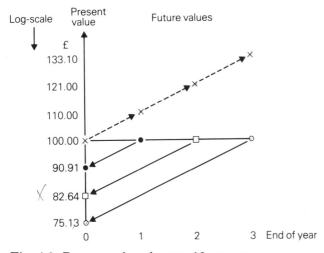

Fig. 4.9: Present value chart at 10 per cent a year.

You should be able to read off Fig. 4.9.:

a. what £300 invested today would accumulate to in two years' time,
b. the 'present value' of £200 receivable at the end of year 3,
c. how long it would take for £82.64 to accumulate to £121.00.
(*Answers are shown at the foot of page 76.*)

4.3.2 The 'Opportunity Cost' of Capital

We have been assuming that we can always invest any sum of money now (say with a bank) to yield an annual return of 10 per cent. In practice it is not always easy to estimate this rate of interest (the 'opportunity cost' of capital), as we shall discuss in more detail in Chapter 7.

★ See Question B1

If the relevant opportunity cost is 10 per cent a year, then that is the **required rate of return** on a capital investment project, also called the **criterion rate**, or 'hurdle rate' or 'cut-off rate'. If money deposited with a bank will yield 10 per cent a year, why invest in any capital project expected to yield *less* than 10 per cent a year? We need to get a higher return from any particular capital project for it to be worth investing in.

Using an annual interest rate enables us to compare money amounts receivable, or payable, at different points in time.

4.4 Discounted Cash Flow Methods

4.4.1 Net Present Value

The **net present value** (NPV) method of investment appraisal calculates a project's profit by comparing cash payments and cash receipts at the *same* point in time. It does so by discounting expected future cash flows *back to the present* (i.e. back to the end of Year 0); and then comparing the total *present value* of the future cash receipts with (the present value of) the cash payment(s) representing the capital investment in the project.

The NPV method multiplies future cash flows by a suitable discounting factor, which is equivalent to dividing by the appropriate compounding factor. The discounting factor depends on two things: the **discount rate** being used, and the number of years in future that the cash flow arises.

Example: A (non-returnable) investment now of £10,000 in Project D is expected to produce £3,000 cash at the end of year 1, £4,000 at the end of year 2 and £5,000 at the end of year 3. Assuming that money could otherwise be invested (e.g. with a bank) to earn 10 per cent a year, should the company invest in Project D or not?

End of year (EOY)	Cash flows (£)		Discount factor (at 10%)	'Present' EOY 0 value (£)	(£)
0	− 10,000	$[\div (1.10)^0] \times$	1.000 =	− 10,000	= − 10,000
1	+ 3,000	$[\div (1.10)^1] \times$	0.909 =	+ 2,727	
2	+ 4,000	$[\div (1.10)^2] \times$	0.827 =	+ 3,308	= + 9,790
3	+ 5,000	$[\div (1.10)^3] \times$	0.751 =	+ 3,755	
				Net present value =	− 210

Fig. 4.10: Net present value of Project D.

Treating cash payments as negative, and cash receipts as positive, we see
that the net present value of Project D is negative. The 'cost' of investing in
Project D is £10,000 now, while the gross present value of the receipts is £9,790.
Thus Project D amounts to a proposal to pay out £10,000 now in order to
acquire the rights to future cash flows which have a (present) value of £9,790.
That is hardly smart business: it represents a loss (in present value terms) of
£210. Because its net present value (NPV) is negative, Project D is not
financially worthwhile.

Note that we round off all amounts to the nearest pound. There is absolutely
no advantage in seeking more accuracy. Our figures for cash flows are usually
no more than estimates; and the discount rate used is nearly always only an
approximation.

The net present value (NPV) method compares cash receipts and payments
expected to result from a capital project. It multiplies them by discounting
factors to translate all the expected cash flows from a project into 'present
values' (i.e. into end of year 0 money terms). This approach can be shown
graphically:

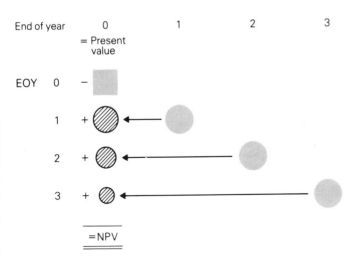

Fig. 4.11: The discounting process in net present value.

4.4.2 Project Valuation

Discounted cash flow (DCF) methods involve forecasting both the *amount*
and the *timing* of **incremental cash flows** (*not* accounting income and expenses) which are expected to result if a particular project is undertaken, but
not otherwise. To tell whether a project is expected to be profitable, we simply
see whether or not the present value of the project's discounted cash inflows
exceeds (the present value of) the cash investment involved.

In other words, we first 'value' the project, and then compare that amount with the project's *cost*. This will often simply be the initial amount of the cash investment, though sometimes projects consist of several cash payments spread out over time, which themselves need to be discounted to 'present value' terms. If the project's value is more than its cost (i.e. if it has a positive net present value), then it is worth undertaking on financial grounds: it will increase the business owner's wealth.

A way of picturing the valuation process is shown in Fig. 4.12.

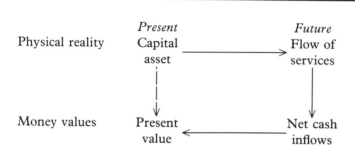

Fig. 4.12: Valuing a capital asset.

The net present value method, in theory, will always give the 'correct' answer – if one assumes that:
a. the amounts and timing of the cash flows are correctly forecast;
b. the opportunity cost of capital is correctly estimated;
c. there are no non-financial aspects to a capital project.
   The sweeping and unrealistic nature of these necessary qualifications makes it clear that in practice no *method of analysis can be guaranteed to give a precisely 'correct' answer.*

4.4.3 Internal Rate of Return

Another method of discounting cash flows is often used instead of the net present value method. This is the **internal rate of return** method (also called the **DCF yield** method).

The net present value method lists the *amount* and *timing* of all the expected future cash flows from a project; and applies a pre-selected (criterion) discount rate, to see whether the *net* total of all the discounted cash flows is positive or negative. If the NPV is positive, then the project is worthwhile; if the NPV is negative, then it is not.

a. £363.00; b. £150.26; c. four years.

In contrast, the internal rate of return method determines, by trial and error, *what is* the (initially unknown) discount rate which, when applied to the same cash flows, will produce a net present value of exactly *zero*. That discount rate is the 'internal rate of return' of the project: it must then be compared with the criterion rate to see whether or not the project is worthwhile.

Example: In Project D, a 10 per cent discount rate produced an NPV of $-£210$. *We know that a* zero *discount rate would produce an NPV of* $+£2,000$. *(This is reached by simply adding up the* undiscounted *cash flows:* $-£10,000 +£3,000 +£4,000 +£5,000 = +£2,000$.) *Therefore, since the sign changes, the internal rate of return (IRR) – which has to produce an NPV of zero – must lie between 0 and 10 per cent. And since* $-£210$ *is much closer to zero than is* $+£2,000$, *the IRR will lie closer to 10 per cent than to 0 per cent.*

Using the 'trial and error' method of finding the internal rate of return, suppose we first try a discount rate of 9 per cent (Fig. 4.13).

End of year	Cash flows (£)		Discount factor (at 9%)	Present value (£)	(£)
0	− 10,000	×	1.000 =	− 10,000	= − 10,000
1	+ 3,000	$[÷ (1.09)^1] = ×$	0.917 =	+ 2,751	
2	+ 4,000	$[÷ (1.09)^2] = ×$	0.842 =	+ 3,368	= + 9,979
3	+ 5,000	$[÷ (1.09)^3] = ×$	0.772 =	+ 3,860	
			Net present value =		− 21

Fig. 4.13: Internal rate of return of Project D.

The net present value of $-£21$ *is close enough to zero; so in practice we would reckon the internal rate of return as being (just under) 9 per cent a year. Since the required rate of return is 10 per cent, Project D's 'internal' rate of return is not high enough to justify investing in it.*

In fact, we could plot the net present value of Project D for a whole *range* of different discount rates, as in Fig. 4.14.

Three values in particular are worth noting:

1. Using a 0 per cent discount rate, the NPV is $+£2,000$. This can be found simply by deducting the (undiscounted) cash outflow from the (undiscounted) total of the cash inflows.
2. Using a 10 per cent discount rate, the NPV is $-£210$. This is the figure we found earlier, when using 10 per cent as the 'opportunity cost' criterion rate.
3. The Net present value is *zero* at a discount rate of 8.9 per cent. This is the 'precise' internal rate of return.

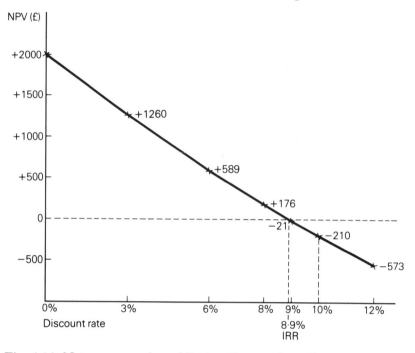

Fig. 4.14: Net present value of Project D at various discount rates.

4.5 DCF Refinements

4.5.1 Investment Outflows

The amount to be included as the 'investment' may be split into two parts:

1. Fixed capital investment (e.g. on factory buildings, machines, etc.), which is usually reduced by **first-year tax allowances**.
2. Working capital investment (e.g. in stocks to support an expansion project). This is usually expected to be recovered at the end of the project (see **4.5.2**).

Cash payments for a project which are spread out over time can be discounted back to present value in the same way as estimates of future cash receipts.

4.5.2 End-of-Project Capital Recovery

Possible limitations to a project's economic life include:

a. Physical exhaustion of equipment.
b. Technical obsolescence of equipment or process.

c. Market factors, such as changing consumer tastes.
d. An arbitrary **horizon** date.

Amounts recoverable at the end of a project's life may stem from:
a. Value of land or buildings.
b. Scrap or second-hand value of equipment.
c. Working capital.

Even when the amount invested is recovered later, as is usually assumed for working capital, the time value of money is still relevant. Capital has an opportunity cost for the period it is invested in a project; so the amount expected to be recovered must be discounted back to present value.

For long projects it is common to use an arbitrary 'horizon' period of 10 or perhaps 15 years, beyond which no cash flows are included even if the project is actually expected to last longer. With a fairly high discount rate this may not make much difference. (For example, with a 15 per cent discount rate, extending the horizon from 15 to 25 years for a project with equal annual cash inflows would increase the present value of all the cash inflows only by 7 per cent. The discount factor would increase from 5.847 to 6.259.)

4.5.3 Tax

As we shall see in Chapter 7, the appropriate discount rate to use as a criterion rate is an *after-tax* discount rate. Hence *after-tax* cash flows should be used in capital project evaluation.

Small companies may be subject to a corporation tax rate of 40 per cent on profits, larger companies to a tax rate of 52 per cent. But many companies recently have been making *losses*, so may not be liable to tax on marginal profits (see 7.1.1).

Unincorporated firms (partnerships and sole traders) pay *income tax* on profits. The basic rate is 30 per cent; but on incomes above £15,000 graduated rates may increase the total income tax rate, to a maximum of 60 per cent on earned incomes above £35,000.

The simplest assumption is to take it that *all* cash inflows and outflows will be subject to tax at the appropriate rate, *except* cash flows relating to working capital. For a small company then, all the before-tax cash flows (except working capital flows) will have to be reduced by the 40 per cent tax rate. In other words, the after-tax cash flows will amount to 60 per cent of the before-tax cash flows.

The *timing* of tax payments is somewhat complicated. A rough estimate would be that tax is payable about one year after taxable profits are earned; but for simplicity this time lag is often ignored.

4.5.4 Risk and Uncertainty

Allowing for risk and uncertainty in capital investment project evaluation is difficult. Strictly, **risk** is the name given to outcomes whose probability of occurrence is *known* (e.g. the odds against the number 5 coming up at roulette); whereas **uncertainty** refers to events whose probability of occurrence is *un-*

known (e.g. the chances of Prince Charles becoming king between 26 March 1982 and 27 July 1991). Business events are usually uncertain: indeed some of the uncertainties may not even be recognised in advance.

No single approach is foolproof, but six different ways of trying to allow for risk and uncertainty may be mentioned:

1. *Conservatism.* Simply making 'conservative' estimates of future net cash flows may lead to rejection of potentially profitable projects. A widely-used variant is to use a deliberately short estimate of a project's life.

2. *Payback.* Payback does not measure profitability (**4.2.2**), since it ignores cash inflows expected to occur *after* payback. But it may be a useful indicator of risk: the faster the payback, the lower the risk.

3. *'Best'/'Worst' forecasts.* Making more than one set of cash flow estimates may give some idea of the spread of possible outcomes (e.g. 'best' or 'worst' outcomes). It requires a consistent approach to the parameters (e.g. is 'best' likely to happen once in ten occasions, or once in a thousand?); it is often difficult to estimate interdependencies (e.g. what is the relationship between advertising expenditure and sales revenue?); and it may be subject to bias, especially to over-optimism in estimating the 'worst' outcome.

4. *Sensitivity analysis.* If one can identify critical assumptions in forecasting future cash flows, one can also test *how much* it changes a project's outcome to vary them. A (difficult) further step would be to estimate *how likely* it is that critical assumptions will vary by specified amounts.

5. *Adjusted discount rates.* If one can classify the 'riskiness' of different types of project, the discount rate used as the criterion rate can be adjusted by allowing for different 'risk premiums' (see **7.2**).

6. *Expected values.* Guessing the likelihood of various possible future events, using 'subjective probability estimates', enables one to compute **expected values** for future cash flows, from which an 'expected' net present value can be derived. This approach is described in more detail in *Production Decisions* by John Powell (in this series). Its value, like that of decision trees, largely depends on the accuracy of one's guesses about unknown future events.

The cash flows for capital projects are usually based on highly fallible estimates, but managers are not merely trying to *measure* levels of risk and return. They are also trying to *manage* projects – either by reducing the risk, or by increasing the return.

We shall be seeing (in **5.2.2**) how *lenders* may seek to reduce their risk, by means of personal guarantees from borrowers, by loan 'covenants', or by taking 'security'. Similarly there are several ways in which business managers may seek to reduce the risks involved in capital investment: such as extensive market research, arranging long-term sales contracts, or ensuring alternative sources of supply.

Managers may also try to increase the returns from a project, by such means as (for example): expanding the volume of sales, increasing selling prices, or keeping careful control of costs. It will be recognised that these are easier to say than to do!

4.5.5 Inflation

The possibility of future general inflation at rates varying up to 25 per cent a year makes it difficult to forecast cash flows more than a year or two ahead. It may also be necessary to forecast *specific* price changes for each kind of cash flow. For example, if general inflation of 10 per cent a year were expected, one might still expect wage costs to rise by 15 per cent a year, say, or raw material costs by only 6 per cent a year.

Two methods of allowing for general inflation are possible:

1. Use actual money amounts expected year by year, with a criterion rate of return which *includes* an allowance for expected inflation. If the 'real' criterion rate (excluding inflation) were 8 per cent a year, then the discount rate *including* inflation would need to be about 18 per cent.
2. Use present-day (Year 0) **constant purchasing power** amounts, with a 'real' discount rate excluding inflation. Any money amounts expected to rise in future by *less* than the general rate of inflation will appear to *fall* in terms of constant Year 0 purchasing power (e.g. lease payments).

In principle it doesn't much matter which method is used (each has advantages); but *consistency is essential*. The rule is: if you use money cash flows, discount them at a money interest rate, including an inflation premium; if you use 'real' cash flows, discount them at a 'real' interest rate, excluding inflation.

4.6 Conclusion

4.6.1 NPV versus IRR

Most businessmen who use DCF prefer IRR to NPV, probably because the result is expressed as an annual percentage rate of return, in a form which is familiar to businessmen. (Though it is potentially misleading to compare an internal rate of return result based on compound interest with simple-interest rates of return.)

Example: It may help to understand the two DCF methods if we compare two mutually exclusive projects. Both Project E and Project F require an initial investment of £25. Project E has cash inflows of £5 a year for 10 years, giving an internal rate of return of just over 15 per cent. Project F produces £1 cash inflow in Year 1, £2 in Year 2, and so on until £10 in Year 10; which gives an IRR of 12½ per cent.

Project E's NPV will be higher than Project F's only if the criterion rate exceeds 6½ per cent (as shown in Fig. 4.15). Given that some criterion rate has to be identified before calculating any net present value, it is clear that the project with the higher NPV will always *be the 'better' one.*

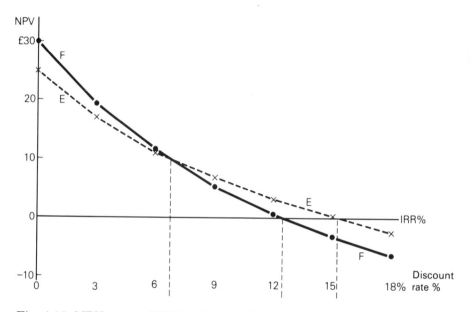

Fig. 4.15: NPV versus IRR for Projects E and F.

But a project with a higher internal rate of return may *not* be better than a project with a lower IRR, for two main reasons. First, the amount to be invested may be different. Is a 50 per cent IRR better than 25 per cent? Not necessarily, if the 50 per cent is earned on an investment of £100, while the 25 per cent is earned on an investment of £10,000.

The second reason is that IRR in effect assumes **re-investment** at the project's own ('internal') rate of return. But this may not be the actual 'opportunity cost' of capital, which can cause problems if the two projects being compared have *different lives*.

4.6.2 The Four Main Appraisal Methods

Discounted cash flow methods of evaluating the profitability of capital investment projects are *theoretically* superior to the traditional methods. The average rate of return on investment method ignores the *timing* of unequal returns (**4.2.1**), while payback ignores amounts received *after* payback (**4.2.2**), so does not measure profitability at all.

Yet both methods of appraisal continue to be used even by large companies. There are probably two main reasons for this. Firstly, few large companies rely on a *single* method of appraisal: many companies use payback as well as IRR or NPV, in an attempt to measure *risk* as well as profit. Secondly, forecasts of future cash flows are often thought to be so unreliable that there is little point in using 'sophisticated' methods of appraisal.

A recent survey of 150 of the largest UK firms in retailing and manufacturing found the methods shown in Fig. 4.16 used in 1980.

Primary[1] *method* (%)	*One method* (%)	*Two methods* (%)	*Three methods* (%)	*Four methods* (%)
a 32	a 11	ab 12	abc 10	abcd 10
b 32	b 8	ac 12	abd 6	
c 41	c 4	ad 6	acd 10	
d 17	d 3	bc 3	bcd 1	
		bd 1		
		cd 3		
122[1]	26	37	27	10

a = Payback   b = Average rate of return   c = IRR   d = NPV

[1] This adds to more than 100 per cent because some methods ranked 'equal first'.

Fig. 4.16: Project appraisal methods used by 150 large UK firms, 1980.

Undoubtedly many cash flow forecasts are subject to wide margins of error. However, this hardly justifies using a theoretically incorrect method of project appraisal. (It does, perhaps, call for special focus on cash flows in the *early* years of a project.)

Some experts believe that the process of estimating the future cash flows arising from a project is the most valuable part of the appraisal procedure; hence that it may not matter too much *which* 'appraisal method' is actually used. (A similar argument is sometimes used in favour of 'decision tree' analysis, where the precise 'probabilities' employed are extremely uncertain as a rule.)

In any case, it would be naive to suppose that only technical financial considerations are relevant in deciding on the commitment of funds which may help shape the whole future of an enterprise. Strategic considerations may be equally, or more, important for large projects. Even where one of the DCF

* See Question B16

methods appears to show that a project will be profitable, it is important for managers to identify the general economic rationale for the project. In other words, *why* can a profit be made on a particular project? If no particular reason can be identified, then the apparent result of the financial evaluation must be questioned.

4.6.3 The Complexity of Capital Investment

In this chapter we have been concerned mainly to identify ways of analysing the desirability of capital investment projects on financial grounds. But other considerations may be even more important.

To summarise the financial approach first. The first requirement is to identify the investment opportunity, whether stemming from replacement of existing equipment, expansion of facilities for making existing products, provision of facilities to make new products, or from some other source. Relevant information must be gathered, feasible alternatives considered, detailed cost and revenue projections worked out for alternatives to be examined in depth. The result of all this work should be the estimation, for each alternative, of expected future *cash flows* (both amount and timing) which will result if a project is invested in, but not otherwise.

Note that in capital investment evaluation by the (theoretically preferable) discounted cash flow method we deal with cash flows *and not* accounting profits. *Hence such non-cash expenses as depreciation should properly be* ignored *in constructing schedules of cash flows in future periods.*

Given an appropriate 'opportunity cost' of capital to use as a discount rate (as discussed in Chapter 7), the estimates of future cash flows are discounted back to 'present value' (that is, into terms of 'End of year 0 money'). Expected inflows and outflows from a capital project can then be directly compared as at the same point in time ('now'). Obviously, if the present value of the inflows exceeds the present value of the outflows, then the project would appear to be *financially* worthwhile.

But financial considerations may not be the only ones, nor even the most important ones. For instance, Pilkingtons are reported to have believed that if they had been a publicly-quoted company at the time they would have been unlikely to have gone ahead with the long-drawn-out development of their 'float glass' process. This was on the grounds that public shareholders might have been unwilling to see such a relatively large investment producing no returns for many years – *even if* the discounted present value of the ultimate cash inflows were expected to exceed the costs of the investment (also discounted).

Similarly certain proposals for automation of manufacturing processes may be rejected, even though on paper they might appear profitable, if they would involve significant redundancies from among the present work-force. A firm may well feel that it owes some loyalty to its workers, as well as to its shareholders; or (more crudely) it may feel that the 'price' to be paid in potential souring of industrial relations may not be worth the 'net present value' of the automation project. (Such decisions are even more complicated than shown here: for example, if competitors are automating *their* manufacturing processes, then our firm's workers may be out of a job anyway if we don't automate too – since our costs may be quite uncompetitive. But by no means all markets are perfectly competitive.)

Another important consideration may be political. Many firms are more or less dependent on selling their products or services to government bodies. Defence firms are perhaps the most obvious; but drug companies sell to the National Health Service, computer firms to government offices, and so on. Long-term strategic considerations may make it difficult to view a particular capital project proposal in isolation from the whole business; hence non-quantifiable judgement may necessarily have to be allowed for. We are not suggesting that 'correct' financial evaluation of capital projects is not worthwhile; merely that *the apparent result of financial evaluation of capital projects is not necessarily* decisive.

4.6.4 Organisation for Capital Budgeting

In addition to a system of evaluating individual capital projects' profitability, companies must have a system of **capital budgeting**. This involves planning the *total* amount of capital spending to be undertaken over the next year or two, in order to arrange necessary financing. It is common for capital budgets to be reviewed and updated quarterly, since both the amounts and the timing of payments can be subject to significant changes.

As far as individual projects are concerned, it is worth repeating: *the most important thing is finding good projects*. Probably some firms spend too much time evaluating projects and not enough *searching* for new business opportunities. To gather *information*, market research is often needed (as described in *Marketing Decisions*, by Peter Tinniswood, in this series).

Once a possible project has been identified, there needs to be some kind of rough 'screening' (for which payback may be suitable), to see that it is not obviously unattractive. The project should also fit in with the company's objectives.

After looking at possible *alternatives* to the project, detailed engineering estimates, market forecasts, etc. will need to be prepared. Many capital investment projects cover the whole range of business: production, marketing, organisation, strategy. Preparing and analysing plans draws on most of the underlying business disciplines: accounting, statistics, operations research, engineering, economics, psychology. Hence large projects involve groups of people, and often cover long periods of time.

In all organisations what goes on *informally* is likely to be at least as significant as the formal system. The 'politics' of capital budgeting is often important. In any case, as was suggested earlier, the quantifiable financial estimates may not be the most critical aspects of capital investment projects.

Even after the final *decision* to invest has been taken, the vital process of *implementing* the decision can not simply be taken for granted. This process can take many months (or even years); and mistakes here may be far more costly than questionable aspects of the financial analysis.

Finally, some companies have a system of **post-project audit**. This may be confined to checking the amount and timing of the capital investment *outflows* only. Or it may involve a full-scale reappraisal after the event to check on the accuracy of the original estimates of both capital expenditure and operating cash flows. The critical assumptions made may also be reviewed, and their realism scrutinised. The purpose is not so much to apportion blame if things have gone wrong, but to learn (if possible) how to make better estimates in future.

In the next chapter we go on to look at the different kinds of funds which a firm can use to finance its long-term investments (both in net working capital and in fixed capital projects). As a rule, companies do not try to relate particular sources of funds to particular projects: they arrange for a 'pool' of funds out of which to pay for their capital spending. Thus companies tend to *separate* their choice of investment projects from the types of funds used to finance them.

Work Section

A. Revision Questions

A1 Is capital investment desirable? Why or why not?

A2 What was suggested as the most important stage in capital investment?

A3 What is the average rate of return on investment method? What is its main disadvantage?

A4 What is the payback method? What is its main disadvantage?

A5 Name two advantages of the payback method.

A6 Why does money have a 'time value'?

A7 Why is the timing of cash flows on an investment project important?

A8 How can use of a rate of interest help a firm to arrange investment projects in a definite order?

A9 How are discounting factors calculated?

A10 How might a company select the appropriate discount rate for a capital project?

A11 How does the net present value method translate expected future cash flows into terms of 'End of Year 0' money?

A12 What assumption does the net present value method make about the 'opportunity cost' of capital?

A13 What is the difference between present value and *net* present value?

A14 Explain the net present value method of investment appraisal.

A15 What basic financial information about a capital project is needed in order to use the net present value method?

A16 Explain how the internal rate of return method works.

A17 What basic financial information about a capital project is needed in order to use the internal rate of return method?

A18 Why is the internal rate of return method sometimes called the 'trial and error' method?

A19 How is interpolation used in the internal rate of return method?

A20 What are the limitations of the DCF approach to project appraisal?

A21 Name three ways of allowing for risk and uncertainty in capital investment project evaluation.

A22 What is the difference between 'risk' and 'uncertainty'?

A23 Why might a cost reduction project be thought less risky than a new product project?

A24 What does sensitivity analysis involve?

A25 What are the two methods of allowing for inflation in project appraisal? (Describe them in sufficient detail.)

A26 What is the difference between 'specific' price changes and 'general' price changes?

A27 What might cause a project's life to end?

A28 Name two items which may constitute capital recovery inflows at the end of a project's life.

A29 What is a 'horizon'?

A30 Why must working capital be allowed for in project appraisal even if it will be fully recovered at the end of the project's life?

A31 Describe the main difference(s) between the net present value method and the internal rate of return method.

A32 Name two reasons why a project with a lower internal rate of return may be better than one with a higher internal rate of return.

A33 What 'reinvestment assumption' is made under the internal rate of return method? Under the net present value method?

A34 If DCF methods are better, why is payback still widely used?

A35 What are the two main kinds of post-project audit?

B. Exercises/Case Studies

B1 Refer to Fig. 4.9 (which is based on a 10% interest rate). Using *only* this chart (on page 73):

a. What would '£200 invested today' accumulate to in three years' time?

b. What is the present value of '£300 receivable at the end of Year 3'?

c. £751.30 is invested at the end of Year 2. When will it have accumulated to £1,331.00?

d. How much would you need to invest today to get £2,420 at the end of Year 3?

e. What would £1,652.80 invested today accumulate to in four years' time?

f. What is the present value of '£5,500 receivable at the end of Year 4'?

B2 a. Calculate the compound interest owing at the end of a three-year period if £100 is borrowed at an annual interest rate of 12 per cent.

b. If you employed *simple* interest, how much less would the total interest amount to?

c. What would be the advantage to a bank of charging interest at 1 per cent a month rather than at 12 per cent a year, over the three-year period?

B3 a. What amount will compound to £2,700 after six years at an interest rate of 20 per cent a year?

b. At what interest rate will £1,500 compound to £2,500 over eight years?

c. What compound interest rate is required to double a sum of money in five years?

d. The Retail Price Index, based on January 1974 = 100, reached 300 in

September 1981. What annual average rate of inflation does this imply?

B4 Calculate the present value of the following future cash flows at the given annual rate of interest (r):
   a. £550 1 year away, r = 10%.   b. £1,728 3 years away, r = 20%.
   c. £251 2 years away, r = 12%.   d. £2,000 9 years away, r = 8%.

B5 At 12 per cent a year, what is the present value of an 'annuity' of £200:
   a. for 8 years?   b. for 20 years?   c. for 50 years?

B6 Which would you rather have (starting at the end of Year 1):
   a. £3,000 a year for the next 20 years, discounted at 20 per cent a year?
   b. £2,000 a year for the next 20 years, discounted at 12 per cent a year?
   c. £1,000 a year for the next 20 years, discounted at 3 per cent a year?

B7 A project requires an outlay of £1,500, and is expected to produce net receipts of £2,000 at the end of Year 5 and £2,000 at the end of Year 10. Should it be undertaken if the firm's cost of capital is:
   a. 12 per cent?   b. 16 per cent?

B8 A firm requires at least 12 per cent a year return.
   a. Should it undertake a project with an initial outlay of £400, which will yield a single cash inflow of £1,000 at the end of Year 10?
   b. What if the same amount were to be received at the end of Year 7?

B9 A firm's cost of capital is 15 per cent a year. A project requires an initial outlay of £6,500 and is expected to yield receipts of £1,000 a year for 12 years.
   a. Should the project be accepted?
   b. Should the firm prefer a modification reducing net receipts to £800 a year, but extending the life to 18 years?

B10 Which would you prefer:
   a. £500 a year for seven years; or b. £700 a year for five years?

B11 A new machine can reduce operating costs (excluding depreciation) by £12,000 a year, and its life is expected to be eight years. Is it worth paying £50,000 for the machine if the firm's criterion rate is 12 per cent?

B12 A project which requires an initial investment of £6,000 will produce cash receipts of £1,000 a year for 10 years. If the required rate of return is 15 per cent a year, is it worth undertaking?
   a. Using the net present value method?
   b. Using the internal rate of return method?

B13 A project is expected to yield £1 million at the end of Year 10. The initial outlay is £410,000. What rate of return does it offer?

B14 A project requiring an initial outlay of £5,400 will yield returns of £1,000 a year for 10 years. (a) What is the rate of return? (b) What annual returns would be needed to yield a 20 per cent internal rate of return?

B15 A project requires an initial investment of £6,000. Its expected cash receipts amount to £2,000 a year.
   a. If its life is five years, what is the highest cost of capital the company can have and still find the project worthwhile?

b. If the cost of capital is 25 per cent a year, for how many years (at least) must the project last to be worthwhile?

B16 Refer to Fig. 4.16 (on page 83). What percentage of the 150 companies:
   a. use more than one method of investment appraisal?
   b. use each of the four appraisal methods? (alone or in combination)
   c. use no discounted cash flow methods?
   d. use only discounted cash flow methods?

B17 Write down a brief description of:
   a. The criterion rate   b. The net present value of a project
   c. Incremental cash flows   d. Sensitivity analysis
   e. Horizon date   f. The re-investment assumption.

B18 What is the present value of:
   a. £1,200 a year receivable from the end of Year 3 to the end of Year 7 at an interest rate of 20 per cent a year?
   b. £4,000 a year payable from the end of Year 5 to the end of Year 10 at an interest rate of 15 per cent a year?
   c. £800 a year receivable from the beginning of Year 4 to the end of Year 8 at an interest rate of 12 per cent a year?
   d. A non-index-linked pension of £5,000 a year receivable from the end of Year 30 to the end of Year 50 at an interest rate of 15 per cent a year?

B19 Mr Smith rents his house to a reliable tenant for £2,000 a year. He can get a return of 12 per cent a year on an investment of similar risk. What is the (present) value to him of the right to receive this rent:
   a. for 20 years?   b. for 50 years?
   c. On a 20-year tenancy, what is the present value of the right to increase the annual rent by 50 per cent after 10 years?

B20 Four projects costing £4,200 each produce a net present value of zero discounting at 6 per cent a year:
   a.   5-year annuity of £997   b. 10-year annuity of £571
   c. 20-year annuity of £366   d. 50-year annuity of £266.
   What happens to *each* project if the rate of interest falls to 5 per cent?

B21 A local council allows rate-payers to pay their rates by equal monthly instalments if they choose. If the rate of interest is 12 per cent a year, how much is such a concession worth to someone who would otherwise pay her £240 rates bill in a single sum at the beginning of the year?

B22 Assuming an interest rate of 12 per cent a year, if a first-class letter (costing 15½p postage) takes one day to reach its destination, while a second-class letter (costing 12½p postage) takes four days, how large does a cheque which you intend to post to your bank manager to reduce your overdraft need to be to justify sending it first class?

B23 Investment in a new mining project is expected to require the following cash payments before operations can begin: 1982 £3m.; 1983 £6m.; 1984 £8m.; 1985 £4m.

Assuming payments occur in a lump at the end of each year, ignoring tax, and assuming a 15 per cent opportunity cost of capital:

    a. what is the present value (at the end of 1982) of the cash payments?

    b. what would the present value of the cash payments amount to if the 'end of year 0' were taken to be the end of 1985?

    c. what is the present value cost (at the end of 1982) if the 1984 payment becomes £10m., the 1985 payment £6m., and £3m. is spent in 1986?

B24 A car licence for 12 months costs £80. For six months, a licence costs £44. How should a motorist who expects to drive throughout the next year decide whether to buy his licence in a 12-monthly payment rather than in two six-monthly instalments? (Assume he can borrow from a bank, if necessary.)

B25 A new toll road is expected to produce net cash receipts of £3.0m. a year when it is completed. Assume that the road will be operational for 25 years. The road will take five years to complete; and the cash outflows are expected to be: £8.0m. at the end of year 0, and £5.0m. a year for years 1 to 5.

What is the project's internal rate of return?

B26 A firm's criterion rate of return is 15 per cent a year. What is the most it should be prepared to invest in a project which is expected to yield £500 a year for seven years:

    a. if the initial investment will *not* be recovered at the end?

    b. if the initial investment *will* be recovered at the end of the project?

B27 a. You purchased, five years ago, a vase for £800. You have just been offered £1,000 for it. If you accept, have you made a 'real' profit, with inflation at five per cent a year during the past five years?

    b. With inflation at 10 per cent a year during the past five years, what price would you need to be offered now in order to break even, in 'real' terms, if you paid £800 for the vase five years ago?

B28 H. Stephenson Limited is considering an investment project which will require the investment of £50,000 in new fixed assets and £12,000 in additional stocks. The annual sales revenue from the project is forecast to be £80,000, and the annual running costs £60,000 (including depreciation of £10,000). The project's life is expected to be five years. Ignoring tax:

    a. Show the cash flows year by year.

    b. Should the project be accepted if the firm's cut-off rate is 20 per cent?

B29 Refer to B28. Additional information is as follows:

    1. Existing assets (being replaced) can be sold for £2,000.

    2. Tax at 40 per cent is assumed payable on profits on the last day of the year in which they are earned.

    3. For tax purposes, depreciation is to be ignored; but a 100 per cent first-year allowance is given against the investment in new fixed assets.

Assume that this can be used to reduce tax on the firm's overall profits in the year in which the investment is made.

a. Show the net cash flows year by year.

b. Should the project be accepted if the firm's cut-off rate is 15 per cent?

B30 As stated in B29, investment in equipment normally carries a 100 per cent first-year allowance for tax purposes. How much worse off would H. Stephenson Limited be if instead straight-line depreciation based on original cost over five years were allowed as a deductible expense for tax purposes? Express this amount as a percentage of the net present value cost under the actual tax rules which now exist.

What would the percentage amount to if one used a 52 per cent corporation tax rate instead of a 40 per cent tax rate?

B31

End of year:	0	1	2	3	4
H cash flows (£)	−1,000	+500	+400	+350	+300
J cash flows (£)	−1,000	+400	+400	+400	+400

a. Which of these two projects has the higher net present value at a discounting rate of 15 per cent a year? By how much?

b. What is the payback period of each project?

c. Chart the net present value of project J at discount rates of 6 per cent, 12 per cent, 18 per cent, 24 per cent and 30 per cent. Estimate the internal rate of return from the chart.

B32 Project T requires an initial investment of £2,000 (which is non-returnable), and is expected to produce cash inflows of £700 a year for five years. Is it worth investing in if the opportunity cost of capital is 15 per cent a year? Calculate your answer using:

a. Net present value method.

b. Internal rate of return method.

c. Graph the project's NPV at discount rates of 6 per cent, 12 per cent, 18 per cent, 24 per cent and 30 per cent. Estimate the IRR from the graph.

B33 Project X requires a cash investment in a new machine of £36,000, which is to be completely depreciated in equal instalments over its expected four-year life. The project's accounting profits are expected to amount to £4,000 a year in Years 1 and 2, and to £7,000 a year in Years 3 and 4.

a. What is the average accounting rate of return on investment?

b. Draw up a schedule of the amount and timing of cash flows for Project X.

c. What is the payback period?

d. If the discount rate is 20 per cent a year, what is the net present value?

e. What is Project X's internal rate of return?

B34 Project Y is expected to produce accounting profits of £24,000 a year
over its eight-year life. The initial investment in fixed capital equipment
is £120,000, and the firm uses straight-line depreciation.
   a. What is the average accounting rate of return on investment?
   b. Draw up a schedule showing the amount and timing of Project Y's
      cash flows.
   c. What is the payback period?
   d. Chart Project Y's net present value, using discount rates from 0 to 30
      per cent inclusive, at 10 per cent intervals.
   e. From the chart, what is Project Y's internal rate of return?
   f. Check your estimated IRR by calculation from the tables.

B35 A company expects to reduce labour costs by £20,000 a year if it invests
£50,000 in new equipment which will last five years. Ignoring tax:
   a. What is the annual increase in accounting profit?
   b. What is the average rate of return on investment?
   c. What is the annual net cash inflow?
   d. What is the payback period?
   e. What is the NPV at 15 per cent a year?
   f. What is the IRR?

B36 Globe Gears Limited is about to choose between three projects. Project A
is for the purchase of a new machine; Project B is for a promotional
campaign to boost sales; and Project C is for the rationalisation of part
of the production department. The cost and expected returns for each
project are set out below:

End of year	Project A (£)	Project B (£)	Project C (£)
0 (Initial outlay)	10,000	10,000	10,000
Cash inflows			
1	1,000	4,000	3,000
2	2,000	3,000	3,000
3	3,000	3,000	3,000
4	3,000	2,000	3,000
5	3,000	—	2,000
6	3,400	—	1,000
Total	15,400	12,000	15,000

   a. Calculate: i. Average rate of return on investment
               ii. Payback period
              iii. DCF rate of return,
               for each project.

b. State with reasons the project you would rank as of greatest value to the firm, on purely financial grounds.

c. What other factors might you consider before making a final choice?

B37 Dragon Paint (see Chapter 3, B15) is planning to extend credit to a customer whose financial standing is weak. Expected cash flows over the next two and a half years are as follows:

End of month 0	Initial investment	−£15,000
End of month 1	Additional outflow	−£ 3,750
End of month 2	Additional outflow	−£ 3,750
EOM 3–30	Net cash inflows	+£ 1,250 per month

At the end of month 30, one of three possibilities will occur:

i. The customer will then pay in full the £30,000 then owing;

ii. The customer will pay £10,000 after a delay of 10 months, and the rest will be a bad debt;

iii. The customer will be unable to pay anything.

a. What is the net present value of the project for each of the three possibilities, assuming a discount rate of 1 per cent a month (and compounding monthly)?

b. What is the payback period?

c. What is the annual rate of return on investment?

d. For possibility (i) – payment in full – what is the approximate internal rate of return on an annual basis?

B38 Refer to B37. Answer each of questions (a) to (d) on the more optimistic assumption that the additional cash outflows in months 1 and 2 amount to £6,250 (not £3,750), but that the net cash inflows from months 3 to 30 inclusive amount to £2,083 per month (not £1,250).

B39 New Supa-calc requires investment in a factory of £2.0 million, in equipment of £1.5 million, and in working capital of £1.0 million. Assume that all cash outflows occur at the same time; that after eight years working capital will be recovered in full, the equipment will be sold for £200,000, and that the factory will then have a value of £500,000. What is the net present value of the capital investment cash flows:

a. Ignoring tax, and assuming a discount rate of 20 per cent?

b. Assuming a tax rate of 40 per cent, an after-tax discount rate of 12 per cent, 100 per cent first-year tax allowances on all the equipment, and 75 per cent first-year allowance on the factory, with the balance being written off for tax purposes equally over the next five years?

B40 Sales volume of new Supa-calc is expected to be 100,000 units in Year 1, 250,000 units in Year 2, and 500,000 units a year for each of the next six years. The selling price per unit will be £6.00 for Years 1 to 4 and £5.00 for Years 5 to 8. Variable costs are expected to amount to (a) production costs of £2.40 per unit in Years 1 and 2, and £2.00 per unit in Years 3 to 8, and (b) selling costs equal to 5 per cent of sales revenue.

Advertising costs will be £100,000 in Year 1, £60,000 in Year 2 and £40,000 per year thereafter.

a. Ignoring tax, set out a schedule of the amount and timing of the operating cash flows, assuming all receipts and payments are for cash (not on credit), and that all cash flows take place at the end of the year to which they relate.

b. What is the net present value of the cash flows, assuming a discount rate of 20 per cent a year?

c. What is the net present value of the after-tax cash flows, assuming a tax rate of 40 per cent and an after-tax discount rate of 12 per cent a year?

B41 Refer to B39 and B40. Using a tax rate of 40 per cent and a discount rate of 12 per cent a year:

a. What is the Supa-calc project's net present value?

b. What is the payback period?

c. What is the internal rate of return?

C. Essay Questions

C1 Why might a company argue that choosing the criterion discount rate for use in DCF investment appraisal was not the most important aspect of its capital investment process? What other aspect(s) might be thought more important, and why?

C2 How, if at all, should a local authority's approach to capital project appraisal differ from that of a commercial business?

C3 How would you try to establish a 'criterion' payback period?

C4 How should a firm using DCF methods of investment appraisal select the discounting rate?

C5 Contrast the four main methods of investment appraisal available to firms. Which method would you recommend, and why? (State any assumptions you have made.)

C6 A large well-known company uses the payback method of investment appraisal. It is apparently fairly successful. Assuming that it is prepared only to use a single method of investment appraisal, write a paper to convince its finance director that the company should change *either* to net present value *or* to internal rate of return. (Choose whichever of these two DCF methods you prefer.)

C7 A firm which changed from payback to net present value a few years ago is now thinking of changing back. It complains that not many of its managers seem to understand NPV, and that anyway its cash flow forecasts are so unreliable that the extra sophistication of DCF hardly seems worthwhile. Try to persuade the company's managing director to stay with NPV.

C8 A firm is thinking of reducing its horizon period from 15 years to 5 years, in view of the apparently increasing uncertainty in the business environment. Write a paper supporting (or opposing) this proposal.

C9 What are the advantages and disadvantages of post-project audits? Why do so few firms appear to carry them out?

C10 In the ten years between 1970 and 1980, real gross domestic product increased by 19 per cent, but while private capital spending rose by 34 per cent in real terms, capital investment spending for which government bodies were responsible *fell* by 27 per cent. Can you account for the fall in government capital spending during this period? What consequences (if any) might be expected?

C11 How would you recommend that a medium-sized manufacturing business should try to allow for risk and uncertainty in capital investment project decisions?

C12 You have been asked by a company's finance manager how his company should allow for inflation in capital investment appraisal. His firm currently uses both payback (mainly to assess risk) and the internal rate of return method. Write an answer which he can circulate to the departmental managers who will actually have to put your advice into effect.

C13 'I prefer IRR to NPV because I can understand about rates of return.' Try to persuade the author of this statement to change his mind.

C14 Should firms use the 'best' method of capital project appraisal? Or are they justified in often using a *combination* of methods? Why?

C15 Should prospective capital investment project evaluation be more closely related to retrospective accounting appraisal of business performance (or vice versa)? Why or why not? If so, how could this be done?

Chapter 5

Types and Sources of Finance

5.1 Shareholders' Funds
5.1.1 Ordinary Shareholders' Funds
5.1.2 Preference Share Capital

5.2 Borrowing
5.2.1 General Features
5.2.2 Risk Reduction
5.2.3 Period

5.3 Financial Institutions
5.3.1 Overview
5.3.2 The Money Market
5.3.3 Banks
5.3.4 Other Institutions

5.4 Small Businesses

5.5 Other Sources of Finance
5.5.1 Equity
5.5.2 Debt
5.5.3 Liquidating Assets

Objective: *To contrast the various kinds of finance and their different risk, return and maturity features; to describe the main UK financial institutions; and to outline the main sources of finance for small and other businesses.*
Synopsis: *Ordinary shareholders have a residual interest in a company's profit or loss. The two main kinds of ordinary shareholders' funds are retained profits (the most important single source of funds) and new issues of ordinary shares.*

Business loans usually contain restrictions, and may be 'secured'; they may be short-term (overdrafts), medium-term loans or long-term (debentures or loan stocks). Short-term borrowing has grown in recent years, as long-term loans have

*declined due to high interest rates; but 'term' loans now form half the banks'
total lending to business.*

*In the capital market, the financial institutions lend personal savings to industry
and to the public sector. Financial institutions normally try to 'match' the maturity
of assets and liabilities: borrowing short and lending long is likely to be profitable
but risky. The insurance companies and pension funds between them now own
half of UK quoted equities.*

*Small businesses may find special difficulty in raising new equity and in long-
term borrowing; so retained profits and bank overdrafts are important sources
of funds for them. Other possible sources of funds include: venture capital companies, leasing, factoring and turning surplus assets into cash.*

The main distinction between types of business finance is between shareholders' funds ('equity') and borrowing ('debt'). Retained profits and new
issues of ordinary shares both increase shareholders' funds, and both are long-
term capital. Borrowing may be either short-term or longer-term.

New sources of funds for UK companies between 1961 and 1980 totalled
about £11 billion a year (in 1980 pounds). Short-term borrowing has increased
recently to make up for the fall in retained profits and in long-term loans
(Fig. 5.1).

		1961–70 (%)	1971–80 (%)
Shareholders' funds	⎰ Real retained profits	62	51
	⎱ New equity issues	8	10
Borrowing	⎰ New long-term debt	14	4
	⎱ Short-term borrowing	16	35
		100	100

Fig. 5.1: UK industrial and commercial companies: new sources of
funds 1961–80.

5.1 Shareholders' Funds

5.1.1 Ordinary Shareholders' Funds

Retained profits are company profits which managers decide *not* to distribute
as cash dividends to ordinary shareholders. Historically they have been the
most important source of funds for UK companies. Retained profits may
fluctuate sharply: indeed, they can even be *negative* if dividends exceed profits

for a period, or if losses are made. In order to cope with fluctuating retained profits as a source of funds, managers may need to adjust the planned amount of new investment, to turn some existing assets into cash, to borrow, or to issue more ordinary shares for cash (as described in more detail in Chapter 6).

Dividends clearly benefit ordinary shareholders, who can also gain from retained profits if the amounts reinvested lead to higher dividends in future. The market value of a company's ordinary shares may rise immediately, if this result is anticipated, thus increasing the wealth of the shareholders. We shall be considering later whether managers always care enough about *shareholders'* opportunities to spend funds retained by a company, which might otherwise have been paid out in cash dividends.

New issues of ordinary shares, like retained profits, are 'ordinary shareholders' funds' (often simply referred to as **equity**). From the *company's* viewpoint, ordinary share capital is *less* risky than borrowing: (a) there is no legal commitment to pay any ordinary dividend (unlike debt interest); (b) no equity capital has to be repaid until the company is wound up (whereas loans must be repaid on the agreed maturity date); and (c) equity capital is free of the restrictive conditions often attached to borrowing (see **5.2.2 b**).

It is the other way round for *shareholders*: owning ordinary shares in a company is more risky than lending it money. In a **liquidation**, ordinary shareholders will get whatever is left over after a company has repaid in full the money amounts owing to all creditors (and preference shareholders). If lenders are *not* repaid in full, because the company has been unsuccessful, then the ordinary shareholders will get nothing. But the liability of ordinary shareholders is limited to the fully-paid **nominal** amount of their shares (hence the name **limited company**). The company cannot call on them for any further contribution. Thus the most that ordinary shareholders can normally lose is the amount they have already invested.

Dissatisfied ordinary shareholders may vote to replace the company's directors at the Annual General Meeting (AGM). But in practice it is far more likely that a disgruntled shareholder will simply sell his shares; though their market value may already have fallen to reflect poor performance. Minority shareholders in **unquoted companies** may be even worse off. They may be unable either to influence the company's policy or to sell their shares (for which there is no public market).

Although ordinary shares are risky for the shareholders, there is no limit on the potential reward if a company is successful. The ordinary shareholders may be regarded as the 'residual owners' of the company: they get anything left over after other suppliers of finance have been paid the agreed amounts due.

5.1.2 Preference Share Capital

Owners of **preference shares** have no legal right to their stated fixed amount of dividend, if a company's directors choose not to declare one. But if preference dividends are paid, they have priority over ordinary dividends.

Most preference shares are now **cumulative**, which means that preference dividends in arrear must be paid in full before any ordinary dividends can be paid. In a liquidation, preference shareholders rank after all a company's creditors (see 8.5.1); but again they have priority over *ordinary* shareholders, in being repaid the fixed nominal amount of the preference shares.

Preference shares have been unpopular with UK companies in recent years, mainly for tax reasons. In 1981, half of the top 500 UK companies had some preference share capital; but in only four of the top 250 companies did it exceed 5 per cent of the market value of the ordinary shares. A recent large issue of preference shares by Chloride was exceptional.

Preference capital may seem an unattractive alternative to debt (Fig. 5.2 column A). It is usually much more expensive than debt after tax, and often appears practically as risky. (There is, however, a big difference between a company being highly embarrassed if preference dividends have to be omitted, and being *liquidated* if debt interest cannot be paid!) But a company near its debt limit may regard preference shares as an alternative to *ordinary* shares (column B) – as a way to increase its financial gearing (see 7.3). Preference capital may then be seen as cheaper than ordinary share capital, yet less risky than debt.

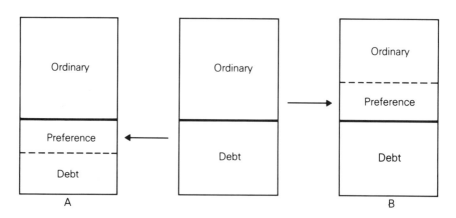

Fig. 5.2: Alternative views of preference capital.

5.2 Borrowing

5.2.1 General Features

A company must repay amounts borrowed (**debt**) when they are due, and regularly pay the agreed amount of interest on the debt outstanding. Failure to do so entitles the lender to take immediate legal action to recover the principal and any unpaid interest. Both lender and borrower will want to see a considerable margin of safety, to enable a company to meet its legal commitments even if things go wrong.

A lender will be concerned with the borrower's honesty and competence. The borrower will have to explain *why* the money is needed, *how much* is required, for *how long*, and how it is planned to *repay* the loan. Many of these questions can be answered by a set of cash forecasts covering the period of the proposed loan (see **2.4**). It may be desirable to have more than one set of forecasts, based on different assumptions.

The rate of interest on loans varies with market conditions from time to time. Recent severe fluctuations in interest rates have led to 'variable-rate' term loans (instead of fixed-rate loans) being widely employed; and bank overdraft interest rates change as market rates vary. As a rule, longer-term loans will carry higher interest rates than short-term borrowing; and smaller or riskier businesses will have to pay a higher rate of interest than larger or more secure companies (see **5.4**).

New issues of long-term debt declined sharply in the 1970s, mainly due to high rates of inflation and heavy government borrowing, which have significantly increased interest rates, and due to taxation factors. A recent £100 million long-term debt issue by Barclays Bank at 16 per cent was exceptional and provoked much comment.

Despite an increased emphasis on shorter-term borrowing, overall **debt ratios** have been falling since the mid-1960s. This is partly due to the rapid 'off-balance sheet' increase in lease financing in the 1970s (see 5.5.2) for tax reasons. It also reflects the sharp fall in real *profitability* of UK industry, which has significantly reduced **interest cover** for many companies.

5.2.2 Risk Reduction

a. *Personal guarantee.* In a limited company the liability of ordinary shareholders is *limited*. In contrast, creditors of partners or sole traders can, if necessary, look for repayment to the private assets of the individual owners. *Their* potential liability is unlimited. Given the risk of loss if the business fails, anyone lending money to a small limited company may want to get a personal **guarantee** of repayment from the main shareholder. This will put the lender in the same position as if the small limited company were a sole trader or **partnership**. *The reverse side of this coin is that* giving *a personal guarantee is a major step. Although it may seem almost a 'free' way of improving a firm's credit rating,* giving *a personal guarantee* fundamentally *changes the legal position of the controlling owner of a limited company.*

b. *Covenants.* Lenders usually insist on certain conditions (**covenants**): either to *prevent* the granting of security to other lenders or the sale of substantial fixed assets; or to *require* the maintenance of certain financial ratios or regular provision of financial information. For smaller businesses there might be covenants restricting dividend payments or directors' remuneration. Breach of covenant can lead to the lender being able to require immediate repayment of the loan.

c. *Security*. Another way for a lender to reduce the risk of loss is to arrange for particular assets to serve as formal **security**. This gives *priority* in using the proceeds of sale from those assets to repay the loan. Anything left over will go into the company's general pool of funds to pay off the **unsecured creditors**. If the proceeds from such assets do not cover the amount of the secured loan, then the creditor will rank as 'unsecured' in respect of the difference.

Debtors, stocks and general (not specialised) equipment can serve as **collateral**, as well as land, buildings, and marketable securities. Legal title to the asset needs to be easily transferable; and the asset's value should be fairly stable, with little risk of physical deterioration or market obsolescence.

Instead of securing a loan on particular assets, a lender may obtain a **floating charge** on all the assets of a borrower. This comes into effect ('crystallises') only when a company goes into liquidation – thus permitting normal selling of assets in the ordinary course of business. But debts which have statutory priority over the claims of unsecured creditors (e.g. certain wages and taxes) also have priority over any floating charges, though *not* over a fixed charge on a specific asset.

5.2.3 Period

Business loans for less than one year are regarded as 'short-term'. 'Medium-term' means from one to five years; and 'long-term' means more than five years. (But for *government* borrowing, any period less than five years is called 'short-term' – see **6.5.1**).

a. *Short-term borrowing*. Bank overdrafts are the best-known form of short-term borrowing. Only the amount actually overdrawn bears interest, though there may be a small 'commitment fee' on the agreed maximum limit. Interest is calculated from day to day, at a rate which varies with market conditions. The bank overdraft is convenient and flexible for borrowers: its main disadvantage is that it is legally repayable 'on demand', so that in theory it can be withdrawn at any time.

b. *Term loans*. **Term loans** are arranged for periods of less than a year to more than five years. A term loan is assured for the stated period, and often matches the time-pattern of assets and liabilities better than a bank overdraft. Sometimes the timing of repayment (or even the rate of interest payable) may be related to the profitability of a project. Term loans, however, may be more expensive than overdrafts, and there will usually be a penalty on early repayment, which somewhat limits flexibility.

Of the total bank loans outstanding to UK industry in 1981, more than half consisted of term loans; and more than 20 per cent of term loans had a *residual* maturity still more than three years away (Fig. 5.3). (Maturities for *new* term loans would be even longer.) Even bank overdrafts, which are nominally short-term, may often in practice amount to medium-term loans.

	£ billion	Per cent
Overdrafts	15.7	46
Term loans:		
1 year or less	7.3	21
1 to 3 years	4.0	12
3 to 5 years	2.8	8
Over 5 years	4.4	13
	34.2	100

Fig. 5.3: Bank loans to industry: residual maturity, August 1981.

c. *Long-term borrowing.* The whole of a long-term loan (**debenture**) is repayable on the maturity date. Where a company's financial position has worsened since the original borrowing, it may be difficult and expensive, if not impossible, to meet this repayment by new borrowing ('re-financing'). **Project finance**, relating to a specific project rather than to the company's business as a whole, may provide for partial repayment at regular intervals.

Long-term loans may be either secured or unsecured, and may be quoted on the Stock Exchange. Public '*quotation*' means that an original lender can be 'repaid' by selling his **loan stock** to another investor. At the **maturity** date (on **redemption**), the borrowing company will repay the principal ('nominal') amount to the then-registered holders of the loan stock. Unquoted loans may be arranged, for example with banks or insurance companies. Where only a single lender is involved, it may be possible to renegotiate certain conditions of a loan if circumstances change.

Companies with overseas interests may choose to borrow in foreign currencies, rather than in sterling. But where such loans are not fully covered by foreign currency earnings, changes in foreign exchange rates can have a serious effect. (This was one of the factors leading to the collapse of Laker Airways in 1982: see problem B6 in Chapter 8.) Following the government's use since 1981 of 'index-linked' securities (see 2.3.2), companies too may seek in future to borrow on an index-linked basis.

Many recent issues of long-term loans are **convertible** into ordinary shares, at the holder's option, on prearranged terms. As long as the loan is not converted, it bears regular fixed-interest payments; but upon conversion it ceases to bear interest and becomes ordinary share capital, ranking for dividends. The potential equity advantage for the lender may reduce the rate of interest payable.

5.3 Financial Institutions

5.3.1 Overview

The main net movements of funds in 1980 between the various sectors of the economy are shown in Fig. 5.4. Personal sector savings go partly to the public sector, but mainly to the financial institutions, who lend on to industry, overseas and to the public sector.

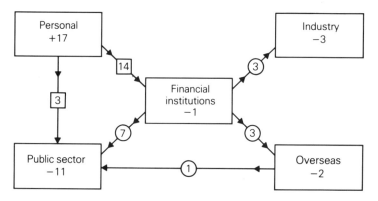

Fig. 5.4: Financial flows between sectors, 1980 (in £ billion).

The largest UK financial **institutions** are banks, building societies, insurance companies and pension funds.

The banks' main function is to provide an efficient mechanism for debt settlement, which they do through the transfer of deposits by cheque and standing order. They are also important financial **intermediaries**, receiving private savings in the form of deposits and then lending out such savings to persons and to businesses.

The **building societies** deal almost entirely with individuals. Their specialised function is to receive savings from individuals, and then to lend other people the money to buy houses. The loan, together with interest, is repaid during the working life of the house-owner.

The **life insurance companies** and **pension funds** receive savings from individuals during their working lives, which they pay out again, together with accumulated interest, during retirement (pensions) or on death (life assurance).

General insurance consists of receiving 'premiums' to cover various risks (such as fire, accident, motor, theft), with payments for claims usually being made within a fairly short time. The 'general funds' of insurance companies, therefore, are invested in shorter-term assets than the long-term 'life funds'.

The banks are the main source of short-term and medium-term loans for business, while the insurance companies and pension funds provide long-term finance, both debt and equity, for larger firms.

5.3.2 The Money Market

The money market deals in short-term liabilities, ranging from money 'at call' or 'overnight' to three-month Treasury Bills and commercial bills of exchange (see **3.4.2**). In addition to the clearing banks, the main institutions in the money market are: (a) the discount houses, (b) the accepting houses and (c) the Bank of England.

a. *Discount houses.* The 12 main **discount houses** represent an important link between the clearing banks and the Bank of England. They help provide liquidity to the financial system by being prepared to quote prices for the government's three-month **Treasury Bills**, and for local authority bills, bank and trade bills, and **certificates of deposit**. The discount houses grew up to invest in commercial bills of exchange, and they attracted deposits accordingly, unlike the clearing banks, whose lending is influenced by the type of deposit they attract.

The discount houses make most profit by borrowing money on terms as short as possible. They represent a convenient home for the clearing banks' very short-term money. 70 to 95 per cent of their borrowing is 'at call' or 'overnight', while they themselves are lending somewhat longer. If necessary the Bank of England will provide them with cash as a **lender of last resort**, possibly at a very high interest rate.

b. *Accepting houses.* The 16 **accepting houses** are better known as **merchant banks**. Their traditional business was 'accepting' bills of exchange; but nowadays they engage in wholesale banking, mainly in foreign currencies. The pattern of their balance sheets is set out in Fig. 5.5. The merchant banks are concerned with investment management, new issues of equity shares, advice on mergers and with corporate finance generally.

c. *Bank of England.* The **Bank of England** is a public corporation: it was nationalised in 1946. The Bank has several important functions: (i) it is the government's banker; (ii) it is banker for the clearing banks; (iii) it is the formal supervisory body for the banking sector; (iv) it has a wider responsibility (partly informal) for watching over the financial system as a whole; (v) it operates the government's monetary policy, and manages the national debt, the note issue, and the Exchange Equalisation Account; and (vi) it advises the government on general financial and economic policy. The Treasury is said to think of the Bank of England as its 'East End branch'; but the Bank tends to regard the Treasury as *its* 'West End branch'!

5.3.3 Banks

The main UK banks are: Barclays, Lloyds, Midland and National Westminster. These four London **clearing banks** account for about 85 per cent of the business of all the UK clearers. The balance sheet summaries shown in Fig. 5.5 show that the banks aim to *match* their sterling liabilities with sterling assets, and the same for other currencies.

	Clearing Banks (%)	Accepting Houses and other UK banks (%)	Overseas and Consortium Banks (%)
Liabilities			
Sterling deposits	63	37	9
Other-currency deposits	24	52	89
Other liabilities	13	11	2
	100	100	100
Assets			
Sterling assets	66	43	10
Other-currency assets	25	53	89
Miscellaneous assets	9	4	1
	100	100	100

Fig. 5.5: Banks in the UK: balance sheets, February 1982.

To a large extent the banks also try to **match the maturity** of their assets and liabilities. Interest rates are often higher on longer-term loans, so it may be more *profitable* to borrow short and lend long. But this is proverbially *risky*, since if too much is lent long the banks may not be able to realise long-term advances in time to repay their short-term liabilities. Hence it is a matter of fine commercial judgement to what extent banks can prudently invest in assets whose maturity is longer than that of their liabilities.

Banks' loans to businesses amount to three and a half times as much as 'retail' loans to persons. Most people's largest asset consists of their house; and at the end of 1981, £50 billion of mortgage loans had been advanced by the building societies, compared with only £15 billion of bank advances to persons. (Though the London clearing banks doubled their personal mortgage lending in the 15 months to February 1982.) In mid-February 1982, sterling advances to UK resident individuals and companies by banks in the UK totalled £71 billion, analysed by borrower, as shown in Fig. 5.6.

	£b'n	*Per cent*
Manufacturing	17.4	24
Other production	7.8	11
Services	22.5	32
Financial and property	8.0	11
Persons	15.5	22
	71.2	100

Fig. 5.6: Banks in the UK: sterling advances to UK residents, February 1982.

Of these advances, 58 per cent were by the clearing banks, 26 per cent by accepting houses and other UK banks, and 16 per cent by overseas and consortium banks. From 1960 to 1973, about 10 foreign banks a year on average opened offices in London: the total increased from 75 to 220. In the eight years from 1974 to 1981 inclusive, more than 20 foreign banks a year opened London offices, bringing the total up to 400 by the end of 1981.

Each of the main clearing banks has subsidiaries in merchant banking, finance houses and in factoring, as shown in Fig. 5.7.

Clearing bank	*Merchant bank*	*Finance House*	*Factors*
Barclays	Barclays Merchant Bank	Mercantile Credit	Barclays Factoring
Lloyds	Lloyds Associated Banking	Bowmaker	Alex Lawrie Factors
Midland	Samuel Montagu	Forward Trust	Griffin Factors
National	County Bank	Lombard North	Credit Factoring
Westminster		Central	International

Fig. 5.7: Main clearing bank associates.

The clearing banks provide a wide variety of financial services in addition to their banking activities: acting as executors and trustees of wills and settlements, managing investment portfolios, providing safe custody facilities, offering tax, insurance and other financial advice, acting as registrars to companies. They also participate extensively in international banking and services.

5.3.4 Other Institutions

Figure 5.8 sets out the pattern of assets of the three largest groups of non-bank financial institutions: pension funds, insurance companies, and building societies. While the banks and building societies own virtually no ordinary shares in UK companies, the insurance companies and pension funds between them own about £40 billion worth.

	Pension funds (%)	Insurance companies		Building societies (%)
		Life (%)	General (%)	
Cash and short-term assets	4	3	11	7
UK government securities:				
Under 5 years	1	1	9	7
5 to 15 years	6	7	10	2
Over 15 years	15	19	5	–
Local authority securities	–	1	1	3
Mortgages and loans	1	6	3	79
Company loans	2	4	6	–
Company ordinary shares:				
UK	44	30	19	–
Overseas	8	4	4	–
Property	17	23	11	–
Other investments	2	2	21	2
	100	100	100	100
★ Total assets (£ billion):	55	54	11	54

Fig. 5.8: Other financial institutions, assets, end 1980.

The £55 billion assets held by the combined pension funds at the end of 1980 were split roughly in the proportion 3–1–2 between (a) private sector

* See Question B3

funds, (b) local authority funds and (c) other public sector funds, including the nationalised industries. ('Other public sector funds' do *not* include the compulsory state retirement scheme. The £14 billion a year payments under this scheme are paid for out of taxation on a 'pay-as-you-go' basis.)

The rapid inflation of the last 15 years has led to significant changes in the proportions of various assets held. There have been large reductions in holdings of UK government and local authority securities, mortgages and company loans (all fixed interest securities). There has been a compensating increase in property and in ordinary shares of companies.

The insurance companies invest their 'life' funds in similar proportions to the pension funds (both being long-term funds); whereas their 'general' funds are invested in shorter-term assets in order to meet ordinary insurance claims becoming due fairly soon.

The building societies borrow short and lend long; but they maintain public confidence and balance inflows and outflows of funds by adjusting the rates of interest offered to depositors and charged to borrowers.

5.4 Small Businesses

In the last 50 years four separate government committees have considered whether there is a particular 'shortage' of funds to finance medium-term projects for smaller firms: Macmillan (1931), Radcliffe (1959), Bolton (1968) and Wilson (1980). In some industries, technical changes have led to economies of scale in research, production and marketing. These have forced some smaller firms to grow in order to compete. And financing working capital has proved difficult for many small firms in the recent years of very high inflation.

As the Bolton Committee said, outside equity capital is available only to the most promising and successful small businesses. New issues of equity are expensive, due to legal and other costs, and because of the high risks and lack of marketability of the shares. Moreover small businessmen usually prefer to avoid new issues of equity for fear of losing control.

Tax policies over many years have also reduced the number of independent investors prepared to invest equity money in small businesses without seeking to interfere in their control (the 'Aunt Agathas'). For tax and other reasons, individual investors have preferred to invest their personal savings in building societies, insurance companies, pension funds and unit trusts; and these financial institutions have been unwilling to put relatively small amounts into unquoted equity shares which could not easily be realised (or even valued). It is true that the 1981 Budget tried to recreate suitable conditions for individual investment; but the scheme has been held back so far by the Inland Revenue's usual obsession with countering 'tax avoidance'.

The high risks and high costs tend to make long-term debt for small businesses unattractive both to lenders and borrowers. Hence, apart from trade credit, the two main sources of funds are retained profits and bank borrowing. High rates of tax and falling rates of profit, together with 'close company' rules until 1980 which tended to require high dividend payments by small companies, combined to put a severe squeeze on retained profits. The Wilson Committee, in respect of medium-sized companies, 'could not find a single individual example of an investment project which had not gone ahead because of the inability to raise external finance ...' but was unable to come to a conclusion on the criticism that, regarding *small* firms, banks tended to be overcautious with respect to gearing and security conditions. A government-backed guarantee scheme may have somewhat improved the position: at the end of 1981 lending under the scheme totalled £64 million.

5.5 Other Sources of Finance

5.5.1 Equity

A number of financial institutions exist to provide **venture capital** and development finance for companies.

As a belated response to the 1931 discovery of the 'Macmillan Gap', the Industrial and Commercial Finance Corporation Limited (ICFC) was set up in 1945 by the Bank of England and the clearing banks to provide funds (both debt and equity) for small and medium-sized firms. At March 1981, ICFC had invested £320 million with 3,400 companies (one sixth needing less than £50,000); of which £80 million represented equity investments with 1,350 companies.

Technical Development Capital (TDC) was set up in 1962 to complement the facilities offered by the National Research Development Corporation (a public corporation founded in 1948). Both these organisations provide finance for research and development by smaller companies. Both TDC and ICFC are now members of the Finance For Industry group (FFI).

In 1976 a consortium of insurance companies and pension funds set up Equity Capital for Industry. It aims to provide equity capital for industrial companies which cannot readily raise new equity from traditional market sources. The fact that by March 1981 its total investments amounted to only £10 million (out of its initial capital of £41 million) suggests that there may not really be much of a 'gap'.

5.5.2 Debt

Several sources of debt finance remain to be noted, which are perhaps of special interest to small and medium-sized firms:

a. *Hire purchase*. Acquiring an asset on **hire purchase** terms involves an initial down-payment of around 20 per cent of the cost, followed by equal monthly instalments (including interest at a fairly high rate) over a period of between one and five years. The purchaser does not become the legal owner until the last payment is made; but the total hire-purchase cost is shown as a fixed asset (subject to depreciation), and all the unpaid instalments – not just those overdue – are shown as liabilities in balance sheets.

b. *Leasing.* **Leases** give the lessee *use* of an asset in return for regular payments of rent to the lessor, who remains the legal owner. It is usual to distinguish operating from financial leases. **Operating leases** are short-term, and often for small amounts. **Financial leases** normally cover the whole of the asset's economic life, may be for large amounts and are non-cancellable. In effect, financial leases put the lessee in almost the same position as if he had purchased the asset outright. The implied interest rate in leases is higher than the cost of ordinary borrowing. Its main advantage is that the lessor can claim tax allowances on the asset, and pass on the benefit in lower lease payments.

c. *Factoring.* **Factors** enable firms to reduce working capital tied up in debtors. The factoring company buys debts from the firm at full value, less a factoring charge, and then becomes responsible for collecting the debts. The service provided may also include sales ledger administration.

d. *Finance houses.* **Finance Houses** finance the purchase of consumer durables, such as motor cars and television sets, by individuals. They also finance industrial leasing, hire purchase and instalment credit; and more than half of their total lending is now thought to be to industry.

5.5.3 Liquidating Assets

Sometimes it may be possible for companies to continue operations while *reducing* the amount invested in certain surplus assets. This could lead to a higher rate of return on capital invested. We have already noted (in Chapter 3) how companies may have too much money tied up in stocks or debtors. Companies may also have surplus fixed assets which can be disposed of.

So far we have assumed that companies may be holding 'surplus' assets. It may also be possible to sell land and buildings to certain financial institutions, and lease them back (**sale and leaseback**). The company continues to *use* the same assets as before; but it *finances* their use by means of leasing (which is really a form of debt). This may not be much different from simply borrowing to finance ownership of the assets.

Finally there is the possibility of **disinvestment** – deliberately choosing to reduce the size of the business. This is quite common after mergers (see Chapter 8). Or a business which has been making losses may find that selling off separate divisions of the business on a 'going concern' basis may raise considerable money (while avoiding all the costs of closing down part of a business, such as redundancy payments). For example, in 1981, Fisons sold their loss-making fertiliser division to Norsk Hydro for £50 million.

Work Section

A. Revision Questions

A1 Why is ordinary share capital less risky for a company than loans?

A2 Define 'retained profits'. In what circumstances can they be negative?

A3 How can ordinary shareholders gain immediately from retained profits?

A4 Why are 'limited' companies so called?

A5 What is the 'cost' of retained profits?

A6 In what respects are shareholders in unquoted companies at a disadvantage compared with shareholders in quoted companies?

A7 What has historically been the most important source of finance for UK companies?

A8 In what respects is preference share capital like ordinary share capital, and in what respects is it like long-term borrowing?

A9 What does it mean for a preference share to be 'cumulative'?

A10 Where do preference shareholders rank in a company liquidation?

A11 Name three important differences between debt and equity capital.

A12 Identify three specific questions an applicant for a loan is likely to need to answer.

A13 Name three different ways in which a lender may try to reduce risk.

A14 What is the effect of a majority owner of a small limited company giving a personal guarantee to a bank granting his company credit?

A15 Give three examples of 'covenants' which might be attached to loans.

A16 In what respect(s) does the position of a 'secured' creditor differ from that of an ordinary (unsecured) creditor in a liquidation?

A17 What are the main characteristics of a bank overdraft? What is its main disadvantage to a borrower?

A18 How does a 'term loan' differ from a bank overdraft?

A19 What is a convertible loan stock? What are its advantages?

A20 Outline, with a simple diagram of a balance sheet, the main ways in which companies can raise money.

A21 Assuming the financial institutions and the overseas sector are in balance, which of the other three sectors (personal, industrial and public) are net lenders and which net borrowers?

A22 Name three functions of the Bank of England.

A23 How is 'borrowing short and lending long' profitable? How is it risky?

A24 What is 'matching maturity' of assets and liabilities? Why is it important for financial institutions?

A25 Why might financial institutions deliberately aim *not* to match their assets and liabilities perfectly?

A26 Why are there different types of lending institutions?

A27 How does a 'merchant bank' differ from a 'clearing bank'? What services do each provide for industry?

A28 Why can pension funds and life insurance companies concentrate on holding long-term assets?

A29 How has the inflation of the last 15 years been reflected in the pension funds' holding of assets?

A30 How can building societies 'borrow short and lend long' while avoiding undue risks?

A31 Why may small businesses find it hard to raise external capital?

A32 Why may small businesses not wish to raise external capital?

A33 Identify two reasons why individual investors may have put less money into buying unquoted company shares in recent years.

A34 What is 'venture capital'? Name three possible sources of venture capital for small companies.

A35 What is the main advantage of financial leasing as a source of business finance?

A36 What is 'sale and leaseback'?

A37 Distinguish between financial leasing and hire purchase.

A38 What is a factor?

A39 In what way do finance houses provide finance for industry?

A40 Name three ways for companies to turn assets into cash.

B. Exercises/Case Studies

B1 A company has issued 250,000 8 per cent preference shares of £1 nominal value and 400,000 ordinary shares of 25p nominal value. The directors retain for future expansion one half of anything that remains once the preference dividend has been paid. Calculate the rate of preference dividend and the amount of ordinary dividend per share if profits are:

a. £20,000;

b. £60,000;

c. £100,000.

B2 A company is declared bankrupt, having assets of £10 million on realisation, and total liabilities of £13 million, as follows:

8 per cent mortgage debenture (secured on the company's £3 million office block)	£ 1 million
9 per cent Unsecured loan stock	£ 1 million
Other liabilities	£11 million.

There are 2 million ordinary shares in issue, of nominal value 25p each. You own £100 nominal value of *each* of debenture stock, loan stock, and ordinary shares.

   a. How much money do you receive in total?
   b. How much would you receive if the assets were worth £4 million more, and the company were still 'wound up'?
B3 Refer to Fig. 5.8. (page 108).
   What proportion of total assets in each case would you consider to be:
   a. Fixed interest?
   b. Short term?

B4 A company reports the following figures in its 1981 profit and loss account:
   Profit before tax £78,000; Preference dividends £3,000; Interest payable £12,000; Depreciation £27,000; Taxation £34,000; Ordinary dividends £18,000.
   a. Draw up a statement showing these items in the order you would expect to find them in a profit and loss account.
   b. How much are retained profits for the year?
   c. How much are net funds generated from operations ('cash flow')?

B5 Fidler Limited has 200,000 Ordinary £1 shares in issue; 60,000 3½ per cent cumulative preference £1 shares; and £80,000 10 per cent debentures, repayable in 1989. Retained profits total £60,000. Calculate:
   a. The debt ratio.
   b. The amount per share the preference shareholders would receive if the company were liquidated and the total assets less the current liabilities realised £125,000 in cash.
   c. The amount per share the ordinary shareholders would receive if the total assets less current liabilities realised £190,000.

B6 Refer to B7 below. For each company calculate:
   a. Current ratio.
   b. Acid test ratio.
   c. Number of days' sales in debtors.

B7 Set out over are 'balance sheet percentages' of six companies in different industries: distilling; mail order; motor vehicle manufacturing; pharmaceuticals; retail store; tobacco. Identify each column of figures with a particular industry. The percentages relate each of the balance sheet items (and annual sales revenue) to net assets (= to long-term capital employed).

	A	B	C	D	E	F
Fixed Assets						
Cost or valuation	101	24	104	26	55	66
Less: accum. depreciation	45	6	3	9	20	33
Net book value	56	18	101	17	35	33
Goodwill and other assets			1	8	23	25
Current assets						
Stocks	61	63	18	72	30	72
Debtors	53	102	4	21	31	35
Cash	32	–	12	9	16	15
	146	165	34	102	77	122
Less: current liabilities						
Bank loans	20	26	5	6	2	23
Creditors	75	52	14	11	23	54
Dividends payable	–	3	4	3	3	1
Taxation	7	2	13	7	7	2
	102	83	36	27	35	80
= Working capital (CA – CL)	44	82	(2)	75	42	42
Net assets	100	100	100	100	100	100
Long-term debt	12	22	8	13	23	39
Deferred tax	4	2				3
Minority interests						17
Shareholders' funds	84	76	92	87	77	41
Capital employed	100	100	100	100	100	100
Sales revenue (annual)	318	310	278	111	151	149

B8 A company going into liquidation has the following liabilities: trade
creditors £172,000; bank overdrafts (secured by a floating charge)
£65,000; bank overdrafts (unsecured, but with a personal guarantee from
the managing director) £48,000; long-term 12 per cent loan (secured on
land and buildings) £80,000.

Ordinary shareholders' funds in the balance sheet are represented by:
Ordinary shares issued (100,000 at 50p each nominal value): £50,000;
Retained profits and other reserves: £112,000;
Preference share capital amounts to £20,000 (in shares of £1 each).
How much will (i) unsecured creditors, (ii) ordinary shareholders, get
a. if all the assets (book value £547,000) realise £750,000 in cash (of
which land and buildings realise £220,000)?

     b. if all the assets realise £500,000 (land and buildings £100,000)?

     c. if all the assets realise £250,000 (land and buildings £50,000)?

B9 Refer to B8 above.

     a. Draw up a list of the liabilities and shareholders' funds.

     b. Draw up a revised list, on the assumption that the long-term loan is convertible into ordinary shares at 160p each, and that the holders decide to exercise their option to convert.

     c. What difference(s) if any does conversion of such a loan into ordinary shares make:

       i. to the company's profit and loss account in future (if it were to continue in business)?

       ii. to the company's debt ratio taken from the balance sheet?

B10 From the latest annual reports of two different companies, study the funds statement, and draw up a brief summary of the sources of funds for each company for each of the two latest years, distinguishing between equity and debt; between retained profits and new ordinary shares; and between short-term and long-term debt.

C. Essay Questions

C1 Why might shareholders object to managements choosing to retain a large proportion of profits in a company? What, if anything, can they do about it?

C2 Discuss the relative advantages and disadvantages to a company of issues of ordinary shares and loan stocks.

C3 Discuss the relative advantages and disadvantages to a company of a bank overdraft and a term loan.

C4 'A banker is someone who will lend you money only when you don't need it.' Discuss.

C5 Why have variable-interest loans become more popular in recent years?

C6 How could a profitable and fairly fast-growing small business hope to finance its need for funds? What would be the advantages and disadvantages of each source?

C7 Why might a medium-sized company choose to factor its debts?

C8 Is there a role for preference capital? Why or why not?

C9 Why might management's interests with respect to sources of funds conflict with those of shareholders?

C10 Why has the market for long-term corporate debt dwindled in the last 10 years? What might reverse this trend?

C11 What would be the advantages and disadvantages to a company of borrowing long-term on an index-linked basis?

C12 Financial institutions such as insurance companies and pension funds now own about half of UK quoted equity shares. Where will this trend lead to? Does it matter? What (if anything) might reverse the trend?

Chapter 6

The Stock Exchange

Objective: *To identify the Stock Exchange's economic functions and to explain how the market works; to discuss the various ways of issuing equity shares, and the main Stock Exchange ratios; to describe the 'gilt-edged' market for government securities; to outline a 'present value' model for valuing securities and to describe other methods of valuing shares.*

Synopsis: *The Stock Exchange functions as a secondary market as well as raising new capital for companies and governments. (Most transactions are in government securities.) The proportion of UK equities held by institutions has grown consistently in the past 20 years.*

An unquoted company can raise new equity capital by 'going public', quoted companies by rights issues to existing shareholders.

Equity investors value company shares by discounting expected future dividends at their after-tax opportunity cost, the key factors being expectations as to future profits, risks and interest rates.

6.1 The Equity Market

6.1.1 Economic Functions

The Stock Exchange is a **market** on which investors can buy and sell **securities** of companies and governments. Many leading international companies' shares are also quoted in London. As we saw in Fig. 5.1, new issues of equity shares are far less important sources of funds for companies than retained profits and bank borrowing. But the Stock Exchange forms the major

	Market value September 1981		Transactions 1980		New issues 1980
	(£b'n)	(%)	(£b'n)	(%)	(£b'n)
UK government, up to 5 years	25	14	75	38	3
UK government, over 5 years	44	24	76	39	12
Other fixed interest	25	14	14	7	–
UK companies, equity shares	88	48	31*	16*	1
	182	100	196	100	16

* Including overseas companies (figures not published separately).

Fig. 6.1: Stock Exchange market values and transactions, 1980.

* See Question B1

market for new government borrowing to finance the **public sector borrowing requirement** (PSBR).

In September 1981 there were just over 100 different British government (**gilt-edged**) securities, with a total market value of some £69 billion. UK quoted equity shares of about 2,000 companies had a market value of about £88 billion: this compares with about 3,000 companies in 1970, with a market value of some £160 billion (in 1981 pounds). The fall in total market value is roughly reflected in the fall in the FT-Actuaries 500-Share Index in real terms between 1970 and 1981 (see Fig. 6.4). The decline in the number of firms is largely due to mergers over the period.

Most Stock Exchange transactions involve the exchange of *existing* securities between investors. Only a small proportion of transactions consists of *new* issues, by companies or governments.

Since investors value liquidity – the ability to sell quickly if they need the money – the existence of a **secondary market** makes it much easier to raise money on the **primary market** than it would otherwise be. Figure 6.2 illustrates the difference between (a) the primary and (b) the secondary functions of the stock exchange. In (a) the company is issuing new shares to A, B, C, and D, and receives the cash. In (b) the *company* is not directly involved in the transactions and *doesn't* receive any cash: shareholder A is not dealing; B is selling shares to D; and C is selling shares to E, at the market price at the time of each deal.

The capital invested by companies and by governments is often represented by fixed physical assets, such as equipment, buildings and roads. Thus workers in a business may tend to be 'anchored' to a particular location or type of business. But if a market exists where shares in the ownership of these assets can be bought and sold, the ultimate investor possesses wealth which is 'mobile'. He can sell his shares to someone else if he needs the cash, or if he wants to invest in another kind of business or in another country.

Stock Exchange transactions by themselves produce neither profits nor losses for investors *as a whole* (ignoring dealing costs). They merely reflect profits and losses arising in trading and manufacturing. It is ultimately *con-*

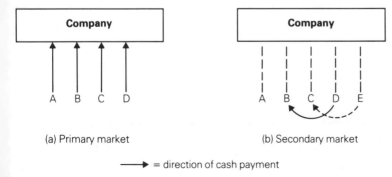

(a) Primary market   (b) Secondary market

⟶ = direction of cash payment

Fig. 6.2: The Stock Exchange: primary and secondary markets.

sumers who determine Stock Exchange prices, by the way they react to productive activities and their costs. Entrepreneurs can buy control of companies on the Stock Exchange (see Chapter 8). If they succeed in satisfying consumers better than other companies, their companies' shares rise in value and they make profits. If they fail, they make losses.

The market is helped by the presence of short-term **speculators**. **'Bulls'** buy securities hoping they will rise in price, while **'bears'** hope that share prices will fall. They either sell shares they do not even own (**'selling short'**), in the hope of being able to buy them later at lower prices than they sold for; or at least refrain from buying yet, in the hope of being able to do so more cheaply later.

If on balance speculators make a profit, the implication is that their views are 'more correct' than other people's. Their activities drive market prices *sooner* to levels they would otherwise have taken longer to reach. The risks connected with Stock Exchange securities exist anyway: *somebody* has to bear them. (In contrast, *gambling* implies the creation of *unnecessary* risks.)

6.1.2 Shareholdings in UK Quoted Equities

In 1980 the Stock Exchange analysed the shareholdings in UK quoted equities. The estimated 1980 pattern of ownership was roughly one third insurance companies and pension funds, one third other institutions and one third individuals. The continuing trend of the past 25 years shows a decline in the proportion of quoted equities held by individuals and an increase in that held by insurance companies, pension funds, unit trusts and investment trusts. A major reason has been tax: both the tax advantages for institutions, and the tax disadvantages for individuals, of holding ordinary shares.

	1957 (%)	1963 (%)	1969 (%)	1975 (%)	1980 (%)
Individuals	68	56	50	40	36
Insurance companies	9	10	12	16	18
Pension funds	3	6	9	17	18
Unit trusts and investment trusts	6	9	10	10	13
Other institutions	14	19	19	17	15
	100	100	100	100	100

★

Fig. 6.3: Listed UK ordinary shares: beneficial ownership, 1957–80.

* See Question B2

The main function of **unit trusts** and **investment trusts** is to invest in ordinary shares on behalf of individuals, who thus get the benefit of a diversified portfolio (see 7.2), expert management and lower dealing costs. A unit trust is 'open-ended': it can expand if individuals wish to purchase more units, or contract if people want to sell back units.

An investment trust is an ordinary limited company, whose purpose is to invest in securities. It is required to distribute nearly all its net income as dividends to shareholders. For reasons which are not entirely clear, the shares of quoted investment trusts usually trade at a significant *discount* from the underlying market value of their shareholdings. It is thought that about three-quarters of the shares in investment trusts are now owned by other financial institutions.

6.1.3 Market Indices

There is interest in the equity market as a whole, as well as in specific industries and companies. Two main equity market indices show how the whole market is performing: the Financial Times Industrial Ordinary 30-share Index, and the FT-Actuaries 500-share Index.

1. *The FT Industrial Ordinary Index.* The 30-share FT Ordinary Index is quoted hourly as an indicator of equity market changes. It contains leading shares from most of the industry sectors; and stood at 570 in March 1982. The index is computed as a geometric average (taking the 30th root of all

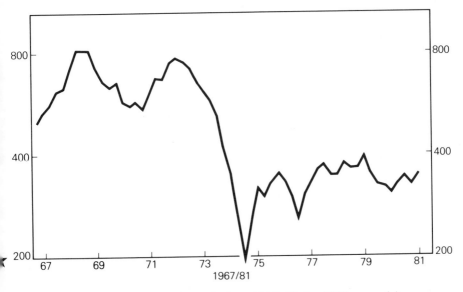

Fig. 6.4: FT-Actuaries 500-share Index, 1967–81 (in 1981 pounds).

* See Question B3

the share prices multiplied together). This makes it unsuitable for comparison over long periods of time. In the short run, however, it gives a fair idea of how leading shares have moved – though quoting it to *two* places of decimals is a nice example of spurious accuracy!

2. *The FT-Actuaries 500-share Index.* The FT-Actuaries 500-share Index was started at 100 in 1962, and gives a wide coverage of UK industrial shares. (There is also an All-Share Index which includes 250 financial and overseas shares as well, making a total of 750 shares.) The 500-share Index, computed as an arithmetical average, is more suitable than the 30-share Index for comparisons over periods of years. Figure 6.4 shows the 500-share Index since 1967, adjusted for inflation. (The published index figures are *not* adjusted for inflation.) Especially noticeable is the very sharp fall throughout 1973 and 1974, only partly recovered during the 1975 rally.

6.2 How the Market Works

6.2.1 Jobbers and Brokers

Stockbrokers are agents for investors buying and selling securities. On the Stock Exchange **jobbers** are the principals (owners of securities) with whom brokers deal. The 4,000 members of the Stock Exchange are organised into about 250 firms of brokers and 20 firms of jobbers.

Stockbrokers make their money by commissions on transactions, jobbers by their '**turn**' – the difference between the prices at which they buy and sell. Firms of jobbers specialise in particular industries, ideally at least three firms to each industry. Since jobbers are prepared to hold stocks (inventories) of the securities in which they deal (or to go 'short' of them), a buyer of shares does not have to wait for another investor to sell.

Example: Mr X wants to buy 1,000 ordinary shares in Lex Service Group Limited. The market price is about 100p a share. Mr X's broker, on the floor of the Stock Exchange, will approach one or more of the motor industry jobbers and ask: 'What are Lex?' To which Jobber A may say: '100 to 102', meaning that he is prepared to buy at 100 or sell at 102. (He does not yet know whether Mr X's broker is buying or selling.) Jobber B may reply: '99 to 101' to the same question. Mr X's broker, being a buyer, naturally prefers the lower price, and agrees to pay Jobber B 101p each for 1,000 Lex shares.

On the same day, Mrs Y's broker is trying to sell 1,000 Lex shares for her. He gets the same quotation from Jobber A as Mr X's broker did, while Jobber C quotes: '98 to 100'. Mrs Y's broker, being a seller, prefers the higher price, and agrees to sell 1,000 Lex shares to Jobber A for 100p each. Although each jobber quoted a 'turn' of 2p, Mr X bought at 101p while Mrs Y sold at 100p. (Indeed, had Mr X's broker happened to approach Jobber C, he could have bought at only 100p.) The position is summarised in Fig. 6.5.

Mr X (buyer) ← Broker 1 → $\begin{cases} \text{Jobber A } 100–102 \\ \text{Jobber B } \ 99–101 \end{cases}$

Mrs Y (seller) ← Broker 2 → $\begin{cases} \text{Jobber A } 100–102 \\ \text{Jobber C } \ 98–100 \end{cases}$

Fig. 6.5: Buying and selling 1,000 Lex shares.

When everyone wants to sell, jobbers quickly reduce their price quotations. Otherwise they would be flooded with large numbers of shares. And when everyone wants to buy, jobbers mark *up* prices to deter people. Thus changes in jobbers' views of supply and demand can affect Stock Exchange prices without any deals occurring. This often happens as a result of overnight news. When there is no imbalance of buyers and sellers, share prices will be stable. Since expert speculators are always on the look-out for profit, even someone who knows nothing about the Stock Exchange can usually rely on the market price as being 'fair'.

6.2.2 Transactions and Costs

Mr X and Mrs Y have to pay certain dealing expenses (**'transaction costs'**): broker's commission, jobber's 'turn', and (for the buyer) stamp duty. Compared with the 'middle price' of 100p for Lex shares, Mr X (the buyer) pays nearly 105p, while Mrs Y (the seller) receives just over 98p.

Mr X – buyer	£	*Mrs Y – seller*	£
Cost of 1,000 Lex at 101p	1,010.00	Sale of 1,000 Lex at 100p	1,000.00
Add: Broker's commission	17.42	Less: Broker's commission	17.25
Stamp duty at 2%	21.00		
Total cost	1,048.42	Net proceeds	982.75

Fig. 6.6: Transaction costs in 1,000 Lex shares.

It is not cheap to buy and sell shares; and clearly it can be expensive to 'turn over' one's equity holdings continually. If Mr X changed his mind as soon as he had bought the Lex shares, he would need to sell them at no less than 107p to avoid making an overall loss. This implies a new 'middle price' of 108p – an increase of 8 per cent in the share price. The costs would be lower for a large transaction; and much lower for government stocks (which are free of stamp duty).

6.3 Issuing Equity Shares

6.3.1 'Going Public'

A company may wish its ordinary shares to be **quoted** on the Stock Exchange for two main reasons: to raise additional share capital from the public; or to enable shareholders to sell some of their shares.

When a company **'goes public'**, it must issue a **prospectus** describing the history of the company, its recent financial results, the names of the directors and certain other details. It must also agree to abide by the rules of the Stock Exchange, concerning announcements about trading prospects, reporting financial results, etc. Normally at least 25 per cent of the ordinary share capital must be offered to the public, in order to ensure a reasonably free market in the shares. (The remainder may continue to be held by the existing shareholders.)

For shares in smaller companies, a new market has recently been set up – the **unlisted securities market (USM)** – some of whose requirements are less stringent than for a full listing. A company would normally need to have equity capital worth at least £1 million to be eligible for the USM; but only 10 per cent of the shares need be offered to the public.

There are four methods of going public:

1. An **offer for sale** (for larger issues) is an issue to the public at large, at a fixed price. The price will normally be above the stated 'nominal' (or 'par') value of the shares: any excess is known as a **share premium**. The shares being issued may initially all be taken up by the **issuing house**, as a preliminary to selling the shares to the public.

2. A **placing** means that a **new issue** (below a certain size) is 'placed' privately by the issuing house (probably a merchant bank) with particular clients, including financial institutions, at a price fixed in advance. A proportion has to be made available to jobbers, to ensure a market. There may be lower expenses than for other methods of issue, but perhaps a higher market discount. There may also be a danger of ending up with concentrated blocks of shareholdings.

3. The **tender method** is a third (rare) method for new issues. Here no fixed price is set in advance. Instead, offers from the public are solicited, and the highest price which will raise all the required money is accepted as the asking price for all successful purchases. The market discount is likely to be small, which discourages **stags** (bulls of new issues).

4. Finally, an **introduction** is used when a company already has a wide spread of shareholders. No new money is raised, nor any shares offered for sale. The purpose is simply to provide a public market in the shares in future.

Pricing new shares may be difficult, especially if there are few directly comparable shares already quoted. If the price of a new issue (fixed some days in advance) is too high, nobody will buy, and the shares will be left with the **underwriters**; but if the price is too low, the issuing company's existing shareholders will find their equity interest **diluted**.

The costs of issuing equity shares to the public can be high. In addition to a price discount (of between 10 and 20 per cent) needed to attract buyers of new shares in a relatively risky little-known company, administrative expenses would be at least $7\frac{1}{2}$ per cent for issues up to £2 million, and 5 per cent or so above that level. These include underwriting costs, fees to professional advisers, printing and advertising costs and capital duty.

6.3.2 Rights Issues

The methods of issue described in the last section applied to companies 'going public', whose shares were previously unquoted. Companies whose shares are already quoted on the Stock Exchange use a **rights issue** to raise more money. This is required by the Stock Exchange as being fairest to existing shareholders.

A rights issue offers extra shares to existing shareholders, in proportion to their holdings, priced at some discount from the current market price per share. In contrast to the importance of the pricing of new issues, in theory it makes *no difference at all* at what price a rights issue is offered. An existing shareholder who is unwilling to take up the new shares being offered can always sell his 'rights' in the market for their 'value', and thus avoid any loss.

Example: A company with 5 million ordinary shares already in issue, with a current market value of 140p each (= total value £7 million), plans to raise a further £2 million by means of a rights issue. Thus the new total value of the equity will be £9 million. Figure 6.7 shows two alternative ways of achieving this: either issuing 1 for 1 at 40p, or else issuing 2 for 5 at 100p.

	1 for 1 at 40p	2 for 5 at 100p
Number of new shares issued	5 million	2 million
New total number of shares (n)	10 million	7 million
New share price (£9m ÷ n)	90 p	128.57 p
Value of the 'rights'	50 p	28.57 p

Fig. 6.7: Rights issue alternatives.

6.3.3 Analysis of Recent Issues

Figure 6.8 analyses methods of raising new capital between 1963 and 1979. It shows three things:
1. The total 'real' amount raised in the 1970s is less than in the previous

★ See Questions B8, B9, B10

10 years. The average for 1978–9 is only just over half as much as in the years 1963–7 (adjusted for inflation).

2. Since 1972, little fixed interest (preference and loan) capital has been raised. The reasons for this were discussed in Chapter 5.

3. Rather than a large number of smaller companies issuing shares to the public for the first time, most new money raised on the stock exchange since 1972 has come by means of rights issue by companies which are already quoted.

Annual averages (September 1981 £s)	*1963–7* (£m.)	(%)	*1968–72* (£m.)	(%)	*1973–7* (£m.)	(%)	*1978–9* (£m.)	(%)
New issues								
Placings	1,525	53	850	31	250	12	135	8
Offers for sale	385	14	460	17	170	9	30	2
Tenders	30	1	90	3	55	3	30	2
Rights issues								
Ordinary share capital	585	20	900	32	1,440	72	1,330	86
Preference and loan capital	340	12	470	17	75	4	25	2
	2,865	100	2,770	100	1,990	100	1,550	100

Fig. 6.8: Methods of raising new capital, 1963–79 (in September 1981 £s).

6.3.4 Bonus Issues and Share Splits

So far we have been discussing two kinds of share issues on the Stock Exchange: new listings, which usually raise new money for the company, but which may merely transfer shares from existing shareholders to new ones; and rights issues, by which listed companies raise new capital from their existing shareholders (or from those who buy the 'rights' to subscribe). Two kinds of share issues which raise *no* new money for companies must also be understood, in order to appreciate the meaning of certain Stock Exchange ratios (described in **6.4**).

1. **Bonus issues** ('scrip issues') represent 'capitalisation' of a company's reserves, by transferring some of a company's **reserves** on the balance sheet to issued share capital. (This is purely a book-keeping entry: the 'reserves' are simply a sub-heading of shareholders' funds in accounts, *not* real assets.) The *total* amount of shareholders' funds remains unchanged, since no new money has been raised; but some of the company's retained profits have now been turned into paid-up ordinary share capital, and are no longer available to be paid out in dividends.

Example: A company with 4 million issued 25p ordinary shares, and reserves amounting to £2.8 million, decides to make a '1 for 2' bonus issue. The position of shareholders' funds on the balance sheet before and after the issue is shown in Fig. 6.9. The nominal issued share capital has risen by £0.5 million, but reserves have fallen by exactly the same amount.

		Before (£m.)		After (£m.)
Issued 25p ordinary shares:	(4m.)	1.0	(6m.)	1.5
Reserves		2.8		2.3
= Shareholders' funds		3.8		3.8

Fig. 6.9: How a bonus issue affects shareholders' funds.

★ *John Higgins owned 1,000 shares before the bonus issue, quoted at 300p each. His total shareholding was worth £3,000. As a result of the '1 for 2' bonus issue, Mr Higgins received an 'extra' 500 shares, so he then owned 1,500 shares. But because there were 50 per cent more shares in issue, while nothing else about the company had changed, each share would be worth only two-thirds (= 100/150) what it was worth before. After the bonus issue, each share would be quoted at 200p. So Mr Higgins would own 1,500 shares worth 200p each, giving a total value unchanged at £3,000!*

2. **Share splits** simply 'split' shares into smaller units, without even affecting balance sheet amounts. Suppose a company has 600,000 ordinary £1 shares in issue, with a market price of £12 each. After the company makes a '4 for 1' split, it will have 2.4 million ordinary 25p shares in issue, each worth 300p. (It may be noticed that a '4 for 1' *split* means 4 new shares *instead of* each existing share held; whereas a '4 for 1' *bonus issue* means 4 new shares *in addition to* each existing share held, making 5 in all.)

★ 6.4 Stock Exchange Ratios

6.4.1 Earnings Per Share
Earnings per share is a company's profit after tax for a period divided by the number of ordinary shares issued. If profits after tax were £2.4 million, with 30 million ordinary shares in issue, the earnings per share would be

★ See Questions B11, B24

8.0p. The absolute amount is of little significance, because bonus issues and share splits can change the number of shares in issue. (In making comparisons over time, they must be adjusted for.) When ordinary shares are issued for cash, a weighted average is used to represent the number of shares in issue during the period.

6.4.2 Price/Earnings Ratio

The current market price of a company's ordinary shares can be divided by the earnings per share to produce a **price/earnings ratio**. With earnings per share of 8.0p, if the market price were 72p, the price/earnings ratio would be 9.0. This can be used as a rough measure of the 'capitalisation rate' of the company's earnings.

If current earnings are *unusually* low, we may expect to see a *high* price/earnings ratio (and vice versa). The market price is looking *forward* to future earnings (or dividends), whereas earnings per share is based on *past* results. Clearly caution is needed in interpreting price/earnings ratios: if a *loss* was made last year, the price/earnings ratio will actually be *negative*! The amount of 'profit' a company reports for a period is not uniquely 'correct': it depends on particular accounting conventions and estimates. (For example, earnings reported on the conventional historical cost basis would often be significantly reduced – if not altogether eliminated! – by inflation accounting.)

6.4.3 Dividend Yield

The **dividend yield** is the dividend per share divided by the current market price. It fluctuates from day to day (like the price/earnings ratio) as the market price changes. Thus if a company pays a dividend of 3.5p cash per share out of its 8.0p earnings per share for a period, and if the market price per share is 72p, one might expect the dividend yield to be 4.9 per cent (= 3.5/72). Unfortunately the position is complicated by tax.

The company is 'deemed' to have deducted basic rate income tax (at 30 per cent) from the 3.5p cash dividend paid. The **gross dividend** is thus 5.0p per share (from which 1.5p tax has been **deducted at source**; and this *gross* amount of 5.0p is the shareholder's dividend income. The dividend yield uses the *gross* dividend per share, so in this case it would amount to 6.9 per cent (= 5.0/72). It is only a *partial* measure of a shareholder's total 'return', since it does not allow for any 'capital gain' if the share's market price rises above original cost.

6.4.4 Dividend Cover

Dividend cover means the number of times that a company's earnings cover its **net dividends** paid. In our example, dividend cover would be 2.3 times – either (a) £2.4m./£1.05m. in total, or (b) 8.0p/3.5p per share. The *reciprocal* of dividend cover is sometimes used, called **dividend payout ratio**: in the example quoted it is 44 per cent (= 3.5/8.0).

A high dividend cover means that even if profits drop sharply, a company may still be able to maintain its dividend out of current profits. If dividends exceed current profits, dividend cover is less than 1.0. (A company may legally pay a dividend even if it makes a loss, as long as it has retained profits available from earlier periods.)

6.5 The Gilt-edged Market

6.5.1 The Market in Gilts

About 75 per cent by value of all Stock Exchange transactions is in UK government securities. The 'gilt-edged' market is important because it reflects the market's view of future interest rates. We have seen how critical these are in many financial decisions. Figure 6.10 shows how discount houses concentrate on dealing in 'shorts', while insurance companies and pension funds tend to hold and deal in 'mediums' and 'longs'.

	Transactions		*End-of-year holdings*	
	Short-term (%)	*Over 5 years* (%)	*Short-term* (%)	*Over 5 years* (%)
Discount houses	31	3	5	–
Banks in the UK	17	7	12	2
Building societies	5	1	17	2
Insurance companies	8	26	7	34
Pension funds	2	12	–	20
Official holdings	11	8	17	11
Other	26	43	42	31
	100	100	100	100

Fig. 6.10: UK government securities split between investors: transactions and end-of-year holdings, 1980.

There are several different kinds of goverment securities:

a. *Maturity*. New government securities are issued with maturity periods varying from three months to more than 25 years. They are distinguished by the outstanding period until final maturity, when repayment of the borrowing becomes due. 'Shorts' have less than five years to run, 'mediums' from five to 15 years, and 'longs' over 15 years (including **irredeemable** securities, which need *never* be repaid).

b. *Coupon rate*. To suit high-rate taxpayers, some government securities are issued with very low **coupons** (nominal rates of interest paid per £100 nominal of stock). They are issued at a large discount from par (£100), thus providing a large element of 'capital gain' to anyone holding until maturity. The capital gain is counted as part of the overall **yield to redemption**, in addition to the regular interest yield (the **flat yield**).

c. *Index-linking*. The British government started in 1981 to issue low-coupon gilts with interest and principal **index-linked** (adjustable by reference to the **retail price index**). By eliminating the risk of inflation, the government is enabled to offer only a very low 'real' interest rate – about $2\frac{1}{2}$ per cent a year. If ordinary 'money' gilts offered a yield of $12\frac{1}{2}$ per cent a year, while index-linked gilts (of the same maturity) offered a 'real' yield of only $2\frac{1}{2}$ per cent a year, then the market must be expecting an average rate of inflation over the period of about 10 per cent a year.

6.5.2 The 'Term Structure' of Interest Rates

The different maturity dates of UK government securities reveal the **term structure** of interest rates. Charting interest yields against the time to maturity (or 'term') of risk-free government securities, may show three different shapes (Fig. 6.11).

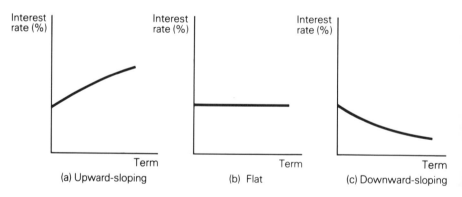

Fig. 6.11: Three kinds of 'term structure' of interest rates.

According to the *expectations theory*, the term structure will be upward-sloping if investors expect that interest rates will rise (perhaps because they expect the rate of inflation to increase), but downward-sloping if they expect interest rates to fall.

The *liquidity preference theory* argues that most lenders want to lend short-term, while most borrowers want to borrow long-term. Hence borrowers have to offer lenders a *premium*, to induce them to lend long; which implies an

upward-sloping term structure reflecting the liquidity premium which has
to be paid on longer-term securities.

6.5.3 2½ per cent Consolidated Stock

Certain UK government securities are irredeemable, carrying a promise to
pay a stated coupon rate each year for ever. Some of these 'perpetuities' have
been in issue for more than 100 years, so they allow long-term comparisons
of gilt-edged prices and interest yields.

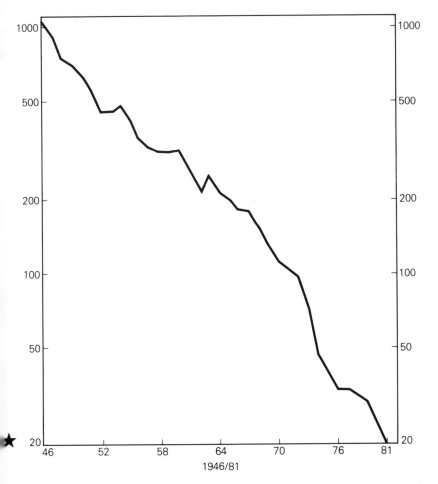

Fig. 6.12: 2½ per cent Consolidated Stock: market price of £100 nominal,
1946/81 (in September 1981 pounds).

★ See Question B4

In the years immediately after the Second World War, interest rates, by modern standards, were low. Indeed, 2½ per cent Consolidated Stock was quoted at par (£100) in 1946, implying a level of interest rates of 2½ per cent. Figure 6.12 shows the market price of £100 nominal of 2½ per cent Consolidated Stock for each year between 1946 and 1981 – adjusted for inflation. This chart dramatically illustrates the single most important financial phenomenon of the post-war years in the UK – continuous, rapid and accelerating government-created **currency debasement**. In 35 years since 1946, the real value of 2½ per cent Consolidated Stock fell by more than 98 per cent!

6.6 Share Valuation

6.6.1 Fixed Interest Securities

In Chapter 4 we saw how to 'value' future cash flows expected from a capital investment project, by discounting them back to 'present value'. The same approach can also be used for valuing shares (or other assets).

Imagine a risk-free government security guaranteeing an annual interest payment of £5 a year for ever (a **perpetuity**). Ignoring tax, what would we expect its market price (i.e. its present value) to be? We know the amount and timing of future cash receipts, so all we need to determine is the appropriate interest rate to use when discounting them. This should be the 'opportunity cost' – the rate of return which could be earned on similar-risk investments.

> *Example: If the current interest yield on risk-free government securities is 12.5 per cent a year, then the present value of '£5 a year for ever' should be £40, since this gives the required interest yield of 12.5 per cent (= 5/40).*
>
> *To find the capital value of a perpetuity, we simply divide the annual amount of interest by the appropriate interest rate. Thus in this case, £5.00/0.125 = £40.*
>
> *If the interest rate fell to 10 per cent a year, our stock's capital value must increase to £50 (= £5.00/0.100). Otherwise nobody would choose to hold other stocks: everyone would prefer to hold our stock (if it were still yielding 12.5 per cent a year). Indeed, people would buy our stock until the price had been driven up to £50, at which point it would yield the 'current' rate of interest of 10 per cent (= 5/50).*

6.6.2 Equity Shares

We can value equity shares in the same way: by discounting the expected future cash receipts from owning the shares, at the opportunity cost of capital. Instead of a regular fixed money annuity, we now have to deal with dividends which can fluctuate. A convenient simplifying assumption which is often made is that, in money terms, the latest annual net dividend per share will grow at a *constant* annual rate in future.

An individual shareholder's 'return' from holding shares consists of two parts: **dividends** plus **capital gain**. Yet the stock market can value a company's equity shares *solely* on the basis of future dividends.

It is true that an individual mortal shareholder (A) (or his estate) will ultimately sell his shares. But he will sell to some *other* shareholder (B), who will presumably value the shares on the basis of future dividends plus ultimate sales proceeds ... Fig. 6.13 shows how we can 'cancel out' the various intermediate purchases and sales on the secondary market, ending up with the value of the shares depending on the stream of future dividends. For simplicity we assume that shareholders A, B, C, D, etc. hold the shares for exactly 10 years each.

Share-holder	Cost of purchase				Sales proceeds
A	Value EOY 0	=	Dividends EOY 1–10	+	Value EOY 10
B	Value EOY 10	=	Dividends EOY 11–20	+	Value EOY 20
C	Value EOY 20	=	Dividends EOY 21–30	+	Value EOY 30
D	Value EOY 30	=	Dividends EOY 31–40	+	Value EOY 40
E	Value EOY 40	=	....		
...					
	Value EOY 0	=	Dividends EOY 1–40 ...		

Fig. 6.13: Valuing shares solely on future dividends.

6.6.3 Calculating Equity Share Values

Applying the present value model to share valuation is straightforward enough in theory, though of course in practice estimating the actual numbers is not easy.

If the latest annual net dividend per share is D, the expected (assumed constant) rate of growth in future dividends per share is g, and the opportunity cost of equivalent-risk equity shares is k, then the present value per share (P) can be found by discounting as follows:

$$P = \frac{D^0(1+g)}{(1+k)} + \frac{D^0(1+g)^2}{(1+k)^2} + \frac{D^0(1+g)^3}{(1+k)^3} + \ldots + \frac{D^0(1+g)^\infty}{(1+k)^\infty}.$$

This can be simplified (see footnote on page 134) to: $P = \dfrac{D^1}{k-g}$.

Example: A share with an expected dividend this year of 11p, an expected future growth rate in dividends per share of 10 per cent a year, and a 15 per cent opportunity cost of equity capital, would be valued at 220p:

$$Value = \frac{11}{0.15 - 0.10} = \frac{11}{0.05} = 220p.$$

*To determine the opportunity cost of equity capital (in this case 15 per cent),
we simply add the assumed constant growth rate of 10 per cent a year to the
net dividend yield of 5 per cent a year based on D^1 – the end-of-current-year
dividend).*

Thus $k = \dfrac{D^1}{P} + g.$

*We must remember, of course, that both 'k' and 'g' are only estimates, so
the difference between them $(k-g)$ is likely to be subject to a big margin of
error.*

6.6.4 Why Share Prices Fluctuate

There can be three kinds of reason why a share's price may fluctuate:

1 There may be a change to the current year's anticipated dividend. Thus
when De Beers unexpectedly cut its dividend early in 1982, the share price
immediately fell by more than 10 per cent. Clearly a change that has *already*
been anticipated by the market will *not* affect the share's market value: only
unanticipated changes will do so. This explains why when a company
announces bad news the share price sometimes goes *up*: presumably the
market was expecting even worse news.

2 The expected future growth rate in dividends per share may vary presumably more or less in line with expected future growth in *earnings* per share.
This may happen for many possible reasons: new management, technological inventions, competitive activity, changes in customer tastes, new
government policies, etc.

3 A change in the 'opportunity cost of capital' could also cause the share price
to vary. This might stem from a change in pure time preference, in risk
premium, or in inflation premium. There are many reasons why the market's
view of the riskiness of a particular company might alter. An analysis of
all the reasons might start by distinguishing between 'business risk' and
'financial risk'. A change in the expected future rate of inflation could
certainly change the inflation premium, but it might affect the dividend
growth rate to the same extent (if both were expressed in money – rather
than in 'real' – terms).

Derivation of expression: $P = \dfrac{D^1}{k - g} :\!—$

Multiply both sides of the equation shown by $\dfrac{(1 + k)}{(1 + g)}.$

Then from the resulting product, subtract the equation shown above, to give:

$$\frac{P(1 + k)}{(1 + g)} - P = D^0 - \frac{D^0(1 + g)^\infty}{(1 + k)^\infty}$$

Since $k > g$, the final term collapses to zero.

Thus any change in the *future* prospects of a business – especially its expected returns or the risks involved – may affect a share's present market value. Since life is uncertain, with new information, new conditions, and new perceptions of the future continually developing, it is hardly surprising that share prices continually fluctuate. *Only in an unchanging world where everything in the future had already been fully and correctly foreseen would this not be so.*

6.6.5 Alternative Methods of Valuation

a. *Price/earnings ratio.* We noted earlier the price/earnings ratio as a method of valuing companies (**6.4.2**). When we *already* knew the market price per share, we divided it by the earnings per share to determine the price/earnings ratio. But for an unquoted company we might know the earnings per share, and want to estimate the value (price) per share.

If we know the price/earnings ratio for a quoted company in the same industry, we could reduce it somewhat, to allow for the extra risk of an unquoted company. We could then multiply the unquoted company's known earnings per share by the adjusted price/earnings ratio, to estimate the value per share. (The same approach applied to a company's total profits after tax could be used to value the company as a whole.)

Obviously the higher the price/earnings ratio, the higher the market value will be for any given level of earnings per share. Implicitly we are assuming either a faster growth rate (g in our formula) in future dividends, or else a lower opportunity cost of capital (k in the formula). But this is fair enough: if we value returns and dislike risk, then we would expect a higher value for a company with either higher returns or lower risks than another.

The price/earnings ratio represents the **capitalising factor** being applied to this year's earnings. But it does not represent literally the 'number of years' future earnings' incorporated in the valuation. The discounting process means that future earnings are worth less than the same amount of earnings this year. Thus a price/earnings ratio of 9.0 does *not* mean that we are looking only nine years ahead: as we know, our valuation formula includes anticipated future dividends *for ever*.

b. *Book value.* Another method of valuation uses **book value**. It simply assumes a company to be 'worth' the amount shown in the latest balance sheet. This is not very satisfactory, since historical cost balance sheets do not pretend to show current values: they merely show the original cost of assets, less amounts written off by way of depreciation. Even **current cost accounting** balance sheets are subject to many drawbacks. Nevertheless, for unquoted companies and for unincorporated businesses (partnerships and sole traders), book values are at least *available*; and despite their disadvantages they are quite often used in practice for purposes of valuation.

c. *Liquidation value.* **Liquidation value** (or **break-up value**) is ultimately the floor value of the assets of a business. If we cannot expect in future to earn cash receipts with a present value more than the assets can now be sold for, then we should sell them now if we want to maximise present value. Thus it may sometimes be appropriate to value a company on the basis of the net realisable value of its separate assets, rather than on the basis of future expected earnings of the going concern.

But presumably whoever is going to *buy* the assets is planning somehow to earn future cash flows from employing them. And presumably he thinks these will produce a present value higher than the purchase price. The fact that he thinks he can use the assets more profitably than we think *we* can is a good enough reason for selling. *Indeed, this economic logic underlies the whole idea of the competitive market combined with private ownership of the means of production. The aim of maximising present value, combined with the freedom of owners to buy and sell assets, leads to the 'best' (most profitable) use of scarce resources.*

Work Section

A. Revision Questions

A1 Roughly what proportion of Stock Exchange *transactions* (by value) is in UK government securities, and what proportion in equity shares?

A2 Roughly what proportion of the *total market value* of listed UK company equity shares is represented by the market value of gilts?

A3 How does the amount of money raised by companies on the Stock Exchange compare with the amount they raise in other ways?

A4 What is the difference between the Stock Exchange's primary and secondary functions?

A5 Since most ('normal') Stock Exchange transactions do not provide finance for companies, what use is the Stock Exchange to them?

A6 How can an individual investor remain 'mobile', while company (and government) assets are often 'fixed'?

A7 What is the difference between Stock Exchange deals and pure gambling?

A8 What is the difference between an investment trust and a unit trust?

A9 Roughly what proportion of UK quoted equities is now held by individuals? Why has this proportion been falling in recent decades?

A10 What are the main differences between the FT 30-share Industrial Ordinary Index and the FT-Actuaries 500-share Index?

A11 Describe how a straightforward purchase of 100 ICI shares by an individual would be carried out.

A12 What do we mean when we say that, in a Stock Exchange transaction, the broker is an 'agent' and the jobber is a 'principal'?

A13 How may transaction costs lead to a conflict of interest between stock-brokers and their clients?

A14 Roughly how much would an equity share have to rise in value soon after purchase before a £5,000 investor could expect to 'break even'?

A15 Why can even ignorant Stock Exchange investors normally rely on Stock Exchange prices being 'fair'?

A16 What are the two main reasons for a company wishing to have its equity shares quoted on the Stock Exchange?

A17 What is the Unlisted Securities Market? What are its two main advantages compared with the ordinary Listed Market?

A18 Name three methods of making a new issue of equity shares.

A19 Why is pricing a new issue of shares important when a company goes public? Why is it difficult?

A20 What are the two main types of expense of issuing new shares when a company goes public?

A21 What is a rights issue? Explain the mechanics.

A22 Why should an existing shareholder not lose whether he takes up his 'rights' or not?

A23 What is a bonus issue of shares (also called a scrip issue)? How does it affect the value of a shareholder's total holding?

A24 How does a bonus issue affect the shareholders' funds section of a balance sheet?

A25 What is a share split?

A26 What is earnings per share?

A27 Why is it not meaningful to compare one company's earnings per share directly with another company's?

A28 What is a price/earnings ratio? Could it ever be negative? Why?

A29 What is dividend yield? Why does it not represent a shareholder's total return from an equity investment?

A30 What is dividend cover? What does a positive dividend cover of less than 1.0 suggest?

A31 Why may some financial institutions prefer to hold and deal in 'short' gilts, while others prefer 'longs'?

A32 What is the difference between the 'flat yield' and the 'yield to redemption' on a government security?

A33 What is an 'index-linked' gilt? Why is the yield so much lower than on ordinary gilts?

A34 What is an 'upwards-sloping term structure' of interest rates? Describe two suggested explanations for its existence.

A35 What has happened to the 'real' value of $2\frac{1}{2}$ per cent Consolidated Stock since the Second World War? Why?

A36 What is the value of a perpetuity of £6 a year if the interest rate is 12 per cent a year? What happens to the value if the interest rate falls to 10 per cent a year?

A37 What will happen to the price of $2\frac{1}{2}$ Consolidated Stock (currently yielding $12\frac{1}{2}$ per cent) if the risk-free interest rate falls to 5 per cent?

A38 In the valuation formula for an ordinary share:

$$P_0 = \frac{D^1}{k - g}$$

what do: D^1, k; and g stand for?

A39 How can we estimate the cost of equity capital (k)?

A40 If an individual shareholder expects his total 'return' from an equity investment to consist of dividends *plus* capital gains, how can it be correct to value the share *solely* on the basis of expected future dividends?

A41 Identify three reasons why equity share prices might fluctuate.

A42 Explain why a company with bad profit growth prospects may experience an above-average rise in its share price in the next year.

A43 Describe three alternative methods of valuation.

A44 Why is 'book value' likely to be unsatisfactory as an estimate of the current value of a share?

A45 Why is it strictly incorrect to regard a price/earnings ratio as representing that 'number of years' future earnings'?

B. Exercises/Case Studies

B1 Refer to Fig. 6.1 (page 118). The *number* of transactions in 1980 was about 1 million for UK government securities, and about 4¼ million for companies' ordinary shares.
   a. Calculate (roughly) the average value of each kind of transaction.
   b. Try to explain why there is such a big difference.

B2 Refer to Fig. 6.3 (page 120). Over the 23 years from 1957 to 1980, what average percentage of total UK listed ordinary shares have individuals as a group sold *each year* to financial institutions as a group? Using Fig. 6.1 (page 118), estimate the annual *value* of the shares thus sold (in terms of September 1981 pounds).

B3 Refer to Fig. 6.4 (page 121), showing the FT-Actuaries 500-share index from 1967 to 1981, adjusted for inflation.
   a. In which year was the highest 'real' level reached?
   b. Roughly what percentage of its peak 1972 value had the index lost
      i. at the end of 1974?
      ii. at the end of 1981?

B4 Refer to Fig. 6.12 (page 131). Roughly what proportion of its 1971 'real' value had 2½ per cent Consolidated Stock lost by 1981?

B5 If the rate of inflation is 12 per cent a year, the FT Ordinary 30-share index is around 600, and the level of equity prices is 'keeping pace' with inflation, how much would you expect the 30-share index to increase *each day*? (Hint: assume 20 working days per month.)

B6 Bill English wants to buy 1,000 shares in Dunlop. His stockbroker gets the following three quotations from jobbers:
      A: '70–72'
      B: '67–69'
      C: '69–71'.
   a. Roughly how much in total would you expect Bill English to have to pay for his 1,000 shares in Dunlop? Show your workings.
   b. Why do you think Jobber B's quotation might be out of line with the others?

B7 How would a jobber react to each of the following events concerning one of his companies:

a. A surprise announcement of a take-over bid for the company at 225p a share (compared with the present price of 170–172p)?

b. Press comment that such a take-over might occur?

c. An announcement of unexpectedly poor results by the company?

d. A government announcement of measures that might be expected to help the industry this company is in?

B8 Refer to the example in **6.3.2** (page 125). For each of the two alternative rights issues, show the position:

a. of a shareholder who takes up his rights;

b. of a shareholder who sells his rights.

B9 Refer to Fig. 6.7 (page 125). Suppose a 1 for 2 rights issue were made at 80p. Complete a third column as for Fig. 6.7.

B10 Refer to Fig. 6.9 (page 127). Suppose a 3 for 4 bonus issue were made (instead of a 1 for 2 issue).

a. Complete a new 'After' column as for Fig. 6.9.

b. What would the position of John Higgins be?

B11 Refer to the John Higgins example in the text (page 127). What would his position be if, shortly after the bonus issue described in the text, the company made a '3 for 1' share split? (Assume that there has been no change either to the post-bonus issue share price or to the number of shares Mr Higgins owns.)

B12 Stuart Tudor Limited's accounts for the year ending 31 December 1981 show the following:

	£'000
Sales	270
Profit before interest	61
Interest payable	9
Profit before tax	52
Taxation	16
Profit after tax	36
Ordinary dividends	24
Retained profits	12

The company has 400,000 ordinary shares of 50p each, with a market value of 120p. The basic rate of income tax was 30 per cent.

Calculate: a. Earnings per share.

b. Dividend cover.

c. Price/earnings ratio.

d. Dividend yield.

B13 Calculate the dividend yield for each of these companies:

	A	B	C	D
Market price	50p	70p	75p	80p
Dividend per share	5p	3½p	4½p	10p

Assuming that dividend yield is the valuation method generally adopted, list the companies in descending order of growth prospects (fastest first).

B14 Refer to B13. Earnings per share for the four companies are:

	A	B	C	D
Earnings per share	10p	10p	7½p	10p

a. Calculate the dividend cover for each company.

b. Calculate the price/earnings ratio for each company. Assuming now that this is the yardstick for valuing shares, list the companies in descending order of growth prospects.

B15 Kay Limited, Tar Limited and Lupus Limited each has an issued ordinary share capital of £120,000 in £1 shares, an accumulated balance of £70,000 on profit and loss account, and no other reserves. The authorised share capital in each case is £200,000.

   The companies make the following ordinary share issues, and you are asked to show the details of share capital and reserves after the issue for each company:

a. Kay Limited issues 20,000 new shares to employees at £1.50 each.

b. Tar Limited makes a 1 for 3 bonus issue.

c. Lupus Limited makes a 1 for 4 rights issue at £2.00.

B16 Refer to B15. If the market price per share for each company were 240p before the ordinary share issue concerned, what would you expect it to be in each case after the issue? Why?

B17 Under what circumstances, if any, would you expect the market price of 2½ per cent Consolidated Stock to rise from its present level of about 20 to a level of about 50 (per £100 nominal of stock)?

B18 The Arcadian government's irredeemable 4 per cent stock stands at 60.

a. What is the rate of interest?

b. What will the price of the stock be if the interest rate is:
   i. 5 per cent?
   ii. 3 per cent?

B19 If the rate of inflation falls from above 10 per cent a year to about 5 per cent a year, what would you expect to happen to the yield on an index-linked gilt which now stands at 2½ per cent a year? Why?

B20 MD Enterprises Limited expects to pay a net dividend this year of 6.0p; and the market expects the dividend to increase by 5 per cent a year. The company's cost of equity capital is estimated at 15 per cent a year. Using the 'present value' formula discussed in the text, what would you expect the company's market price per ordinary share to be?

B21 Refer to B20. MD Enterprises has run into trouble. The company's policy is to pay out a constant proportion of its earnings in dividends each year; but earnings per share are now expected to grow by only 2 per cent a year for the foreseeable future. Instead of 6.0p a share, the company is now planning a dividend of only 4.0p this year. The prospects for the industry look gloomy, and the risk premium applicable to the company has increased, so that the cost of equity capital is now reckoned to be 20 per cent a year. What combined effect will all these changes have on the company's market price per ordinary share, as calculated in B20?

B22 Whizzo Limited, an unquoted company planning to go public, wants to raise £2.0 million additional capital net of all expenses. The two controlling families own 40 per cent of the 6 million ordinary 50p shares currently in issue: they plan to sell one third of their combined holdings. The shares can be sold on the market at 160p, and it is thought that 150p per share will be left after underwriting commissions and certain other costs. In addition, printing and advertising costs, together with professional fees, are expected to total £100,000.

Questions

a. How many shares will be offered to the public?

b. If the shares go to a 10 per cent premium over the issue price, what will the market value of the enlarged equity amount to?

c. If a net dividend of 4.0p per share is expected to be paid on the enlarged capital, with a dividend cover of 2.5 times, what is the envisaged price/earnings ratio based on the issue price?

B23 In February 1982, 50 million shares in Amersham International Limited were offered for sale at 142p per share, on behalf of the British government (which was selling its 100 per cent holding as part of its programme of 'privatisation') The issue was 'over-subscribed' 24 times (meaning that in total applications for 1,200 million shares were made). When Stock Exchange dealings started about a week later, the market price settled down at about 180p; and press comment suggested it might have been better to use the tender method of issuing the shares.

Questions

a. How much cash (ignoring issue expenses, and the small part of the proceeds going to increase the company's capital) would the previous owners of the shares in Amersham International receive as a result of the offer for sale?

b. How much (approximately) would you expect the previous owners to have received if the tender method had been used? Why?

c. Who gained and who lost as a result of what actually happened?

d. Why do you suppose the government chose to use an offer for sale rather than the tender method?

    e. Can you draw a 'demand curve' (relating price on the vertical axis to quantity on the horizontal axis)? (Hint: we know the quantity actually demanded at the offer price; and we know the actual market price of the number of shares available once dealings started.)

B24 Of the four Stock Exchange ratios discussed in **6.4**, which one would *not* be affected by inflation accounting? Explain why each of the other ones would be affected.

C. Essay Questions

C1 Could industrial companies function without a Stock Exchange? What consequence(s) might follow?

C2 'The Stock Exchange now meets only a small part of companies' needs for financing industrial investment.'
    a. Is this true? If so, why?
    b. What is the Stock Exchange's economic importance? Whose needs does it meet? How does it meet them?

C3 The Stock Exchange is sometimes called a 'casino'. In what respect(s) is this a fair comparison, and in what respect(s) unfair?

C4 'Abolishing stamp duty would significantly reduce Stock Exchange transactions costs, and thus improve the working of the stock market at very little net loss to the Exchequer.' Comment.

C5 The tender method is said to have significant advantages to a company issuing new shares. So why isn't it more widely used?

C6 'In a rights issue, companies should offer shares at a large discount, and thus avoid any need to pay underwriting commissions.' Comment.

C7 'The "price/window ratio" is calculated by dividing a company's market price per share (in pence) by the number of windows in the chairman's office. It is calculated, like the price/earnings ratio, by dividing one number by another; and it is probably equally useful.' Discuss.

C8 'It's absurd to call a government stock like $2\frac{1}{2}$ per cent Consolidated Stock "risk-free" when it has lost more than 98 per cent of its real value since 1946.' Discuss.

C9 'In making money on the Stock Exchange, what matters is not whether the particular company in which you buy shares is "good" or "bad", but the *price* you have to pay.' Discuss.

C10 'I'm fed up with holding my shares in Imperial Chemical Industries Limited; but unfortunately I bought when the price was much higher than it is now, and I can't afford to take a loss.' Discuss.

C11 Why do different companies have different share prices?

C12 Why, if at all, might the directors of a public company be worried by a sharp fall in its share price?

C13 'It's impossible to denationalise loss-making companies, and unfair to the taxpayer to sell off profit-making nationalised companies.' Discuss.

Chapter 7

Long-term Finance

Objective: *To identify the costs of debt and equity capital, and to show how they can be combined to establish the required minimum rate of return on investment; to note some major implications of modern portfolio theory; to describe how financial gearing works and how it affects the market values of firms; and to discuss dividend policy and some of the main factors in choosing long-term finance.*
Synopsis: *Debt costs less than equity because debt interest is tax-deductible and the investor's risk is less. The 'cost of equity' is the shareholders' opportunity cost. Debt and equity costs can be combined, weighted by their respective market*

values, to produce an overall cost of capital. This is the rate at which to discount future cash flows in evaluating capital investment projects. Alternatively, a risk premium representing only market *risk can be added to the risk-free rate of return.*

How it invests funds determines a company's business risk; how it finances them, its financial risk. The traditional view of financial gearing suggests an optimal range: 'Not too little and not too much'. Shareholders with different tax positions are likely to view dividends differently; but as long as a company explains its dividend policy, underlying profits are more important in influencing market value.

7.1 Cost of Capital

A firm's **cost of capital** is 'that rate of return which its assets must produce in order to justify raising the funds to acquire them'. In this section we discuss the costs of the two main kinds of capital, debt and equity. They form the basis for a 'criterion rate' for capital investment projects, which we used in Chapter 4.

7.1.1 Cost of Debt

The 'cost' of borrowing (debt) is the regular payment of interest to the lender. Debt interest is an 'allowable expense' in computing the borrower's tax on profits, so the 'after-tax' cost of debt is usually less than the nominal rate of interest. (Similarly, most personal mortgage interest is deductible for income tax: hence it is cheaper than other personal borrowing, which is not.)

If a company pays loan interest of 15 per cent a year, and if corporation tax on its profits is 52 per cent, then the after-tax cost of debt is 7.2 per cent:

$$15\% \times (100\% - 52\%) = 15\% \times 48\% = 7.2\%.$$

A similar loan to a higher-risk small company might cost 16 per cent. If that company were subject to the 40 per cent 'small company' tax rate, the after-tax cost of the debt would be 9.6 per cent:

$$16\% \times (100\% - 40\%) = 16\% \times 60\% = 9.6\%.$$

Many UK companies cannot benefit from the tax-deductibility of debt interest because they are not currently subject to corporation tax. For them, the after-tax cost of debt is the same as the before-tax cost. There are two main reasons why companies may *not* be subject to corporation tax on marginal profits:

a. They may currently be making *losses* in the UK. These can be 'carried forward' and set against subsequent taxable UK profits; but any benefit will not be received until later.

b. They may be receiving tax allowances (exceeding taxable profits) for:
   i. fixed capital investment (100% first-year allowances);
or ii. **stock relief**.

There is a further complication. The tax laws do not recognise inflation accounting: they refer to monetary units and not to **units of constant purchasing power**. So the 'real' gain to the borrower in respect of inflation *is not taxable*.

Suppose a 15 per cent interest rate comprises: (a) 2 per cent pure time preference; (b) 5 per cent risk premium; and (c) 8 per cent inflation premium (assumed correct). Then the **purchasing power** needed to repay the loan will be 8 per cent a year *less* than that originally borrowed. This is a 'real' gain to the borrower; but the tax system allows for the inflation *premium* payable but *not the actual inflation itself*. So the borrower deducts from taxable profits the whole money debt interest paid, but is *not* taxed on his 'real' gain resulting from the actual inflation. Hence in after-tax terms there is a **negative real interest rate**:

Before-tax interest rate	15.0%
Less: corporation tax at 52%	− 7.8
= after-tax interest rate	7.2
Less: actual inflation at 8.0%	− 8.0
= 'real' after-tax interest rate	− 0.8%

7.1.2 Cost of Equity

For equity capital there are no cash payments analogous to interest on debt capital. (Dividend payments do *not* represent the whole cost of equity capital, since equity capital would still have an 'opportunity cost' even for a company paying *no* dividends.) What *is* the opportunity cost of equity capital? What the shareholders could otherwise have done with the money. Hence it is the discounting rate they (presumably) apply to the future dividends anticipated from holding the shares.

We saw in **6.6.3** that: $k = \dfrac{D}{P} + g.$

In words: the cost of equity capital (k) is the expected current-year net dividend yield (D/P) plus the annual (assumed constant) rate of growth (g) in dividends per share. A company paying *no* dividend will still have a positive share price, representing suitably discounted expected *future* dividends. (Because shareholders have different tax positions, estimating the 'after-tax' amount of dividends per share can be difficult.)

Example: Phillipson Limited's expected current-year net dividend is 9.0p per share. Dividends per share are expected to grow at 10 per cent a year, and the current market price is 150p per share. Then Phillipson's cost of equity capital is 16.0 per cent:

$$k = \frac{9}{150} + 10.0\% = 6.0\% + 10.0\% = 16.0\%.$$

7.1.3 Overall Cost of Capital

We have discussed in outline how to calculate a company's after-tax cost of debt capital and its cost of equity capital. Combining these gives the company's *overall* cost of capital, sometimes described as its **weighted average cost of capital** (WACC). This establishes a basic discount rate to use in evaluating capital investment projects.

For example, if a company had equity capital with a market value of £12 million, and debt capital with a market value of £4 million, then weights of three-quarters and one-quarter would be applied to the cost of equity and cost of debt respectively. Using the costs of 16.0 per cent (equity) and 7.2 per cent (debt) from the previous two sections, the result would be an overall cost of capital of 13.8 per cent. (This is simply (three-quarters × 16.0 per cent) plus (one-quarter × 7.2 per cent), which comes to 12.0 per cent plus 1.8 per cent.) In practice, we would round this up and use 14 per cent as the discount rate.

We are trying to establish what it *costs* a company to raise more capital in order to find out the minimum rate of *return* that needs to be earned on any capital investment of funds. But it is worth emphasising that nearly all the numbers we need to estimate can only be *approximate*: the future cash flows relating to a capital project (both their amount and their timing), the costs of debt and equity capital, and their market values.

One further point should be noted. As a rule, businessmen think in terms of a 'pool' of funds. They *separate* the question (a) whether a project is worth investing in or not, from the different question (b) if a project *is* worth investing in, how it should be financed.

The consequence is that even if a particular project is going to be financed by means, say, of debt capital, the relevant criterion rate is still based on the company's *overall* cost of capital. Otherwise projects promising identical returns would be accepted or rejected for investment depending on how they were to be financed. This could clearly lead to inconsistent decisions. As a matter of fact, companies often don't *know* the source of the funds used to finance a particular project. All their receipts, from whatever source, are simply added to the 'pool of funds', and all payments reduce the pool.

7.1.4 Adjusting for Risk

Rather than use WACC for *all* capital projects (the horizontal line in Fig. 7.1 below), we may choose to adjust the WACC upwards (= 'require a higher return') for 'high-risk' projects, *and to adjust the WACC downwards for 'low-risk' projects.*

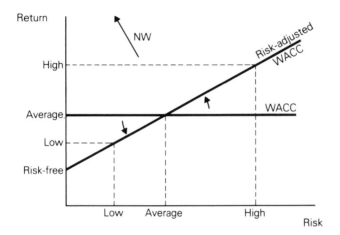

Fig. 7.1: Risk-adjusted weighted average cost of capital.

How to adjust for risk in the context of WACC is a matter of guesswork (usually referred to as 'judgement'). The cash flows for capital projects are usually based on highly fallible estimates; and managers are not merely trying to measure levels of risk and required return. They are also trying to *manage* the projects, in order to 'move' their position to the 'north-west' – either to the 'west' (by reducing the risk) or to the 'north' (by increasing the return).

We saw in 5.2.2 how *lenders* may seek to reduce their risk (by personal guarantees, by loan covenants or by taking security). Similarly, business managers might aim to reduce risk by various means, such as: extensive market research, arranging long-term sales contracts, or ensuring alternative sources of supply. Managers might also try to increase returns, for example by: expanding the volume of sales, increasing selling prices or keeping careful control of costs. (These are, of course, easier to say than to do!)

7.2 Modern Portfolio Theory

7.2.1 Shareholder Diversification

Modern portfolio theory (MPT) is based on the idea that business investment is subject to two different kinds of risk: market risk and unique risk. **Market risk** stems from all the uncertainties of the economy as a whole. There is no way for an equity investor to avoid it. **Unique risk** relates to a *particular* company or project: it can be **diversified** away by investing in a number of different kinds of projects (or shares).

Research suggests that an investor splitting his equity holdings equally among as few as a dozen different shares can diversify away about 60 per cent of the *total* risk he would bear by investing all his funds in a single equity share. In effect, the unique (or **'specific'**) risk of the shares can be 'averaged out' by investing in a **portfolio** of different shares. About 35 per cent of the total risk of a single security *cannot* be diversified away however many shares are held. It represents the residual market risk (**non-diversifiable risk**) to which all shares (and projects) are subject. Increasing the number of holdings beyond about 12 investments makes very little further difference in reducing unique risk.

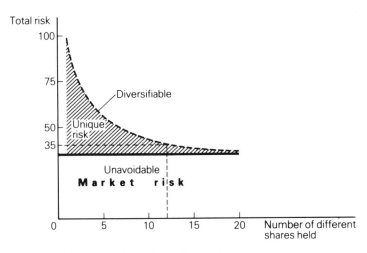

Fig. 7.2: Unique risk and market risk.

7.2.2 The Risk Premium

Modern portfolio theory says that no investor *needs* to assume unique risks: he can get rid of them by diversifying his portfolio, and holding shares in several *different* companies. *Hence* only *'market risk' will be compensated for by market returns.* Based on actual past results over many decades, an investment in the equity market as a whole is reckoned to require a risk premium of about 8 per cent – on top of the 'risk-free' rate of return available on government securities.

The return on any particular investment is thought to bear a definite relationship (known as **'beta'**) to the return on an investment in the 'market' as a whole. Estimated betas for quoted companies are published regularly; but as yet there is no satisfactory way to establish at all accurately the beta for a particular capital project.

An investment with a beta of less than 1.0 is *less* 'risky' than the whole market; with a beta of more than 1.0, more risky. ('Risk' in this context means the volatility of a share's returns.) The *required* rate of return for a particular investment is found by adding a risk premium to the **risk-free rate of return**. In MPT, this risk premium is simply the whole market's required risk premium (estimated at 8%) *multiplied by the investment's beta.*

*Example: Project C (which might be an ordinary share in Company C) with
a beta of 0.5 will have a required risk premium of 4.0 per cent, while Project
D with a beta of 2.0 will have a required risk premium of 16.0. Assuming
the required risk-free after-tax money return is 6.0 per cent, the required project
rates of return will be:*

Project	Required risk-free return	+	(Beta	×	Required market return	=)	Required risk premium	=	Required project return
C	6.0%	+	(0.5	×	8.0%	=)	4.0%	=	10.0%
D	6.0%	+	(2.0	×	8.0%	=)	16.0%	=	22.0%

These results are portrayed in Fig. 7.3, in which the **capital market line**
(CML) shows the linear relationship between market risk and required rates
of return: it quantifies the risk premium required for any given level of market
risk (as measured by beta). We assume that Project C has an expected return
of 12 per cent, and Project D of 18 per cent. Thus Project C is acceptable,
but Project D is not.

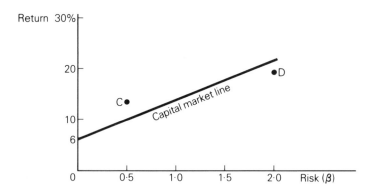

Fig. 7.3: The capital market line.

The Capital Market Line in Fig. 7.3 starts from the 'risk-free rate of return',
and adds for all risky projects a 'risk premium' found by multiplying the
estimated 'market' risk premium of 8.0 per cent by the project's estimated
'beta'. The CML's beta refers *only* to 'market risk'. It ignores a project's
'unique risk', on the grounds that it can be eliminated by any investor holding
a diversified portfolio.

This points to an important difference of outlook (see **8.4.3**) between
managers of a company and its shareholders. *Managers* (like workers) are
committed largely to a particular company, and may therefore be concerned
with its 'total risk' (that is, *both* 'market risk' *and* 'unique risk'). *Shareholders,*

on the other hand, are 'mobile' (see **6.1.1**), and presumably hold diversified portfolios: so they need be concerned *only* with market risk.

7.3 Financial Gearing

7.3.1 How Financial Gearing Works

A company's **business risk** is determined by how it *invests* funds, its **financial risk** by how it finances those investments. A company's management can adjust its financial risk (**'gearing'**) by changing the proportions of debt and equity in its total capital structure:

Equity
$\left\{\begin{array}{l} \text{(1) by retaining profits or paying dividends} \\ \text{(2) by issuing new shares or buying back shares in issue} \end{array}\right.$

Debt   (3) by borrowing more or repaying existing debt.

Financial gearing means borrowing to finance business operations, rather than using only equity capital. If the rate of return on assets financed by borrowing is greater than the cost of the debt, any surplus is added to equity earnings, and thus benefits the ordinary shareholders. The other side of the coin is that debt interest must be met, even if the rate of return on assets is *less* than the rate of debt interest. In that event, the net result is a *loss* from borrowing.

We want to relate the level of gearing (as measured by the debt ratio, the proportion of debt capital to total capital employed) to the benefit to ordinary shareholders, which is measured by **return on equity** (computed by dividing profit after tax by shareholders' funds). When operating profit is high, then high gearing will benefit shareholders; and vice versa.

Example: Green Limited and Brown Limited are similar except for their gearing.

	Low gearing Brown £'000	High gearing Green £'000
Gearing		
Equity	90	50
Debt (at 20% interest)	10	50
= Capital employed	100	100
Debt ratio: $\dfrac{\text{Debt}}{\text{Capital employed}}$ =	10%	50%

In Year 1, the before-tax return on capital employed is 40 per cent – well above the 20 per cent rate of debt interest payable. As a result, the return on equity for high-geared Green is much higher than for low-geared Brown:

	Brown £'000	Green £'000
Year 1 Results		
Earnings before interest and tax	40	40
Debt interest payable (at 20%)	2	10
Profit before tax	38	30
Tax (at 50%)	19	15
Profit after tax	19	15

$$\text{Return on equity:} \qquad \frac{19}{90} = 21\% \qquad \frac{15}{50} = 30\%$$

Although Brown's total profit after tax is somewhat higher than Green's (£19,000 against £15,000), Brown has more equity capital, so its rate of return on equity is lower (21% against 30%).

We can also see another way to measure 'gearing' (known as interest cover), by relating earnings before interest and tax to debt interest payable. Obviously, higher gearing means a lower interest cover; and vice versa.

$$\text{Interest cover:} \quad \frac{\text{EBIT}}{\text{Interest payable}} \quad \frac{40}{2} = 20 \qquad \frac{40}{10} = 4$$

In Year 2, the before-tax return on capital employed is only 10 per cent – half the 20 per cent rate of debt interest payable. This time, the return on equity for low-geared Brown is higher than that for high-geared Green.

	Brown £'000	Green £'000
Year 2 Results		
Earnings before interest and tax	10	10
Debt interest payable (at 20%)	2	10
Profit before tax	8	—
Tax (at 50%)	4	—
Profit after tax	4	—

$$\text{Return on equity:} \qquad \frac{4}{90} = 4\tfrac{1}{2}\% \qquad \frac{0}{50} = 0\%$$

$$\text{Interest cover:} \qquad \frac{10}{2} = 5 \qquad \frac{10}{10} = 1$$

We have looked at only two years' results; but in Fig. 7.4 (given our assumptions) we can plot return on equity (on the vertical axis) against any rate of return on capital employed (on the horizontal axis).

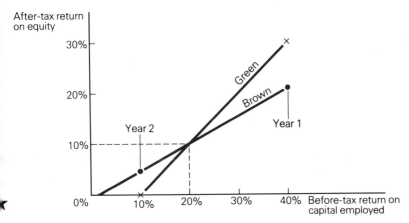

Fig. 7.4: The effect of financial gearing.

The after-tax return on equity is the same for both companies at 10 per cent; which relates to a before-tax return on capital employed of 20 per cent. This is what we would expect, since 20 per cent is the rate of debt interest payable. Once the rate of return (on total capital) exceeds that level, a high-geared company's shareholders will do better. But if the rate of return on total capital is below the rate of interest payable on debt, then a low-geared company's shareholders will do better (or 'less badly'). It is important to recognise that gearing works in both directions.

7.3.2 Gearing and Market Value

The 'traditional' view of gearing is that there is an 'optimal range' of capital structure, and that a company can increase its total market value by moving towards it. Over a significant range of moderate gearing, where the overall cost of capital is almost flat, a firm's market value is not very sensitive to minor changes in gearing. Outside the range, however, a company may have too much debt or too little. In either case, it can increase its overall market value by adjusting its financial gearing (Fig. 7.5).

Debt is normally cheaper than equity (after tax), so using debt instead of equity should reduce a company's overall cost of capital (WACC). By reducing the discount rate applying to future cash flows, this means increasing its overall market value. If there is 'too much' debt, however, then because of the increased risks the cost of both debt and equity will start to rise, and at some

---

* See Question B9

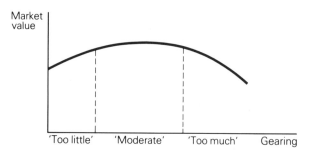

Fig. 7.5: Gearing and market value.

point the firm's market value will start to fall. Unfortunately there is no satisfactory theory saying at what level of gearing there is 'too much' debt.

7.4 Dividend Policy

7.4.1 The Nature of Dividends

Ordinary dividends are cash payments by a company to its shareholders. Only realised profits are legally distributable as dividends, and only to the extent that they exceed cumulative realised losses. Dividends represent the difference between profits and *retained* profits: they are thus an important *link* between the profit and loss account and the balance sheet.

UK companies normally pay an interim dividend and a final dividend each year. The ratio between the two varies widely, with the final dividend usually being larger. The variation sometimes makes it hard to tell what annual 'rate' of dividend is to be expected (unlike most American companies, which pay equal quarterly dividends).

At an annual general meeting (AGM), shareholders may vote to *reduce* the amount of a final dividend proposed by a company's directors, but they cannot *increase* it. Holders of a majority of voting shares can dismiss directors if they dislike the policy, but it is hard to change the policy and keep the directors. In fact, open opposition to a company's dividend policy is quite rare. Hence it caused some surprise when 12-year-old Jacob Rees-Mogg (a shareholder) told the managing director, Lord Weinstock, at GEC's 1981 AGM that the company's dividend policy was 'pathetic'!

7.4.2 Taxes and Dividends

In a **'perfect' capital market** with no taxes, dividend policy would not affect shareholders' wealth. Dividends would transfer cash to shareholders, but any retained profits would be precisely reflected in the market value of the shares. If shareholders could sell shares with no taxes or transaction costs, in effect they could 'declare their own dividends'. Thus a company's actual dividend policy would be irrelevant.

In reality, the tax positions of various shareholders can be widely different – with tax-exempt pension funds (**'gross funds'**) at one extreme and high-rate individual taxpayers at the other. This makes it difficult for companies to know what dividend policy is best for 'shareholders as a whole': it hardly makes sense to 'average' them!

Pension funds may want regular and growing dividend income to help meet their regular and growing commitments: they can *reclaim* from the Inland Revenue the income tax deducted at source from dividends, thus ending up with cash receipts equivalent to the *gross* dividend.

On the other hand, some individual shareholders may be liable to graduated rates of income tax and/or the investment income surcharge. Over and above the basic 30 per cent rate already deducted at source (**advance corporation tax**), they then have to pay the Inland Revenue the additional tax due, calculated on the *gross* dividend. Such shareholders end up with cash receipts equivalent to *less* than the *net* dividend paid by the company. Hence they may want to avoid dividends and prefer high retained profits, which (if reflected in higher share prices) would ultimately be subject at most to 30 per cent capital gains tax.

7.4.3 Choosing a Dividend Policy

Should a company fix its dividend first, and regard any profits left over (retained profits) as a residual? Or should it first choose how much to re-invest (retained profits), and then treat *dividends* as the residual? Most companies take the former course: they base the current year's dividend on last year's dividend, possibly plus an increase (which may or may not keep pace with inflation).

In most years between 1966 and 1979, **dividend controls** limited the increase in annual cash dividends to a percentage increase lower than the rate of inflation. As a result, companies were forced to *reduce* their 'real' dividends paid by about one third during the 13 years.

If it were not for tax and transaction costs, one might argue that companies should always pay out *all* their real profits in dividends, and then seek to raise new money from shareholders explicitly for expansion projects. (Rights issues could be regarded as 'negative dividends'.)

In the real world, it is hard to say what percentage of inflation-adjusted profits a company should pay out in dividends. A company with few profitable investment opportunities probably ought to pay out more than a company with many. It would be difficult to justify retaining profits in a company if the resulting increase in market value were less than the after-tax equivalent of the potential dividends withheld from shareholders. Ultimately it is expected future *profits* which influence market values.

Probably the best that can be suggested on dividend policy is to follow two general rules. First, tell shareholders clearly what a company's dividend

policy actually is; and second, try not to change it unexpectedly. Then shareholders who like the policy will be attracted to the company's shares, and
those who don't can avoid them.

7.5 Choosing Long-term Finance

7.5.1 Debt versus Equity

★ *Example: Rutherfords Limited's current level of earnings before interest and tax
(EBIT) is £15 million; current debt interest payable is £3 million a year; and
40 million ordinary shares are outstanding. Earnings per share (EPS) are 15p.
The company requires £20 million of new capital to finance investment projects
which are expected to produce profits of £4 million a year before tax. We assume
there are only two alternatives: (a) to issue 10 million ordinary shares at 200p
each, or (b) to borrow £20 million at 12 per cent a year interest. Should Rutherfords choose debt or equity? How can the company decide between the two methods
of finance?*

*We can easily calculate what EPS would amount to under each alternative
(Fig. 7.6):*

| | Now | With increased capital | |
| | | Equity | Debt |
	(£m.)	(£m.)	(£m.)
EBIT	15.0	19.0	19.0
Interest payable	3.0	3.0	5.4
Profit before tax	12.0	16.0	13.6
Tax (at 50%)	6.0	8.0	6.8
Profit after tax	6.0	8.0	6.8
Ordinary shares issued (m)	40	50	40
Earnings per share (pence)	15	16	17

Fig. 7.6: Earnings per share calculations.

*Thus if EBIT does increase by £4 million as expected after raising the
new capital, the new EPS would be 16p if 10 million equity shares were
issued, and 17p if £20 million were borrowed.*

★ See Questions B5, B11

Borrowing often appears *cheaper* (after tax) than equity capital; but the *risk* still has to be allowed for. We are *not* entitled to assume that the market value of each ordinary share will be higher with debt merely because EPS is higher. That would imply the *same* price/earnings ratio. But debt, being riskier, might result in a *lower* price/earnings ratio than equity.

We can always establish the 'break-even' EBIT level, where EPS is the *same* under the two alternatives. In the Rutherfords example, the break-even point comes at an EBIT of £15 million:

$$(\text{Debt}) \quad \frac{50\% \ (x - 5.4)}{40} = \frac{50\% \ (x - 3.0)}{50} \ (\text{Equity})$$

$$
\begin{aligned}
50 \ (x - 5.4) &= 40 \ (x - 3.0) \\
50x - 270 &= 40x - 120 \\
10x &= 150 \\[2ex]
x &= 15
\end{aligned}
$$

Above the 'break-even' level of EBIT, EPS will be higher with the debt alternative (due to gearing); *below* it, EPS will be higher with equity. In practice, uncertainty about the price at which equity shares can be sold may be important (see **6.3**); more than one debt package may be available; and preference shares issues may be another alternative. The most difficult problem is not calculating the numbers (on particular assumptions). It is exercising commercial judgement about balancing risks and returns. For example: how *likely* is EBIT in future to fall below the break-even level? how much does it matter if that sometimes happens?

7.5.2 Short-term versus Long-term Debt

The choice between short-term and long-term borrowing depends on comparing the relative costs and risks. To avoid uncertainties, a firm might try to 'match' the period of its borrowing to the period for which the money was needed. Thus long-term needs (say for a new plant expected to last 15 years) would be financed by long-term money, and short-term needs (say to finance temporarily high raw material stocks) by short-term sources.

But a company may not be sure how *much* money is required, nor for *how long*. Estimates of the amount and timing of capital projects can be subject to wide margins of error. It may often make sense to think of a company's needs as consisting of a long-term 'base load' which can be forecast with reasonable certainty, and a fluctuating balance of short-term needs whose size will vary depending on the nature of the business. Many companies, for example, find that their working capital needs fluctuate during the year, perhaps because of seasonal sales or seasonal production patterns. How should they finance short-term seasonal working capital peaks?

Figure 7.7 shows two approaches to this problem. A company may aim to finance its *maximum* level of working capital by long-term funds, which will leave surplus liquidity during the off-peak period. Or it may finance only its *minimum* level of working capital with long-term funds, which will leave it needing short-term finance during the seasonal peak.

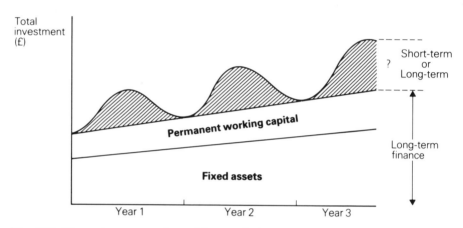

Fig. 7.7: Financing seasonal working capital.

7.5.3 **Control and Flexibility**

Decisions about which method of long-term finance to employ are not solely a matter of 'scientific' calculation. Many of the estimates can only be approximate. Moreover there are two other aspects of long-term finance which cannot easily be quantified, but which may be of paramount importance: control and flexibility.

a. Control. For small and medium-sized companies, the question of *control* of the company's equity capital is often over-riding. The current majority shareholders (probably members of one or two families) may be unable to subscribe for their share of any proposed rights issue. If so, they may be unwilling to see an equity issue which would dilute their own equity interests.

'Control' need not refer only to the ownership of voting equity shares. Certain borrowing arrangements may involve more restrictive covenants and other restraints on a company's future actions than the managers think acceptable. As a result, some companies might prefer to cut back on their investment plans and on their proposed rate of expansion – even at the cost of shareholders forgoing large potential profits.

b. Flexibility. Even in larger companies (where no small group owns a controlling interest in the equity capital), management will usually be concerned about *flexibility*. Most managements would like to keep open a number of alternative courses of action in future if at all possible. Thus they might be unwilling to borrow all the way up to some theoretical 'optimum' level of gearing, if that would make it virtually impossible to borrow any more for a number of years.

It must be borne in mind that a company which makes a *loss* necessarily reduces its accumulated retained profits, and therefore its balance sheet equity. (The same is true, of course, of paying dividends.) An apparently acceptable debt ratio can soon be turned into an unacceptably high one by a combination of (a) one or two years' losses, and (b) further borrowing in order to provide finance for current operations.

It is not surprising, then, if managements sometimes appear rather cautious to the outsider. In practice many company managements – both of large and of smaller firms – often seem to prefer safety and flexibility to profit.

Work Section

A. Revision Questions

A1 How may tax considerations affect the choice of financing method?

A2 Name two reasons why a company might not pay tax on its marginal profits.

A3 Why might borrowing be a sensible reaction to inflation?

A4 What is a 'negative real interest rate'?

A5 Name two reasons why the cost of borrowing might be higher for a small company than for a large one.

A6 What is the difference between market risk and unique risk?

A7 Why does diversification reduce shareholders' risk?

A8 What is 'beta'?

A9 How is 'beta' used to determine a risk premium?

A10 Identify two differences between risk-adjusted WACC and the capital market line.

A11 What is the difference between financial risk and business risk?

A12 What is 'financial gearing'? Give a numerical example.

A13 Name three ways in which a company can adjust its level of gearing.

A14 Explain how financial gearing can 'work both ways'.

A15 What is the 'traditional' view of gearing?

A16 Why do dividends matter: (a) to companies? (b) to shareholders?

A17 In what respect is the effect of paying a dividend like that of making a loss?

A18 How do taxes affect dividends?

A19 What is 'deduction at source'? How does it apply to dividends? In what ways may it be modified by the overall income tax system?

A20 What two practical rules were suggested as a guide to dividend policy? What is the reason for them?

A21 Why might a company *not* choose the debt/equity alternative producing the higher earnings per share at the expected level of EBIT?

A22 What two alternative approaches were described for financing seasonal working capital needs? What are the advantages and disadvantages of each?

A23 How does making a loss affect financial gearing?

A24 How could issuing debt affect the control of a company?

A25 Which two non-quantitative aspects of finance were suggested as often being important? Why may each be important?

B. Exercises/Case Studies

B1 The nominal rate of interest on a five-year loan is 15 per cent. What would the after-tax cost be for:
   a. A large loss-making company?
   b. A small profit-making company?
   c. A sole trader subject to basic rate income tax?

B2 Refer to B1. What would the 'real' after-tax cost be in each case if inflation is running at 10 per cent a year?

B3 The risk premium on the whole equity market is estimated to be 8.0 per cent a year, after tax.
   a. What will the required after-tax market return be if risk-free government securities yield 6.0 per cent after tax?
   b. What will be the required after-tax return for a company with a beta of 1.5?
   c. What will it be for a company with a beta of 0.8?

B4 F. G. Porter Ltd, with an issued share capital of £7½ million in 25p ordinary shares, is paying a final dividend of 14p per share.
   a. What is the cash cost to the company of the dividend?
   b. How much will Robert Jacks, who owns 2,000 ordinary shares in F. G. Porter Limited, receive in respect of the dividend?
   c. How much income tax will be deemed to have been 'deducted at source' from the dividend paid to Mr Jacks?
   d. How much extra tax will Mr Jacks have to pay if his marginal tax rate is 75 per cent?

B5 Refer to the Rutherfords example (7.5.1). With reference to the algebraic calculation of the 'break-even' level of EBIT, confirm that EPS is the same under both debt and equity alternatives at an EBIT level of £15 million; and calculate what EPS would be.

B6 Refer to the 'negative real interest rate' example on page 146.
   a. What would the real interest rate be if the inflation premium, and the actual inflation rate, were not 8 per cent but 18 per cent a year?
   b. What if, in the original example, the tax rate were not 52 per cent but 40 per cent?

B7 Refer to the 'negative real interest rate' example on page 146.
   a. What would the real interest rate be if the inflation premium were 12 per cent and the *actual* inflation rate were 6 per cent?
   b. What would the real interest rate be if the inflation premium were 6 per cent and the *actual* inflation rate were 12 per cent?

B8 Davis Ltd and Higgins Ltd, two companies in the same industry, are similar in most respects, but have different financial gearing. In 1981 each company made an operating profit of £40,000, in 1982 each made £150,000. Each company has capital employed in each year of £1.0

million (including 2 million ordinary 25p shares in issue); but Davis has a debt ratio of 5 per cent, Higgins one of 40 per cent. The debt in each case carries an interest rate of 15 per cent a year.

Questions

a. Prepare a table similar to page 152, showing the after-tax return on equity for each company for each year. Assume a 40 per cent tax rate.

b. What is each company's earnings per share for each year?

c. Draw a chart similar to Fig. 7.4, showing the effect of gearing on return on equity for each company. What is the 'break-even point? Why?

B9 Refer to Fig. 7.4. Redraw the chart on the basis of an interest rate of 10 per cent a year and a tax rate of 40 per cent.

B10 Kit Somerville Limited's latest profit and loss account is summarised as follows:

	£m.
Earnings before interest and tax	17.2
Interest payable	4.0
Profit before tax	13.2
Tax	5.7
Profit after tax	7.5
Preference dividends	0.3
Available for ordinary shareholders	7.2
Ordinary dividends	4.8
Retained profits for the year	2.4

The company has 120 million 10p ordinary shares in issue and 10 million £1 6 per cent preference shares. £25 million 16 per cent long-term debentures are outstanding. Retained profits amount to £37 million: there are no other reserves. The price/earnings ratio is 15.0.

Calculate:

a. Interest cover.

b. Debt ratio.

c. Earnings per share.

d. Dividends per share.

e. Dividend cover.

B11 Refer to the Rutherfords example (7.5.1). Draw an 'EBIT chart' showing the EPS in pence at various levels of EBIT in £ millions for both the debt and the equity alternatives. Show EPS on the vertical axis and EBIT on the horizontal.

(Hints: 1. We know that the 'cross-over' (or 'break-even') point comes at an EBIT level of £15 million.
2. We have already calculated what EPS will be under each alternative at an EBIT of £19 million.
3. At what level of EBIT in each case will EPS be *zero*?)

B12 *GRANT INDUSTRIES LIMITED*

Early in April 1980, Mr Gerald Morgan, newly-appointed finance director of Grant Industries Ltd, was considering what recommendation to make about the 1979 final ordinary dividend at the board meeting on 11 April.

Grant Industries was a medium-sized group in the electrical engineering industry. Summarised financial statistics since 1974 are shown below:

Year ending 31 December	*1974*	*1975*	*1976*	*1977*	*1978*	*1979*
per share (pence)						
Earnings	13.71	15.81	17.40	24.02	27.00	31.70
Dividends (net):						
Interim	2.68	2.60	2.92½	3.30	3.63	4.20
Final	3.90	4.55	4.95	5.36	6.16	
Share price:						
High	149	165	182	251	261	299
Low	63	70	127	164	207	234

Profit margins were contracting in the home market, though Grant had managed to double its sales revenues in the last five years. Exports represented about 15 per cent of total sales. Overall return on investment had been squeezed as inflation added to working capital needs, and the board now regarded it as worryingly low – with little prospect of improvement.

Following the stock market collapse in 1974, Grant's share price had slowly recovered over the next few years, reaching its 'all-time high' the day after the Conservative General Election victory in May 1979. One of the early actions of the new government had been to abolish dividend controls, but this had not affected Grant's interim dividend of 6.0 gross declared in October 1979. It had been agreed to review the compnay's dividend policy when the full year's results were available in the spring.

Grant Industries had 40 million ordinary 25p shares in issue, of which about 40 per cent were held by various instittutions, and most of the rest by individuals. The directors in total held less than 1 per cent of the shares. At the end of March 1980 the share price stood at 260p, some 10 per cent below the May 1979 high. The current gross dividend yield, at 5.7 per cent, was somewhat above the sector average of 4.2 per cent (which, however, was pulled down by the very low yields on the two largest companies, GEC 2.4 per cent and Racal Electronics 2.5 per cent).

Having arranged informal discussion with a number of directors, Mr Morgan found at least three separate groups with different strongly-held views about dividend policy. (Other directors regarded dividend policy as relatively unimportant.)

Most of the executive directors favoured increasing the dividend as little as possible. They wanted to conserve resources for a difficult year or two ahead, and preferred a final net dividend of about 7.0p per share. Typical of this group was Mr Travers, the personnel director: '*There's no point paying out more than we've got to. If we bump up the dividend too much now, we'll just have to make a rights issue in a year's time to ask the shareholders to put up new money. You know how much that will cost in terms of underwriting expenses and so on. And if things do get worse, as some of us rather expect, the share price will probably then be a good bit lower than it is now.*'

Mr Hughes, the technical director, agreed: '*Actually it's in the shareholders' own interests. They'll gain far more in after-tax terms from capital gains than they would from dividend income.*'

Mr Robertson, the marketing director, also thought dividends should be kept low, with the HC cover about the same as in 1978: '*You weren't around then, Gerald, but I can assure you we were all jolly glad to see dividend controls over the past few years. They gave us a watertight excuse for retaining all the earnings we wanted. Now we're free to pay whatever we like, you'll just have to earn your salary by thinking up some convincing reasons why we can't afford to increase the payout.*'

A second group, which was small, but included the chairman, Lord Southwell, thought the stock market was expecting a final net dividend of about 9.8p. They were afraid that anything less might be taken to signify lack of confidence in the company's prospects. Lord Southwell was nervous about disappointing shareholders now that dividend controls had been lifted. '*After all, the extra cash cost of paying 9.8p instead of 7.0p is only about a million pounds. It's not worth risking a slump in the equity price for that. The whole group's now valued at about £100 million. If we don't come up to scratch with this dividend I wouldn't be surprised to see the shares fall below 200p. Far better to pay a decent dividend and keep the share price up. Then even if we do have to make a rights issue in a year's time, we won't need to sell too many new shares.*'

A third group of directors wanted to *raise* the final dividend substantially, to as much as 14.0p net. They included two non-executive directors (Messrs Ancastle and Hossell), who tended to carry weight in questions of external financial policy.

Mr Ancastle argued that Grant's limited investment needs could partly be financed by reducing working capital. Moreover he believed the company's debt ratio (31%) would permit extra borrowing if necessary. (In the December 1979 balance sheet, debt, including bank overdrafts, totalled £52 million.) '*It's clear we won't be increasing capacity before 1982 at the earliest, given the sales weakness we expect over the next year or two. In fact, our rate of return on investment is looking so sick at the moment I'm not sure we can really justify retaining any earnings at all!'*

Mr Hossell agreed, but for different reasons. He thought government policy was likely to change within 18 months. '*The unions show little sign of holding down their wage claims, whatever this monetary policy is supposed to do. The government will have to bring in an incomes policy of some kind by 1982 – with or without Mrs Thatcher. And when it happens they're quite likely to reimpose dividend controls. We'd be fools not to jack up the payout as much as we can while we've got the chance. That will establish a higher base before the controls come on again.'*

Mr Travers drew a different conclusion: '*If we raise the April dividend by anything like 50 per cent over last year's final, what do you think the effect will be on wage claims? The unions are bound to use it to justify asking for even more.'*

Mr Morgan knew that some academics said dividend policy didn't matter, but he believed that this conclusion was reached by assuming no taxes. He was unsure exactly how taxation in the real world might affect optimal dividend policy.

On 31 March 1980 the accountancy bodies finally produced a Statement of Standard Accounting Practice on Current Cost Accounting (SSAP 16). Until now Grant Industries, like many other companies, had rather ignored inflation accounting; but now they would be required to publish CCA figures (as supplementary) from 1981. Mr Morgan reckoned that Grant's historical cost profits might be reduced by about half on a CCA basis.

Questions

a. For each of the three final dividends mentioned, calculate:
   i. the cash cost
   ii. the dividend cover
   iii. the dividend yield.
b. As Mr Morgan, what do you think are the most important considerations to be taken into account in deciding on a final dividend for the year 1979?
c. As Mr Morgan, what would your recommendation be about the final dividend? What dividend *policy* would you propose?

B13 *HASTINGS MANUFACTURING LIMITED*

In November 1981, Mr Watson, finance director of Hastings Manufacturing Ltd, was considering how the company should finance its £$3\frac{1}{2}$ million expansion programme. After some disagreement at a recent board meeting, Mr Sidney, the company's chairman, had asked Mr Watson to evaluate the various arguments and make a definite recommendation to the board at its next meeting.

Hastings made containers for industrial and commercial use. The level of sales and profits had fluctuated over the years, but the company had shown a profit nearly every year since 1952. A significant volume of sales related to small tins for packing delicate instruments, used in aircraft. The company had recently gained contracts to supply several pharmacutical firms with tins for pills and small bandages, which had helped to add a needed element of stability to demand.

Years ending 31 March		1977	1978	1979	1980	1981
Sales	£m.	28.3	41.6	43.2	36.8	49.3
Profit before tax	£'000	1647	3271	2553	3047	4033
Profit after tax	£'000	1044	1981	1697	1968	2420
Earnings per share	p	8.70	16.51	14.14	16.40	20.17
Dividends per share	p	8.00	8.00	8.00	8.00	10.00 gross
Market price High	p	101	162	148	164	217
Low	p	53	94	113	108	136

Late in 1981 the Hastings management decided to modernise and enlarge a small plant near Walsall which had been acquired in 1965. New fixed assets would require £2.1 million, and extra working capital £1.4 million. The proposed investment was expected to net £1.0 million in extra profits before tax. Originally it had been hoped to provide the funds from retained profits, but a general inflationary increase in working capital requirements made this seem inadvisable. It was therefore planned to seek the necessary capital from external sources. Management policy had traditionally avoided long-term debt; and in 1981 the company's balance sheet contained no fixed indebtedness of any kind.

For some years both Mr Sidney and Mr Watson had been disappointed in the market price of Hastings shares. They believed the possibility of more stable earnings in future might justify a change to the company's established practice of avoiding long-term debt.

Descendants of the company's founders still retained a large shareholding, but more than half the shares were publicly held, though there was only a thin market. Mr Watson thought that a rights issue of ordinary shares could probably be sold at 185p per share, to leave the company net proceeds of 175p per share after underwriting expenses and other fees. Thus raising £3½ million would require issuing an extra 2.0 million equity shares.

Balance Sheet, 31 March 1981

	£m.
Fixed assets (net)	14.9
Current assets:	
Stocks	8.0
Debtors	5.8
Cash	1.8
	15.6
Less: Current liabilities	6.3
	9.3
	24.2
Ordinary 50p shares	6.0
Retained profits	18.2
	24.2

Alternatively, the company could raise the £3.5 million from institutional investors through the sale of 15-year 18 per cent debentures. Repayment of £200,000 of the issue would be required every year, leaving £500,000 outstanding at maturity. Mr Sidney viewed the 18 per cent interest rate as equivalent to 10.8 per cent after 40 per cent corporation tax (which was the rate the company used in all its forward planning). In contrast, he reckoned that the share issue at 175p per share, and with a 10p gross dividend, would cost the company only 5.7 per cent a year. But he wondered whether the debenture issue might be desirable, after allowing for expected inflation. (The current level of inflation was just over 10 per cent a year.)

The board had agreed to the proposal to enlarge the Walsall plant, if satisfactory financing could be arranged; and early in November 1981 Mr Sidney decided to sound out board sentiment on debt financing. To his surprise an acrimonious discussion developed.

Mr Hartley calculated the annual 'sinking fund' payment to be 10 per cent of the average size of the debenture issue over its 15-year life: to him, the cost of the share issue seemed much less than that of debt. He emphasised the cash outlay called for in the debenture programme, and the £500,000 maturity, and argued that the extra risks from borrowing would make the ordinary shares more speculative, and cause greater variation in the market price in future.

On the other hand, Mr Harris claimed that ordinary shares were a 'giveaway' at 175p. Past retention of profits had built up book value to more than 200p per share. Even this understated the true worth of the business, because at today's prices Hastings would be quite unable to replace fixed assets at anything like balance sheet net book value. He concluded that the sale of ordinary shares at 175p would give new buyers a substantial part of the real value attributable to the company's present shareholders. (He dismissed as 'academic' Mr Bartholomew's suggestion that existing shareholders would be unaffected by any supposed rights issue 'discount' from the current market price.)

Two other directors, Messrs Gilbert and Lonsdale, compared debt and equity in terms of earnings per share. At the anticipated level of profits (£5.0 million a year, before interest and before 40 per cent tax – including the extra £1.0 million from the Walsall plant expansion), they calculated that earnings per existing share would become 21.43p with a rights issue netting 175p. In contrast, the sale of debentures would produce earnings per share of 21.85p. They didn't think it mattered that the annual repayment of debt would amount to 1.67p per share.

Mr Wilkinson argued for an equity issue because simple arithmetic showed the company could net £600,000 after tax a year from the new investment. Yet if 2.0 million ordinary shares were sold, the dividend requirement at the present rate of 10p per share would amount to only £200,000 a year gross (= £140,000 net cash required, after deducting 30% basic rate income tax). He couldn't see how selling equity shares would hurt the interests of present shareholders.

Mr Joseph, a long-serving director, confessed he didn't fully understand all the calculations. But he was uneasy about changing the company's established policy towards borrowing, especially as the UK economic environment seemed likely to remain difficult for the next year or two at least. His motto was: 'Better safe than sorry.'

Questions:

a. Calculate the 'break-even' level of EBIT,
   i. algebraically
   ii. by drawing an EBIT chart (as described in B11)
   iii. confirm the algebraic calculation of the break-even level of EBIT under the two alternatives by calculating EPS at that level for both debt and equity alternatives.
b. Critically evaluate each of the arguments put forward in the case by a director. Explain in each instance whether or not you agree with the argument, giving your reasons.
c. As Mr Watson, the finance director, what recommendation would you make to the board about financing the Walsall plant expansion? Why? How would you attempt to persuade the other directors?

C. Essay Questions

C1 How, if at all, might a small unquoted company's attitude to financial gearing differ from that of a larger quoted company? Why?

C2 Why have many companies increasingly come to rely on short or medium term bank borrowing? Why might this be risky?

C3 How may inflation affect a company's financing policy?

C4 How may taxation affect a company's financing policy?

C5 Given its tax advantages, why should a company limit the amount of debt in its capital structure?

C6 What are the main sources of funds available to companies, and what are the main considerations in choosing between them?

C7 How might the finance director of a group of companies view the riskiness of a particular capital investment project differently from a manager of a division of the group? How might a shareholder's view of a project's riskiness differ from both of them?

C8 'A properly diversified portfolio will have a beta of 1.0. But you can't beat the market by holding the market.' Discuss.

C9 How would you expect inflation accounting to affect each of the two conventional measures of gearing? (Hint: Assume the main change to assets will be a substantial increase in the book value of depreciable fixed assets.)

C10 How should a company choose its dividend policy?

C11 What, if anything, can shareholders do if they dislike the dividend policy of one of their companies?

C12 In answer to the question: 'How much debt should a company have in its capital structure?', the traditional answer is quite definite: 'Not too little, and not too much!' Discuss.

C13 'Financial markets are relatively "efficient", so it makes little difference how a company finances its activities.' Discuss.

C14 Why should managers seek to maximise the wealth of their existing shareholders:
a. in their own interests?
b. in the interests of society as a whole?

C15 Discuss what influences are at work to change the pattern of how companies finance their operations. What changes would you expect to see in future? Why?

Chapter 8

Mergers and Reorganisations

Objective: *To discuss types of mergers and acquisitions, and economic reasons for and against them; to outline the process of valuation and bargaining, and some of the management, human and financial consequences; and to describe other forms of business reorganisation, including liquidation and 'de-mergers'.*
Synopsis: *Most business combinations are acquisitions of one entity by another, horizontal mergers (between companies in the same business) being the most common. Mergers may produce economies of scale and transfer resources to more*

*capable management, but they may also lead to monopoly and reduced competition.
Shareholders in companies being acquired have (on average) received a 20 per
cent premium, but the profitability of merged companies appears to have declined.
Mergers provide an example of possible conflict between management and shareholders. Other important forms of business reorganisation include liquidation and
'de-mergers'.*

8.1 Types of Merger

8.1.1 Mergers and Acquisitions

Mergers and acquisitions both imply combining two (or more) formerly
independent business units into a single enterprise, with a common top
management and common ownership.

A **merger** may be defined as: a business combination in which holders
of substantially all the ownership interests in the constituent companies
become the owners of a single company which owns the assets and businesses
of the constituent companies. In a merger, M and N pool their assets and
liabilities, with each of their shareholders receiving shares in a new **holding
company**, MN, in exchange for their former shares in M and N respectively.

An acquisition may be defined as: a business combination where a significant
part of the ownership interests in the acquired company is eliminated (as,
for example, when the price is all cash). In an acquisition, the acquiring
company buys either most of the equity *shares* in the acquired company or
its *assets*. There may be left **minority interests** in the **subsidiary** of a holding
company.

Where (as is usual) one of the constituent companies is clearly dominant,
then the transaction is presumed to be an acquisition rather than a merger.
Nevertheless, for convenience the term 'mergers' will generally be used from
now on.

8.1.2 Economic Types of Merger

From an economic viewpoint, there are three main types of merger: (1)
horizontal; (2) vertical; and (3) conglomerate:

1. **Horizontal mergers** combine firms in the same business; for example,
   a daily newspaper merging with a Sunday. About 80 per cent of mergers
   are of this kind. Horizontal mergers are most likely to yield economies of
   scale; but they are also most likely to lead to problems of concentration
   and monopoly.
2. **Vertical mergers** combine firms in the same industry, but involved at
   different stages of the overall production process. Thus a manufacturer
   of soft drinks might combine with a company making containers for drinks,
   or with a firm which distributed drinks. Vertical mergers have been rather
   rare in the UK since the mid-1960s. Their purpose might be: to secure

better control over quality; to ensure sources of supply; or to move closer to the ultimate market for a firm's products.

The different nature of horizontal and vertical mergers is illustrated in Fig. 8.1.

	Horizontal	*Vertical*
Primary sector	A ------ B	G K
Secondary sector	C ------ D	H I L
Tertiary sector	E ------ F	J M

Fig. 8.1: Horizontal and vertical mergers.

3. **Conglomerate mergers** combine firms in different industries, often with no obvious connections; for example, a steel company buying an oil company, or a mining company merging with a hotel chain. Conglomerate mergers now form only a small proportion of all mergers, though a few large ones hit the headlines from time to time. Naturally it can be very difficult to interpret the **consolidated accounts** of conglomerate groups.

8.2 Reasons for Mergers

8.2.1 Economics Pros and Cons

From the viewpoint of the economy as a whole, the main economic arguments for mergers are: the possibility of economies of scale (which vary significantly between different industries), and the transfer of resources from the control of a less competent to that of a more competent management.

The main arguments against mergers are: they may result in monopolies in particular markets, possibly leading to restriction of output and monopoly pricing, or they may cause inefficiencies by reducing the pressure of competition, but this depends on barriers to entry.

In looking at 'concentration', one needs to look at relevant *markets* – including imports – not merely at domestic *production*. Nor is it clear whether increased concentration will reduce or increase *competition*.

8.2.2 Government policy

Proposed mergers in the UK may be referred to the Monopolies and Mergers Commission (MMC) for investigation, where:

a. the gross value of assets being transferred exceeds £5 million; or

b. the merger would create or enhance a monopoly share (25% or more) of the relevant market in a substantial part of the UK.

If the MMC finds that a merger would operate against the public interest, the government may prevent it, or allow the merger, perhaps subject to certain conditions. The MMC tries to maintain and promote effective *competition* between suppliers, and the interests of *consumers* in respect of the prices and quality of goods and services.

Only about four mergers a year on average have been referred to the MMC between 1965 and 1981. Of these 70-odd references, one third were abandoned on being referred to the MMC, one third were found to be against the public interest, and the other one third were found *not* to be against the public interest.

The government may *favour* mergers, to strengthen UK competitiveness against foreign companies, both at home and abroad, and to gain economies of scale. On the other hand, it may *oppose* mergers where they lead to monopoly, in order to protect consumers. Thus in any particular case it may be difficult to predict the government's view.

Many of the most powerful UK monopolies are government-*created*. Establishing nationalised industries by merging formerly independent competitors under state ownership has led to monopolies in many of the 'commanding heights' of the UK economy: for example, in transport, communications, power, steel and shipbuilding. And there are state monopolies in education and health services.

8.2.3 Reasons for Acquisition

The acquiring company may want *expansion*. This can often be gained more effectively, and nearly always more *quickly*, by purchasing a going concern rather than by internal growth. The existence of 'under-valued' assets may constitute a tempting prize; but the acquiring company must be able both to *detect* and to *make use* of them. There may be a desire to avoid outside control: it is much harder for governments to interfere with intra-company transactions than with market deals between autonomous companies.

UK tax rules have encouraged some acquisitions. Between 1965 and 1973 dividend payments were penalised, so companies with few profitable expansion opportunities in their own industries sometimes used retained profits to acquire other companies, either in the same or in different industries. After 1973 the UK tax system penalised companies whose profits arose mainly abroad, thus encouraging them to acquire companies with UK earnings. This probably explains BATs acquiring International Stores, Consolidated Gold Fields acquiring Amey Roadstone and (more recently) Beechams acquiring Bovril.

There are many possible commercial reasons for acquisitions, as shown in Fig. 8.2.

Production
1. Acquiring technical skills
2. Expanding capacity
3. Economies of scale
4. Vertical integration

Marketing
5. Acquiring patent rights
6. Extending product range
7. Gaining entry to new markets
8. Expanding market share
9. Eliminating a competitor

Miscellaneous
10. Acquiring management skills
11. Diversifying business risk
12. Preventing a *competitor* from acquiring the target company
13. Making the acquiring company itself less attractive as a target
14. Temporary stock market opportunity:
    a. target company's shares under-priced
    b. acquiring company's shares over-valued
15. Tax advantages

Fig. 8.2: Reasons for Acquisition.

8.2.4 Reasons for Selling

Many commercial assets are for sale if the price is right. People who have founded a business may want either to *retire*, or to diversify their risk by accepting cash, or shares in a larger concern. If a major shareholder dies, his shares may have to be sold in a block to pay capital transfer tax, which might lead to a sudden unwelcome change in control. An agreed merger leading to a market quotation means that major shareholders can gradually dispose of their holdings on an orderly and unhurried basis.

Another reason for disposing of a business may be *management* problems, either management succession or the ability to manage an expanded business following a period of growth. The death or retirement of one or two key men can often reveal a need for new management. Or selling an ailing business may simply be 'a civilised alternative to bankruptcy'.

8.3 The Process of Merging

8.3.1 Valuation

Financial evaluation of a potential acquisition can be treated like a capital investment 'project' (see Chapter 4). The total net amount to be invested is computed by adding to the formal 'purchase price' any additional investment needed immediately, and by deducting the expected proceeds from the sale of any surplus assets. The anticipated cash inflows year-by-year in future are estimated by adjusting the 'existing' operating cash flows to allow for any **synergy** (or other anticipated changes), and for any additional investment required each year in future.

The internal rate of return on the proposed investment can then be calculated in the usual way, by finding the discount rate which equates the various annual cash inflows to the initial total net investment required. Alternatively, the 'maximum purchase price payable' can be found by: (a) discounting the estimated annual cash inflows at the *required* rate of return, and (b) adjusting to allow for any extra capital investment needed immediately after acquisition, or for the proceeds from sale of any surplus assets. If desired, an estimated 'terminal value' at the horizon date can also be incorporated in the valuation.

8.3.2 Bargaining

If a seller (S) *wants* to sell, naturally the buyer (B) will try to discover why. Are there adverse future factors anticipated by S, but unknown to B? Are there personal reasons for selling? Will the motivation of S's top managers be affected when they have sold their shares? Similarly, S will seek to discover B's motives. Is there some aspect of the business which B values more highly than S? Is it valuable to *other* potential bidders, or only to B? Both B and S should keep an eye on possible *alternatives*: B on alternative acquisitions, or on internal growth; S on alternative buyers, or on continued ownership.

Both B and S may have in mind a range of 'acceptable' prices before negotiations begin. If these ranges overlap, a deal should be possible. In practice, however, the 'acceptable' range may alter during negotiations. In the excitement of a contested take-over bid, the 'successful' buyer sometimes ends up paying far more than he would have contemplated at first. Hence the 'losing' bidder may find the market price of its own shares *rising* when it drops out of the auction.

Basing part of the purchase price on future profits not only defers part of the payment, but insures the buyer against expected profits failing to materialise. It may also provide an incentive for former owner-managers to continue contributing to profitable operations.

There are certain methods of defence against unwanted take-over bids. But the interests of the 'victim's' (V's) top management may not coincide with those of V's *shareholders*. For this reason, the City Code has been developed to govern take-over practice. The main theme is the duty of the directors of a company for which an offer is made (whether welcome or not) to provide full information to enable the *shareholders* to make a decision.

Where V's directors control at least 10 per cent of the shares, they can prevent the compulsory acquisition of such a large dissenting minority. Sometimes V can itself take over another company, either to make itself too large to be taken over, or at any rate less attractive than before. There is usually not time to raise the dividend hurriedly (though this was a factor in Courtaulds' successful defence against ICI in the early 1960s). Or V's directors may argue that the acquisition would be against the public interest; or suggest that none of V's senior management would be prepared to serve under the buyer's control.

8.3.3 Consequences

a. *Management organisation.* The UK joined the European Economic Community in 1973, but genuinely international mergers have remained rare. Transactions usually have to be for cash, and there are several complicating factors: differing national legal systems, tax systems, accounting practices, languages and cultural patterns.

This last factor also affects domestic mergers. Over time most companies do develop a 'culture' of their own, and it can be difficult to combine two organisations if their cultures are not reasonably compatible. The car industry has provided several examples: Austin and Morris; BMC and Jaguar; BMC and Leyland. And several of the nationalised industries have found it very difficult to integrate the formerly separate organisations.

Even if two organisations can be merged successfully, it often takes more time and effort than expected. In order to make the most of new profit opportunities, the combined group's top management will probably want to look in detail at every major aspect of the new business: each product line, every plant, the main markets, all senior personnel. This takes a great deal of management time. And other necessary consequences of a merger can be troublesome, such as integrating two different accounting systems. 'Rationalisation' can be difficult and long-drawn-out: according to *The Economist*, as late as 1982: 'Perhaps British Aerospace's most onerous legacy from premerger days (i.e. before 1977) is two design teams, more competing than complementary.'

b. *Workers.* We have been looking at mergers from top management's point of view. But many human problems can arise among other employees. 'Economies of scale' may mean that one man can do two men's jobs. Other people will be effectively demoted; or may have to move to a new office or factory, perhaps hundreds of miles away from their present homes and friends. Such 'redeployment' may often be economically desirable; but it requires great skill, understanding, tact and investment of time and energy on management's part. Inevitable fears and uncertainties have to be soothed away; and delicate personal decisions must be taken and communicated without upsetting too many people.

c. *Financial structure.* Financial structure may be significantly changed by a merger. Some financial decisions (dividend policy, for example) usually make only a minor impact on overall capital structure; but a large acquisition can make a big difference. For instance, a company with a 35 per cent debt ratio which acquires another company half its own size could end up with a 23 per cent debt ratio if the purchase consideration consists of equity shares, or a 57 per cent debt ratio if the acquisition were paid for entirely by loan stock.

d. *Accounting treatment.* In accounting for an acquisition, the assets and liabilities (other than shareholders' funds) are simply added together in the **group accounts**. Where one company acquires all (or most of) the shares in another company, any excess of the purchase price, whether in cash or shares, over the book value of the various assets acquired appears in the group balance sheet as **goodwill**.

At present in the UK, goodwill is either (a) left permanently on the balance sheet at cost, or (b) written off directly against reserves. But new EEC rules may soon require goodwill to be: (c) written off ('amortised') against profits in future on some reasonable basis (like depreciation of fixed assets).

This third treatment of goodwill would obviously reduce the reported after-tax profit. (Revaluing upwards the acquired company's fixed assets would produce a similar result.)

8.4 Results of Mergers

8.4.1 Pattern of UK Mergers

A summary of purchase considerations in UK mergers of industrial and commercial companies between 1969 and 1981 is shown in Fig. 8.3.

	Annual averages			*Method of payment*		
	Number of mergers	*Cost per merger* $(£m.)^1$	*Total cost* $(£m.)^1$	*Cash* $(\%)$	*Equity* $(\%)$	*Debt* $(\%)$
1969/73	1,000	5.2	5,100	28	51	21
1974/81	450	3.0	1,400	61	34	5
[1] September 1981 £s.						

Fig. 8.3: Method of payment: UK mergers, 1969/81.

The 13-year period splits into two parts:
1. Five years from 1969 to 1973, when there were many mergers (some of them very large), and cash was relatively unpopular.
2. Eight years between 1974 and 1981, with fewer mergers, when debt was not often used as a method of payment.

There have been only four 'large' mergers (over £150 million 1981 pounds) since 1974, compared with as many as 31 in the previous five years.

8.4.2 Profitability of Mergers

Most studies looking at company performance after mergers suggest that in general mergers have *not* been profitable. In estimating 'success', one must look at results for several years after the merger, not just the first year or two (in which there may be special factors). If there is added monopoly power, profits reported after a merger may tend to overstate increased 'efficiency'.

Again there is widespread agreement about returns to shareholders. Shareholders in companies being acquired have received a premium above the pre-merger market price averaging between 15 and 25 per cent; while shareholders in the acquiring companies have neither gained nor lost on average.

Unfortunately the results appear to be inconsistent with each other! If one of the two parties to a merger gains, and the other doesn't lose, then on balance it would seem that there *have* been net gains from mergers. But studies of accounting measures of profitability show the opposite.

The evidence suggests that most mergers do not benefit shareholders in the *acquiring* firm. This does not mean that mergers are economically unjustified: but the premium which has to be paid to shareholders in the acquired company may absorb all the economic gains. Given a likely premium of about 20 per cent, an acquiring company clearly needs to identify definite areas for significant improvements in profits.

8.4.3 Managers versus Shareholders

One reason for mergers may be a desire to reduce a company's total risk. According to modern portfolio theory, however, this reason makes no economic sense to the *owners* of a company, since they can easily arrange to hold diversified portfolios of shares (see 7.2.1). They will already have diversified away most of the 'unique' risk of any particular company in which they own shares; and they do not need that company to turn itself into a diversified conglomerate on their behalf. Managers, however, may take a different view. They necessarily have all their eggs in one basket. So reducing the riskiness of that basket may well seem desirable to them, even if it won't pay off for the shareholders.

Only where there are expected to be economies of scale or other improvements in profitability can a merger be justified in theory. Mere reduction of business risk is not enough. Indeed, many of the 'reasons' for making acquisitions (in Fig. 8.2) do not seem to provide sound economic reasons for mergers.

We discussed earlier the cost and difficulty of merging two different organisations. It should be noted that *this* cost is borne substantially by managers, and only indirectly by shareholders. It may therefore be expected to loom large in managers' minds.

One practical question is whether capital market 'imperfections' may cushion managers who fail to maximise shareholder wealth. In theory such managements ought to be vulnerable to a take-over bid for control of their company if they fell far short of what a more capable management could achieve. That would yield large profits for anyone who organised such a take-over bid (and then ran the company well). Some companies, however, may be largely exempt from this ultimate market discipline. Unquoted companies, for example, are not easy to buy control of; very large companies may be too big to be taken over; and there may be little incentive to take over very profitable companies, since the required acquisition price might be too high, and the chance of substantially increasing profits remote. Another feature may be the tendency of institutional shareholders to support existing managements.

Even so, there are surely plenty of small to medium not-very-profitable quoted UK companies. But it may be difficult in practice to improve their profits if they are in declining industries, or face problems that are really difficult to overcome. And with about 500 mergers each year among UK industrial and commercial companies, the market for corporate control is not completely inactive.

On balance, however, it seems quite likely that the interests of managers and shareholders often *do* diverge significantly.

8.5 Liquidation and Reorganisation

8.5.1 Liquidation

Bankruptcy is the name for personal inability to pay debts due. The same thing for companies is liquidation (often referred to as **'winding-up'**).

Liquidation is a legal process, triggered by **insolvency** (failure or inability to pay debts due). It involves:

a. the appointment of a liquidator (either by the courts or by the firm's creditors);

b. the realisation of all the assets for cash; and

c. the distribution of cash between creditors and shareholders, according to their legal rights.

Except when members of a company voluntarily *choose* to wind up their company (without having to, for reasons of insolvency), the effect of liquidation is to remove resources from the control of managements which have failed to operate profitably, or which have hopelessly mismanaged their finances.

(We know that lack of *profit* is not necessarily the same thing as lack of *cash*.) Of course, not all firms which make losses go bankrupt: the higher the proportion of equity in the capital structure, the less the risk of liquidation.

'Compulsory' liquidations in the UK (i.e. other than members' voluntary liquidations) have increased in the second half of the 1970s; from over 3,000 a year from 1970 to 1974 to over 5,000 a year from 1975 to 1979, and rising to 8,500 in 1981.

When a firm goes into liquidation, its assets do not all disappear in a puff of smoke. They are realised for cash, admittedly often for amounts considerably less than their balance sheet book values. Then the proceeds have to be distributed according to the priorities listed in Fig. 8.4.

---

1. The costs of the liquidation
2. Creditors secured by a fixed charge on property
3. 'Preferential' creditors:
   a. One year's taxes due to government
   b. Wages of employees
4. Creditors secured by a floating charge
5. Unsecured creditors
6. Preference shareholders

7. Ordinary shareholders

Fig. 8.4: Priority of distribution in a liquidation.

8.5.2 Capital Reorganisation

As we have seen, 'liquidation' means ending the life of a company, by realising all the assets for cash, paying creditors according to a definite order of priority and distributing anything left to ordinary shareholders (after preference shareholders, if any, have been repaid).

Capital structure may be adjusted in the ordinary course of business, through retained profits, positive or negative, or through issuing new equity shares or borrowing. More important than the change to capital structure may be how any extra funds are *invested*.

There are three other kinds of formal capital 'reorganisation' for a company which is to continue in business: (1) merging, (2) 'de-merging' or (3) formal reduction of equity capital.

1. *Merging.* We have already discussed most of the details of merging. A combination of two formerly separate companies is likely to increase the equity 'cushion', and thus to reduce the risk attaching to any loans from existing creditors. (The terms of any *future* loans will presumably reflect the lower risk.) Indeed, merging – by reducing the *total* risk of an enterprise (though not necessarily the 'market risk', see 7.2.2) – may encourage managements to increase financial gearing.

2. *'De-merging'*. 'De-merging' (the opposite of merging) has been encouraged by recent changes in company and tax law. There are two versions:

a. Management buy-outs, where the managers of a loss-making subsidiary arrange to acquire all, or most of, the equity, often heavily assisted by institutional venture capital. If this prevents liquidation of the subsidiary, it suits the management, who get continued employment as well as the chance of a large capital gain. It may also suit the former parent company, which eliminates continuing losses of the subsidiary, while avoiding possibly heavy costs of liquidation.

b. Split-offs to shareholders, where the shares in a profitable subsidiary are simply distributed pro rata to shareholders in the holding company. Separating the two businesses may be justified on the grounds that they are not closely enough related to be managed as a single enterprise.

3. *Formal reduction of equity capital.* This has to be agreed by the courts, as a rule, because of the obvious danger that the interests of creditors may be harmed. There are three main types:

a. Substituting debt capital for preference share capital was common in the years after 1965, for tax reasons. It was usually possible to satisfy all parties, since there was a net gain to the company 'at the expense of' the Inland Revenue – which could be shared out on suitably agreed terms between ordinary shareholders, former preference shareholders, and new loan creditors.

b. Repaying to ordinary shareholders any liquid resources surplus to the company's needs has been difficult in the past, for tax reasons. The repayment might have been treated as taxable income in the hands of shareholders. Yet it seems clearly desirable that scarce resources should not be hindered from flowing to where they can be more profitably employed.

One of the factors leading to conglomerate mergers between 1967 and 1973 may have been the existence of large retained earnings (dividends being limited either by formal controls or by tax penalties) for which there were insufficient uses within the industry. An extra pressure to use resources profitably could be introduced by allowing ordinary shareholders to vote to *increase* the ordinary cash dividends (*reduce* retained earnings) proposed by a company's directors. At present this is not possible.

c. Recognising that part of the capital has been permanently lost is potentially troublesome (because it is losses, not gains, which are being shared between the interested parties). But it may sometimes be necessary as a preliminary to new capital being introduced.

Explicit recognition of losses is most often seen in the nationalised industries, where huge losses are 'written off' equity or debt capital. Reported (historical cost) write-offs totalling some £4 billion in the last 20 years probably exceed £20 billion on an inflation-adjusted basis in 1982 pounds. But since the government is usually the major loan creditor as well as the equity owner, no conflict of interest usually arises between investors.

Work Section

A. Revision Questions

A1   What is the difference between a 'merger' and an 'acquisition'?

A2   Which of a company's issued securities *must* be acquired for it to be 'taken over'?

A3   What is the difference between a 'horizontal' and a 'vertical' merger? Give one example of each.

A4   What is a 'conglomerate' merger?

A5   What kind of merger is most likely to yield economies of scale?

A6   From the point of view of the whole economy, what are two main economic arguments in favour of mergers?

A7   From the point of view of the whole economy, what are two main economic arguments against mergers?

A8   Name two production reasons for a company to make an acquisition.

A9   Name two marketing reasons for a company to make an acquisition.

A10 Name two reasons for wanting to sell a company.

A11 What incentives are there to take over poorly-managed companies?

A12 Explain why 'defensive' mergers take place.

A13 Why may takeover 'victims' support a merger?

A14 What has been the overall result of the 70-odd references since 1965 to the Monopolies and Mergers Commission?

A15 Why does the government have mixed feelings about mergers?

A16 How may the employee and/or the consumer (a) suffer and (b) gain from a merger?

A17 Why will an acquiring company probably need to find ways of substantially increasing profits in order to make a take-over pay?

A18 What alternatives are likely to be open to a buyer? to a seller?

A19 What defences are open to the directors of a company receiving an unwelcome take-over bid?

A20 In which three ways may 'goodwill' arising on an acquisition be treated: (a) in the group balance sheet, (b) in the profit and loss account?

A21 Which method of payment for acquisitions has been most common since 1974, and which (of the main methods) least common?

A22 Who seems to gain from mergers in financial terms?

A23 Why might managers and shareholders take a different view towards a company policy of diversification by merger or acquisition?

A24 Which 'cost' of merging is borne directly by managers?

A25 Why may the 'market for corporate control' not work as efficiently as theory would suggest: (a) for small companies; (b) for large ones?

A26 How does the existence of known priorities in the event of liquidation help companies to borrow?

A27 Why is a company with plenty of equity capital less likely to go into liquidation than one with little equity capital?

A28 What happens to assets disposed of on a liquidation?

A29 Name two possible reasons for 'de-merging'.

A30 Why might a company wish to *reduce* its equity capital?

B. Exercises/Case Studies

B1 Goliath Limited acquired 100 per cent of David Limited for 3 million £1 ordinary shares valued at £4.00 each on 31 March 1982, when their respective balance sheets were as summarised below:

	Goliath (£m.)	David (£m.)
Issued £1 ordinary shares	15	2
Retained profits	35	5
	50	7
Long-term debt	10	3
	60	10
Fixed assets, net	35	5
Working capital	25	5
	60	10

   The acquisition method of accounting is to be used. Show the consolidated balance sheet after the acquisition:

a. if any resulting goodwill is left on the balance sheet.

b. if any resulting goodwill is written off against reserves.

B2 Hollyhock Limited is proposing to acquire all the equity capital of Snapdragon Limited. Future cash inflows for Snapdragon as a separate company are estimated at £400,000 a year after tax; but Hollyhock's management reckons that economies of scale can add a further £200,000 a year after tax, to achieve which an immediate capital investment of £500,000 (which is stated net of tax allowances) will be required.

   Regular fixed capital investments needed to maintain Snapdragon's profits are to be taken as equal to the company's present current cost depreciation of £250,000 a year. Surplus Snapdragon assets to be sold immediately after acquisition (without significantly affecting profits) are expected to realise £100,000 net.

If the appropriate after-tax discount rate is 12 per cent a year, what is the maximum purchase price for Snapdragon that Hollyhock should be prepared to pay:

a. using a horizon period of 10 years?

b. using a horizon period of 15 years?

B3   Runge Limited is planning a major acquisition costing £5.0 million. The company's present capital consists of 10 million 50p issued ordinary shares, £4.0 million retained profits and £3.0 million 10 per cent Secured Debentures.

Runge can pay for its acquisition either by (a) issuing 4 million ordinary shares at £1.25 each, or (b) issuing £5.0 million 12 per cent Loan Stock. Present EBIT of £2.5 million a year is expected to rise to £3.5 million as a result of the acquisition.

For each of the two alternatives, compare (i) debt ratio, (ii) interest cover, (iii) earnings per share after the acquisition with Runge's present position. Assume a tax rate of 50 per cent.

B4   Bridge Steel Limited has been trading unprofitably for several years. A potential investor, George Simpson, is prepared to put up another £2 million of new equity capital to try to restore its fortunes, on condition that there is a capital reconstruction. It is reckoned that the net assets would realise just under £1.0 million now if the company were put into liquidation.

The present capital employed appears on the balance sheet as shown:

	£m.
Ordinary shareholders' funds	
5.0 million ordinary £1 shares in issue	5.0
Less: Accumulated losses	(4.0)
	1.0
8 per cent £1 cumulative preference shares	0.5
Add: five years' dividends in arrears	0.2
12 per cent Loan stock	1.2
	2.9

Losses have been running at £500,000 a year, but Mr Simpson believes he can turn the company round and earn at least £300,000 a year before tax and interest from now on. (Tax losses brought forward exceed £3.0 million.) He proposes the following scheme of reconstruction:

1. The present ordinary shares to be written down to 20p each.
2. The preference shareholders to waive the dividends in arrear.
3. The loan stock to be reduced to £1.0 million, still at 12 per cent a year.
4. The new equity capital of £2.0 million to be subscribed in return for 2.5 million new 20p ordinary shares.

Questions

a. Draw up a summary of capital employed for Bridge Steel Limited after the proposed capital reconstruction.
b. Does the scheme seem reasonably acceptable, from the viewpoint:
   i. of the loan stockholders?
   ii. of the preference shareholders?
   iii. of the existing ordinary shareholders?
   iv. of Mr Simpson?

B5 *NORTHERN STORES LIMITED*

Refer to problem B15 in Chapter 3 (Dragon Paint).

On 7 April 1982, Mr Simon, the credit manager of Dragon Paint Limited's north-east region, received a credit report on Northern Stores Limited, a potential new customer. The report indicated slow payment to several trade creditors, in a way which had not been experienced before.

Mr Simon had also learned that Northern had an overdraft with one of the clearing banks, up to a limit of £150,000. The account was unsecured, but was personally guaranteed by Mr Joseph Hamilton, Northern's main shareholder and managing director. The bank overdraft had originally been repayable on 31 March 1982, but a temporary extension had been granted. This was to allow Northern to raise about £70,000, the estimated amount which the company had lost through operations for the year ending 28 February 1982. It was understood that this was to be achieved by the end of June 1982.

Northern's stock position at the end of March was reported to total more than £300,000 despite vigorous attempts to liquidate a surplus of television sets and major appliances in late 1981 and early 1982. The bank was reported to be dissatisfied with this stock, having concluded that substantial investment rested in types of goods which were moving too slowly. Furthermore the bank was thought to be unhappy about a new store opened in November 1981, when funds were known to be needed to bolster a weak working capital position. (All Northern's stores were leased; but equipment and stock was needed when a new one was opened.)

Mr Simon was considering whether Dragon Paint Limited should extend its thin market coverage in the north-east by granting credit to Northern Stores. This would probably consist of £20,000 for initial stocks (on a three-year credit basis) plus the normal 60 days' credit on 'fill-in' orders. Mr Simon was anticipating business with Northern in excess of £60,000 a year; but Mr Hamilton was talking in terms of 'over £100,000 a year'.

Mr Hamilton showed Mr Simon a draft summary balance sheet at 28 February 1982, as shown below. He said he wished to keep the figures confidential until they were made public in about 10 days' time.

Northern Stores Limited
Balance Sheet – 28 February 1982

	£'000
Equipment and fixtures (net)	63
Current assets:	
Stocks	363
Debtors	36
Cash	13
	475
Current liabilities:	
Bank overdraft	138
Creditors and accrued charges	121
Tax payable	13
Shareholders' funds	203
	475

Sales in the past three years (£m.):	1980	2.2
	1981	2.8
	1982	3.1

Although Northern had suffered a loss of more than £50,000 in 1981 as a result of a drop in television and major appliance sales, this was fairly typical of the retail trade, which had had a very bad year. Mr Hamilton said that although the television and major appliance inventory had reached a peak during the last year of more than £150,000, the position at the end of March 1982 was less than £100,000.

He also stated that the gross profit on television sales throughout the country had dropped considerably between 1980 and 1981. For Northern this drop was reckoned to have caused a loss of £70,000, in spite of the fact that sales volume and gross profit on most other items sold by the company remained level. About 90 per cent of all sales were for cash.

Mr Hamilton said he hoped the worst of the recession was now over; and he was looking forward to a recovery of Northern's previous trend of rapid expansion, especially since the newest store of the Northern chain was just getting established.

Questions:

a. Try to estimate what are the chances of Northern Stores going bankrupt within the next 12 to 18 months.

b. What would be the position of an unsecured creditor like Dragon Paint, if the required credit was extended, if Northern did go bankrupt?

c. What difference would it make if the bank's position were secured?

d. In the context of problem B15 in Chapter 3 (Dragon Paint), would you, as Mr Simon, extend credit to Northern Stores Limited?

B6 *LAKER AIRWAYS*

On 5 February 1982, at the request of the company, the Clydesdale Bank appointed Messrs Mackey and Hamilton (of Ernst & Whinney) as joint receivers of the Laker companies. The appointment followed more than six months of negotiations between Laker Airways, its bankers and aircraft manufacturers to resolve continuing and mounting cash flow difficulties. Within a week two of the Laker subsidiaries, Arrowsmith Holidays and Laker Air Travel, had been disposed of, to Greenall Whitley (a brewery company) and Saga Tours respectively.

It was thought that Sir Freddie Laker himself (who together with his wife owned all the equity shares in Laker Airways) would probably lose a relatively modest amount compared with the losses of his financial backers. Laker's three Airbuses were mortgaged to a banking consortium headed by Midland Bank, and its 11 DC–10s were similarly mortgaged to a consortium of largely US banks.

One important reason for the crash had been changes in the dollar/sterling foreign exchange rate:

At 31.3.80 £1.00 = \$2.16; at 31.1.82 £1.00 = \$1.88. The average rate for the year ended 31.3.81 had been £1.00 = \$2.35.

At the time of the crash, the most recent Laker accounts available were for the year ended 31 March 1980. They are summarised below:

Laker Airways (International) Limited
Balance Sheet at 31 March 1980.

	1980 (£m.)	1979 (£m.)
Shareholders' Funds		
Issued ordinary £1 shares	5[1]	5[1]
Foreign exchange fluctuation reserve	5	3
Profit and loss account	13[2]	5
	23	13
Secured US dollar loans (\$235m.)	109[3]	61
Sterling loans	3	—
Current liabilities	31	22
	166	96

Fixed Assets

Aircraft and spares (net of acc. depn. 20)	136[4]	74
Other	10	8
Current Assets	20	14
	——	——
	166	96
	══	══

1. Adjusted (retrospectively) for a 9 for 1 bonus issue in September 1980, which increased issued share capital from £½m. to £5m.
2. Including prior year adjustments of +£8m.
3. (a) $235m. loans translated at 'closing rate' of $2.16 = £1.00.
   (b) $41m. loans repayable within next 12 months.
4. Capital commitments (relating mainly to new aircraft): £275m.

Laker Airways (International) Limited
Profit and Loss Account, year ended 31 March 1980.

	1980	1979
	(£m.)	(£m.)
Sales turnover	111	92
	══	══
Profit before depreciation	13	10
Depreciation (aircraft & spares: 5½)	7	5
	——	——
Earnings before interest and tax	6	5
Interest payable	6	2½
	——	——
Profit before tax[1]	—	2½[1]
	══	══

[1] In both years, no tax charge or ordinary dividends.

Questions:
a. As at 31 March 1980:
  i. what is the current ratio?
  ii. what is the debt ratio?
b. Assume:
  i. A loss of £11 million was incurred in the 22 months ended 31 January 1982, exactly equalling depreciation charged on aircraft and spares in that period;
  ii. New American loans of $611 net were incurred during the year ended 31 March 1981, to buy new aircraft.
Note: The above assumptions are deliberately over-simplified. They do *not* purport to represent actual financial events.
  i. Prepare an estimated balance sheet for Laker Airways as at 31

January 1982. (Use the 'closing rate' method of translating $s.)
ii. What is the debt ratio?
iii. What were estimated foreign exchange losses over the 22 months?
c. What alternative financial arrangements might have been desirable for Laker Airways after March 1980?
d. What went wrong? Could it have been prevented?

C. Essay Questions

C1 What is the purpose of conglomerate mergers?

C2 Early in 1982 it was rumoured that Distillers might make a takeover bid for the Royal Bank of Scotland. How could such a merger possibly be justified?

C3 Is there any need for a Monopolies and Mergers Commission? Why or why not?

C4 Do the reasons for which mergers are undertaken suggest that they should be encouraged?

C5 Most cigarette companies have been diversifying into other industries. How does this affect their shareholders?

C6 Which treatment of 'goodwill' in group accounts would you recommend in order best to show a 'true and fair view'?

C7 In what ways can a merger fundamentally alter the bidding company's financial position?

C8 Why may it be difficult to value the net benefits to be expected from a merger?

C9 Why do 'merger booms' appear to come in waves?

C10 Why has debt become an unpopular way of paying for acquisitions?

C11 Discuss possible conflicts between managers and shareholders with respect to: (a) financial gearing; (b) dividend policy; (c) mergers.

C12 Are there enough company liquidations to allow the efficient allocation of economic resources?

C13 'Mergers and acquisitions are, among other things, a civilised alternative to bankruptcy.' Discuss.

C14 Why might 'de-mergers' be desirable?

C15 Is it desirable for companies to be allowed to buy back some of their own issued equity shares? What 'safeguards' (if any) might be necessary? Why?

Part III Case Studies

Chapter 9

Park Products and Langley Engineering

This chapter contains a number of exercises, problems and questions concerning two companies, Park Products Limited and Langley Engineering Limited. There are 30 questions, broadly matching Chapters 2 to 7 of the text. (Chapter 8 is largely covered by the Burmah Oil case in Chapter 10.)

Park Products Limited is a small but rapidly-growing engineering company owned by three brothers who are also its top management. Colin Park is the production director, Gordon is in charge of marketing, and James is the financial director. The company has borrowed substantially from the bank, but its problem has been to borrow fast enough to provide the machinery it needs to expand output in line with market opportunities. The company's shares are all owned by the three brothers (and their families): as yet they are not quoted on the Stock Exchange, nor, therefore, are they available to members of the public. Park Products has a high return on capital, and on the whole it is a company that takes risks to gain its objectives.

Langley Engineering Limited is a medium-sized company, supplying various capital goods firms. It has a cautious but steady growth record, and its shares can be bought and sold through the Stock Exchange by members of the public. Most of the shares are still held by members of the Langley family, although the recently-appointed managing director is not one of them. Langley relies substantially on its own retained profits to finance its growth; when it does borrow, it tends to do so for specific projects rather than for general expansion. The company owns its offices and factory. Its return on capital is about average for the industry. Langley is in the same industry as Park, but has less export business and deals with less technically-advanced products.

Managing Cash

Park Products faces a seasonal demand for its products. At the start of its financial year, James, the financial director, has prepared a cash budget showing expected sales and purchases, cash receipts and payments.

The company's seasonal pattern of sales is matched (though, of course, earlier) by the pattern of purchases and of wages paid, the latter reflecting overtime worked. Park pays for goods one month after their arrival (fairly promptly, because it does not wish to annoy the suppliers); and it receives payment from customers two months after delivery (in its competitive business, generous credit terms help attract customers). Various other payments are also scheduled for the next year, as shown in the table below:

(£'000)	Transactions		Cash receipts	Cash payments		
Month	Sales	Purchase	Sales	Goods	Wages	Other
April	100	60	50	50	40	—
May	120	60	60	60	50	—
June	150	60	100	60	50	—
July	180	60	120	60	50	30 (m)
August	160	50	150	60	50	—
September	140	50	180	50	40	—
October	110	40	160	50	40	50 (m)
November	80	40	140	40	30	—
December	70	40	110	40	30	20 (d)
January	50	40	80	40	30	90 (t)
February	50	50	70	40	30	—
March	60	50	50	50	40	—

(d) = dividends to the owners; (t) = taxes on profits;
(m) = investment in new machinery.

Questions:
1   Draw up a further table to show the net cash flow (receipts less payments) for each month; and the cumulative effect, month by month, on the company's bank overdraft, which at the beginning of the year stands at £300,000. As James Park, the financial director, what ceiling on the overdraft would you try to agree with the bank?
2   a. How much would each of the following events (separately) affect Park's overdraft position during the next year?
        i. Wages are increased by £10,000 monthly, but strict price controls prevent the company from passing this on to customers.
        ii. All payments for sales are received from customers one month later than had been expected.
        iii. Economic uncertainty means that all planned purchases and sales are put back by one month in April, so that all subsequent purchases and sales are one month later than forecast.
    b. How adequate would a bank overdraft ceiling of £500,000 for the year prove in the face of all three events occurring *in combination*?

Langley Engineering expects to have the following pattern of sales in its next financial year (figures in £'000s):

July	300	January	450
August	350	February	400
September	400	March	350
October	450	April	300
November	500	May	300
December	500	June	300

In the current year, May sales were £350,000, and June sales £300,000. The company's sales are on two months' credit. Raw materials (estimated to cost 40 per cent of final sales revenue) are purchased three months in advance of expected sales, on one month's credit. Factory labour costs account for 20 per cent of final sales revenue, and the work is done in the month before dispatch of goods.

Rent of £30,000 is paid every quarter, starting in September. Regular monthly payments are: maintenance of £10,000; administrative salaries and expenses of £40,000; and research and development expenses of £20,000. The company's only advertising expenditure is £60,000 a month from August to October. Dividends are expected to be £120,000 in September. Capital expenditure on machinery of £400,000 is planned, with £100,000 being paid in October and the balance in March.

The bank overdraft is at present £600,000; and interest is added each month at the rate of 1 per cent of the *previous* month's closing balance.

Questions:

3 Draw up a detailed table showing the company's estimated cash flows in each month, with the resulting level of the bank overdraft. The present agreed overdraft limit is £1,000,000. Would you advise the company's finance director to renegotiate this limit? If so, to what amount? What assumptions have you needed to make?

4 The bank agrees to raise its overdraft facility limit, but to a figure £70,000 below what you expect the overdraft to be at the end of October. Assuming that it is impossible for Langley to borrow money from any other source, what action do you recommend for the coming year?

5 At the beginning of July, Langley is informed that the price of all supplies has risen by 25 per cent. The company will raise its own selling prices by an average of 10 per cent to match this increase, but will not be able to until the higher-priced raw materials are themselves, in their finished form, for sale. How will this affect Langley's cash needs:
a. this calendar year?
b. over a longer period?

6 A strike in a supplier's firm means that deliveries cease in October. Assuming that production is maintained as long as possible, what is the likely effect on Langley's overdraft?

Managing Working Capital

Park Products is wondering whether to cut back on sales to 'Class C' customers, whose credit rating is less satisfactory than most customers. (This relates more to the *time* they take to pay than to the likelihood of their eventually becoming 'bad debts', by failing to pay at all.)

Gordon, the marketing director, is keen to sell to anyone who will buy; but James, conscious of the limited finance available, feels that at least reducing sales to Class C customers of lower-profit product lines might be sensible. He reckons that the variable expenses on the lower-profit lines amount to as much as 90 per cent of sales revenue; yet they tie up about two months' worth of stock, and often take up to three months, or even longer, to pay for goods (with Class C customers). With interest rates running at more than 12 per cent a year, he is not sure whether this kind of business is really profitable. (Assume that selling lower-profit products to Class C customers accounts for 5% of total sales revenue.)

Questions:

7 a. Estimate the average 'investment' in stocks and debtors needed to service the low-profit Class C-customer business. (For this purpose, assume that sales run at a level £100,000 each month.)

   b. How much net contribution to profit, after financing costs, does such business make in a year?

   c. Do you tend to agree with Gordon or with James? Why? How would you try to persuade the other?

At the end of last year (sales £3.6 million), Langley's stocks stood in the balance sheet at £1.5 million, and debtors at £900,000. Cost of sales amounted to about 60 per cent of the selling price of Langley's products, half in wages, half in materials. Trade credit terms allow one month's credit, but the company has been taking two and a half months on average, and is anxious to reduce this to at most one and a half months. Of the £400,000 'creditors' figure on the most recent balance sheet, £175,000 relates to taxation and accrued charges (other than trade credit from suppliers of materials) – and it is not expected that this amount will change significantly

More as a result of inflation than genuine growth in volume of output, the current year's sales are expected to be about 25 per cent up on last year. Langley's finance director is worried about how much extra finance may be needed to support working capital by the end of the financial year. (Fixed capital expenditure is budgeted separately.) As a starting point, he decides to assume that the level of stocks and debtors relative to sales will remain the same as now; and for simplicity he plans to work on the basis of level monthly sales.

Questions:

8 Estimate the likely amount of each item of working capital (other than the bank overdraft) at the end of the current financial year. How much extra money will be needed to finance it?

9 Assuming a marginal after-tax contribution of 20 per cent on sales, and a dividend payout ratio of 50 per cent, how much extra money would be needed to finance an extra £100,000 sales per year if trade creditors could be reduced to one and a half months?

Long-term Investment Projects

Colin Park is enthusiastic about a new German machine, which he thinks would enable Park Products to reduce operating costs by £20,000 a year (before tax). The machine costs £60,000, and would be eligible for 100 per cent first-year tax allowance. (Assume that all tax effects occur at the same time as the related cash payments or receipts; in other words, ignore any possible time-lags.) At the end of its expected five-year life the machine could probably be sold for about £5,000. The company normally requires a return of at least 20 per cent a year (after-tax) on this kind of investment.

Question:

10 Should the German machine be bought? (The tax rate may be taken as 50 per cent.)

Park Products did go ahead and buy the German machine (G); but a month later Colin Park visited Japan in order to keep abreast of the latest technical developments. While he was in Tokyo he learned about an even better machine (J), which would cut Park's operating costs by a *further* £12,000 a year by replacing machine (G). Machine (J) would last five years, with not much salvage value at the end, and would cost £60,000. Unfortunately machine (G) would have to be sold, and would realise only £25,000.

Questions:

11 a. Should machine (J) be purchased?

b. If machine (J) *is* purchased, presumably it was a mistake to buy machine (G) in the first place. How much did this mistake cost? How did it come about?

Langley's products were regarded as 'capital investments' by many of their customers, who tended to be small engineering companies which used the 'payback' method of project evaluation. After reading about discounted cash flow methods, Langley's marketing director decided to compare project evaluations for a typical Langley product – which tended to be a long-life cost-reduction type of investment – with a product from a competitor like

Wilson Machines, which would produce larger savings each year, but over a much shorter working life.

For simplicity the marketing director decided to ignore any salvage value at the end of a machine's life (which would only be small in either case). One of Langley's larger machines might cost £10,000 and produce savings of £2,000 a year for 20 years. In contrast, a £10,000 machine from Wilson would last only eight years: it might save £4,000 operating costs in the first year, but this would have declined to before-tax savings of only about £1,200 by the eighth year.

Questions:

12 Assuming that Langley's customers would use an after-tax discount rate of 12 per cent, and be able to claim 100 per cent first-year tax allowances on the machines purchased, compare the £10,000 machines of Langley Engineering and Wilson Machines from the customer's point of view:
   a. using the payback method
   b. using the average return on investment method
   c. using the net present value method.
   What conclusions can you draw?

13 Why do the three methods above not all give the same ranking for Langley and Wilson machines? Does it matter? Why should Langley's marketing director bother himself about a technical question like the particular method of project evaluation used by his customers?

Types and Sources of Finance

Questions:

14 Without knowing more than we already do about the two companies, contrast the likely attitudes of the management of Park Products and Langley Engineering towards raising £200,000 by:
   a. Selling ordinary shares to outsiders.
   b. A term loan.
   c. Increasing their bank overdraft.
   d. Trade credit.
   e. Leasing assets.
   f. Raising funds from assets.

The Stock Exchange

As part of his longer-term planning of the company's finances, James Park has been wondering whether the time has yet come for Park Products to 'go public' by issuing shares to members of the public, on the Stock Exchange. A number of difficult policy questions arise, but James is anxious to get some idea of the likely market price of each ordinary share in that event. Park is too small for a full listing; so if it were to go public, it would be on the Unlisted Securities Market. One advantage would be that no more than 10 per cent of the equity would need to be made available to 'outsiders'.

Some of the relevant financial information is shown below:

Shareholders' funds: 200,000 issued 25p shares	£ 50,000
Retained profits	£150,000
Annual pre-tax profits:	£160,000
Annual growth rate in profits (approx.)	15%
Latest annual dividend (net of tax)	£ 20,000

Typical price/earnings ratios and dividend yields for the industry:

	P/E ratio	Net dividend yield (%)
A fast-growing company	15	3
A medium-growth company	10	6
A poor-growth company	7	9

Questions:

15 Assuming a 50 per cent corporation tax rate, what would you expect might be the quoted Stock Exchange price of each ordinary share if Park Products were to go public?
   a. Based on price/earnings ratio?
   b. Based on dividend yield?
   c. Based on book value of assets?
   d. Based on the dividend growth formula? (Assume the cost of equity capital is estimated at 25% a year.)

As a result of his calculations on working capital (see Questions 8 and 9 above), Langley's finance director was thinking about ways for the company to raise money. One obvious possibility was a rights issue of ordinary shares to existing shareholders. Langley's 4 million 25p ordinary shares issued were currently quoted on the Stock Exchange at 40p each; and in order to raise £350,000 the finance director was considering a 1 for 4 rights issue at 35p. (See also the balance sheet on page 197.)

Questions:

16 What is Langley's current:
   a. earnings per share?
   b. price/earnings ratio?
   c. net dividend per share? (see question 3 above)
   d. net dividend yield?

17 What would Langley's 'shareholders' funds' on the balance sheet consist of after the proposed rights issue?

18 Does it matter that Langley's market value of equity is considerably less than the balance sheet book value? Why or why not?

19 Consider the position of two Langley shareholders, each holding 4,000 shares at present. Mr Smith would take up his rights, while Mr Jones would sell his on the market.
   a. How much money would Mr Smith have to put up in subscribing for his rights under the proposed issue?

b. How much money would Mr Jones receive for selling his rights under the proposed issue?

c. What would Mr Smith's shareholding in Langley be worth after the rights issue?

d. What would Mr Jones's shareholding in Langley be worth after the rights issue?

20 In the end, Langley decided *not* to make the proposed rights issue. Why do you think the company may have come to this decision? Identify as many relevant factors as you can.

Long-term finance

Summarised balance sheets at the end of June for Park Products and Langley Engineering are set out below, together with figures for the most recent year's sales and profits.

Balance Sheets (end of June) (£'000)		Park Products		Langley Engineering
Shareholders' funds			200	3,000
Long-term loan			200	–
= Capital employed			400	3,000
Fixed assets				
Buildings			–	600
Machinery			300	1,000
			300	1,600
Current assets				
Stocks	200	1,500		
Debtors	300	900		
	500	2,400		
Less: Current liabilities				
Bank overdraft	300	600		
Creditors	100	400		
	400	1,000		
Working capital		100		1,400
= Net assets			400	3,000
Latest year's sales			1,200	3,600
Latest year's profits (after tax)			80	240

Questions:

21 Consider Park and Langley each raising £200,000 for investment in machinery. Discuss, with reasons, whether one company might be particularly influenced by cost, while the other's choice might be dominated by questions as to flexibility.

22 Might one company have wider access to sources of finance than the other? Why?

23 How do Park's and Langley's needs differ? How might these different needs be reflected in their approach to borrowing?

24 How do Park's objectives appear to differ from Langley's?

25 Which of the two companies is more highly geared? Which would like to be?

26 How 'well balanced' would you say each of the two companies is financially?

27 How would you expect that Park Products and Langley Engineering might differ in their reaction to an unexpected period of rapid inflation?

The directors of Park Products and Langley Engineering are now considering their plans for the next five years. Park expects to double sales and profits in real terms; Langley expects that each should rise by one third.

Questions:

28 Assuming that the £200,000 mentioned earlier has *not* been raised, calculate how much cash (in terms of present purchasing power) each company will need to raise to support its operations, given that they aim as follows:

	Park Products	*Langley Engineering*
Machinery:	one-third of annual sales	one-third of annual sales
Stocks:	two months' sales	four months' sales
Debtors:	three months' sales	three months' sales.

29 For each company, retained profits will help to finance investment in fixed assets and working capital. Over the five years, how much (in terms of today's purchasing power) will they contribute to the funds of each company? What assumptions do you need to make to calculate this?

30 Your answers to Questions 28 and 29 above should produce estimates of how much further cash each company will need over the next five years, and how much retained profits will contribute (both expressed in terms of present purchasing power). How should each company raise the difference? Draw up estimated balance sheets for each company as at the end of five years (in terms of today's purchasing power), assuming that each raises extra finance as you suggest.

Chapter 10

Burmah Oil

The year 1974 was a watershed in Burmah Oil's history. This chapter contains six case studies: three leading up to 1974, one describing what happened in that year, and two dealing with subsequent events. Questions are set out at the end of each section.

Prologue

On 8 May 1901 the Shah of Persia, for £20,000 cash, gave William Knox d'Arcy, an Englishman who had made his fortune in the Australian goldfields, the exclusive right to prospect for oil throughout the Persian Empire for a term of 60 years. His party endured dysentery, plagues of locusts, and an outbreak of smallpox. But they found no oil; and after three years even d'Arcy's purse was beginning to feel the strain of failure.

Meanwhile a small group of British naval officers led by Admiral (later Lord) Fisher became convinced that to sustain the navy's supremacy against the German threat, its coal-fired boilers must be replaced by oil-fired. This meant that a source of the new fuel must be found. On the whole, Britain's imperial territories looked unpromising, but southern Persia was under effective British control, so d'Arcy's lone venture in the Persian desert acquired fresh significance. Prodded eagerly by Fisher, the British government agreed to find d'Arcy a partner to help him stay in business. They lit upon the Burmah Oil Company, a consortium of Scotsmen whose discovery in Burma had given them resources to invest elsewhere. With Burmah's aid d'Arcy carried on for another three years, but without success. By 1908 nearly £1 million had been spent on exploration with no tangible results.

Early in May 1908 a telegram arrived at the rig at Masjid es Suleiman, some 130 miles north of the Gulf coast, to say that no more funds were available. But the head of the drilling team decided to ignore the instruction to stop drilling, until a confirming letter arrived. Just before dawn on 26 May 1908 he was woken by excited shouting, and arose to see a fifty-foot column of oil gushing into the sky. So began the Anglo-Persian Oil Company (later renamed British Petroleum – BP); and that is how the Burmah Oil Company came to own a large shareholding in BP. D'Arcy got his money back, plus £900,000 worth of Burmah shares.

Another important year for Burmah Oil was 1942, when the company's own employees destroyed its Burmese installations in order to prevent them from falling into the hands of the Japanese enemy. After the Second World War, the Burmese fields were nationalised, and the company's trading operations were confined to India and Pakistan. Burmah Oil was subsequently involved in a famous legal argument with the British government, which in 1965 passed the War Damage Act retrospectively preventing the company from seeking to claim damages from the Crown in respect of the Burmese installations.

10.1 **Strategic Objectives**

In 1961, Burmah Oil's operations continued in India and Pakistan; but the company's largest single asset (worth £126 million) was its holding of some 77 million ordinary shares in British Petroleum (just under 25% of BP's issued shares).[1] Burmah also held some 16 million ordinary shares (worth £23 million) in Shell Transport and Trading (about 3½% of the issued capital). At the end of 1961, Burmah Oil's own 82 million £1 ordinary shares were quoted at £1.56 each on the Stock Exchange.

Burmah included in its profit and loss account only the dividends received from its large investments in BP and Shell (rather than its pro rata share of their trading profits). By arrangement with the Inland Revenue, the company did not pay tax on the BP and Shell dividends, but undertook to pass them straight on to its own shareholders in the form of a Burmah Oil dividend. Figures 10.1 and 10.2 show the relative importance in 1961 of Burmah's trading operations and its investments in BP and Shell.

Burmah Oil had been built up on the basis of its oil and gas operations on the Indian sub-continent. But by 1961 there were stringent limitations on its business there, foreign exchange controls on the remittance of cash to the UK, and increasing pressure to transfer the operations into local ownership. Political instability in its main area of operations, and the strong possibility of nationalisation, led Burmah Oil's directors in the early 1960s to consider a number of alternative strategies for shaping the company's future.

---

[1] Burmah's holdings in BP were 76.9 million £1 ordinary shares, until in 1964 5.9 million extra shares were bought (on a rights issue by BP), making a new total of 82.4 million BP shares which were held up until the end of 1974.

	£m.
Issued £1 ordinary shares	82
Reserves	19
	___
= Ordinary shareholders' funds	101
Preference share capital	4
Long-term loans	4
	___
	109
	═══
Fixed assets and trade investments	31
Investments in BP and Shell (at cost)	60
Net working capital	18
	___
	109
	═══

Fig. 10.1: Burmah Oil, Balance Sheet, 31 December 1961.

	£m.
Operating income	4
Income from trade investments, etc.	4
Dividends on BP and Shell shares	12
	___
Profit before tax	20
Tax	9
	___
Profit after tax	11
Ordinary dividends	9
	___
Retained profits for the year	2
	═══

Fig. 10.2: Burmah Oil, Profit and Loss Account, 1961.

One suggestion was to allow trading operations to run down, and to turn the company (in effect) into an investment trust – with its primary holding in BP. Few of the board liked this idea: most directors agreed that it would be folly to throw away Burmah's considerable expertise in the oil business.

Several directors, noting that the bulk of the Stock Exchange value of Burmah Oil's shares was accounted for by the investment in BP, believed that the stock market was seriously undervaluing Burmah's own trading operations. They wanted to distribute the BP shares to Burmah shareholders, since they expected this would immediately increase the value placed by investors on Burmah's trading operations. As the third largest independent oil company in the UK (after BP and Shell), with widespread expertise in exploration and pipeline technology, Burmah might become a very attractive acquisition prospect for several foreign oil companies if it could thus cut itself free from BP. But the idea of being taken over was not generally popular among Burmah's directors.

Another group on the board pressed for expansion of Burmah's trading operations, by developing new reserves of oil and gas in the Western hemisphere to counterbalance its investments on the Indian sub-continent. The company should not only diversify geographically, they argued, but it should also reduce its risk by diversifying out of oil. In particular, there were exciting opportunities in the fast-growing petrochemicals industry, and in a number of businesses supplying the motorist. These areas were logical extensions of Burmah's traditional activities.

Since it had undertaken to pass all the BP dividends straight on to its own shareholders, Burmah had insufficient internally-generated funds to finance any major expansion. But the expansionists were opposed to distributing the company's BP shares themselves to Burmah Oil shareholders, arguing that the large BP holding should be used as backing to raise debt finance for expanding Burmah's trading interests. They felt a sensible target debt ratio would be around 30 per cent. In this way, they believed, Burmah's shareholding in BP could be used to obtain for Burmah Oil shareholders greater benefits than would be available to them as direct holders of the BP shares.

Questions:

1 Identify the main alternative financial and investment opportunities open to Burmah Oil at the end of 1961.
2 What do you see as the advantages and disadvantages of each?
3 On balance, what combination of financing and investment strategies do you prefer? Why?
4 In 1961, what value is the stock market apparently placing on Burmah Oil's business apart from its investments in BP and Shell shares?
5 How would you try to establish a sensible target debt ratio for Burmah?

10.2 Diversification

Burmah Oil's directors were still debating alternative strategies when in 1962 the opportunity arose to acquire Lobitos Oilfields, joint operator of a large oil concession in northern Peru. Lobitos was involved in all aspects of supplying oil products for the Peruvian market. It also owned two small refineries in the UK – at Barton and at Ellesmere Port – which handled crude produced in excess of domestic Peruvian demand; as well as some small marketing companies which handled the refinery output. The decision to acquire

Lobitos signalled that the expansionists had won the day. Burmah would keep its 77 million BP shares and use them as backing for geographical and product diversification.

The company's next major opportunity came in 1966, when it became known that Castrol, a leading British producer of speciality lubricants, was looking for a merger partner. Castrol was a soundly managed firm with a well-known product line, which also fitted well with Burmah's intention to develop a speciality oil business in the Western hemisphere. But it faced a similar problem to Burmah: it was in danger of being squeezed out of one of its principal markets. The oil majors were keen to promote their own oils, and the development of solus petrol stations left Castrol in an exposed position.

Burmah had been considering a £9 million plan to expand the Ellesmere Port refinery, acquired with Lobitos. After 1966, the decision was taken to extend Ellesmere Port further to supply a large part of Castrol's needs. As the company was separately considering entering the petrochemicals field, it also seemed sensible to build some extra flexibility to increase the output of light fractions. The scale of these proposed developments made it economical to close down the small Barton refinery and to concentrate all Burmah's UK refining at Ellesmere Port. The revised £30 million plan was approved in January 1969, but due to poor costing and site troubles the actual cost finally exceeded £40 million. To make matters worse, after abortive discussions with Laporte Chemicals in 1970, severe overcapacity emerged in the industry and Burmah decided to drop any plans to produce petrochemicals.

Non-oil Diversification

The Ellesmere Port development led to other acquisitions. In 1968, Burmah bought Petrocarbon Developments, a company involved in the design and construction of petroleum and petrochemical plant. The prospect of a five-fold increase in fuel and lubricants from Ellesmere Port led Burmah to expand its marketing and distribution operations to handle the additional output. During 1968 and 1969 several garage chains and oil distributors were acquired to safeguard outlets. And in 1970, Burmah bought Halfords, the motorists' accessories chain. The Halfords deal not only linked Burmah with a 'household name', but was considered important because it afforded 'security of outlet to Castrol because of the increasing tendency for lubricants to be sold through the supermarket and the high street shop'.

Burmah's acquisitions of Lobitos and Castrol also led towards product diversification. With Lobitos, Burmah had inherited Dussek Brothers, manufacturers of electrical insulating compounds, and Campbells Technical Waxes. The Castrol acquisition had brought with it Expandite, which manufactured products for the building industry, Atlas Preservatives, and Edwin Cooper (chemical additives). Since Burmah saw little prospect of further acquisitions of the calibre of Castrol in the UK oil sector, it decided on a policy of 'acquiring market leaders in the fields into which Castrol and Lobitos had themselves diversified'. This policy led to the purchase in 1969 of Rawlplug, manufacturers of building products and masonry fixtures, which complemented the activities of Expandite. In 1972 Burmah acquired Tabbert, a German manufacturer of caravans, and Quinton Hazell, which manufactured car components, and in 1973 Carruthers, a heavy crane producer.

In 1970 the non-oil industrial operations were organised into four major

£m.	1967	1970	1973
Sales turnover	126	236	496
Operating profits:			
Oil products: India and Pakistan		13	15
Other overseas		10	21
Burmah Oil Tankers		–	18
Non-oil products: Castrol		(1)	1
Quinton Hazell		–	3
Halfords		2	3
Edwin Cooper		1	1
Burmah Industrial		2	3
Burmah Engineering		–	1
Unallocated central expenses		(2)	(4)
= Net operating profit	21	25	62
Dividends: British Petroleum[1]	15	18	12½
Shell[1]	2	3	1½
	38	46	76
Interest payable	3	6	19
	35	40	57
Taxation	7	10	11
Profit after tax	28	30	46
Minority interests and preference dividends	3	2	2
Profit for ordinary shareholders	25	28	44
Ordinary dividends[1]	19	22	17
Retained profits for the year	6	6	27

[1] All dividends expressed gross in 1967 and 1970; and net in 1973.

Fig. 10.3: Burmah Oil, Profit and Loss Accounts, 1967, 1970, 1973.

groups: Halfords; Edwin Cooper; Burmah Industrial Products; and Burmah Engineering. The Burmah Industrial Products group was formed from (a) the old Lobitos subsidiaries, Campbell and Dussek; (b) the former Castrol subsidiaries, Atlas and Expandite; and (c) Rawlplug. Burmah Engineering was composed of Flexibox (which manufactured mechanical seals), Dynaflex (garage equipment) and Petrocarbon Developments. Despite the nationalisation of much of Burmah's Eastern business, as late as 1970, oil and gas operations in India and Pakistan still accounted for half the group's profits other than the dividends from BP and Shell.

Burmah's four major acquisitions had been paid for by issuing ordinary shares, the others mostly for cash. In 1966 Burmah issued £15 million 7¼ per cent cumulative redeemable preference stock to finance the 5.9 million BP ordinary shares allotted to Burmah (at 250p each) on a BP rights issue.

		£1 shares (m.)
	1.1.62: Shares in issue	82.4
1962	Lobitos	11.6[1]
		94.0
1964	1 for 4 scrip issue	23.5
		117.5
1966	Castrol	6.4[2]
		123.9
1968	Rawlplug	4.9
		128.8
1969	Major (distributors)	0.4
	Conversion of £5.9m. 7½% Loan Stock 1981/86	1.8
		131.0
1970	Halfords	3.4
		134.4
1972	Quinton Hazell	9.3[3]
1972/4	Conversion of warrants	0.3
	Shares in issue: 31.12.74 (and 31.12.80)	144.0

[1] Tangible Lobitos assets £17.1m.: the difference of £5.5m. was credited to share premium account.
[2] Plus £21.2m. partly-convertible 7½% loan stock 1981/6
[3] Plus £4.5m. 8½% loan stock 1991/6. To the *nominal* price of £13.8m. was added £27.8m. share premium.

Fig. 10.4: Burmah Oil, issued ordinary shares, 1962 to 1980.

Some of the directors were unhappy about the company's general acquisi-tion policy: they felt that Burmah was becoming known to investors as a conglomerate that always paid too much and got too little. (Premiums over market price paid for Castrol, Rawlplug, and Halfords were 30%, 46% and 26% respectively.) But the managing director strongly resisted such sugges-tions: Burmah's diversification strategy was carefully controlled; acquisitions were concentrated in oil-related industries; and the company's new divisional structure ensured close control over its subsidiaries.

In addition, by the early 1970s Burmah had established its own fleet of oil tankers and had been expanding its oil exploration activities in Australia, Canada, the Gulf of Mexico and the North Sea (see case 10.3). All these developments did not appear to have put excessive strain on Burmah's balance sheet (see Fig. 10.5), with the debt ratio at the end of 1973 remaining within the company's self-imposed target of 30 per cent. At the end of 1973 the board had approved future capital expenditure of £174 million.

£m.	1964	1967	1970	1973
Issued £1 ordinary shares[1]	118	124	134	144[1]
Reserves[2]	192	254	409	461[2]
= Ordinary shareholders' funds	310	378	543	605
Preference share capital	4	19	19	19
Minority interests	8	14	15	42
Loan capital	13	31	106	186
Deferred tax, pensions, etc.	–	4	6	53
	335	446	689	905
Properties and operating assets, net	30	60	129	304
Investments: Trade and associates	38	58	61	71
BP and Shell shares (m.v.)	245	310	445	469[3]
Current assets	52	68	155	272
Less: Current liabilities[4]	(30)	(50)	(101)	(211)[4]
	335	446	689	905

[1] Quoted at year end, per share: (p)   240   338   313   374
[2] Including surplus on BP and Shell shares revalued at current market prices (done in *published* accounts only from 1969)
[3] Including Shell shares (m.v. £m.)   35   51   66   26
[4] Including bank overdrafts (£m.)   1   8   24   84

Fig. 10.5: Burmah Oil, Balance Sheets, 1964, 1967, 1970, 1973.

Questions:
1. Estimate the total cost of each of the five major acquisitions between 1962 and 1973: Lobitos (1962), Castrol (1966), Rawlplug (1969), Halfords (1970) and Quinton Hazell (1972).
2. How did Burmah Oil manage to finance its extensive programme of diversification between 1962 and 1973 without putting excessive strain on the balance sheet? What additions did the acquisitions cause in total to (a) ordinary shareholders' funds?, (b) long-term borrowing?
3. Classify each of the acquisitions mentioned as horizontal, vertical or conglomerate. How do you see each of them fitting in to Burmah's diversification strategy?
4. Does it appear to you that Burmah 'got too little' from its acquisitions? How can you judge?
5. At each of the four balance sheet dates shown in Fig. 10.5, at what amount was the stock market apparently valuing all Burmah's assets other than the BP and Shell shares?
6. (a) On the BP rights issue in 1966, what alternatives were open to Burmah instead of issuing £15m. 7¼ per cent preference shares to pay for the 5.9 million BP shares allotted to it at 250p each? (b) Given a BP dividend in 1966 (on the expanded capital) of 11.67p per share, what would have been the net effect of the whole transaction on Burmah's profit and loss account?

10.3 Oil-related Operations

By 1970 Burmah realised that the Ellesmere Port scheme incorporated a serious flaw, in that profitability was tied closely to the transportation costs of the crude landed there. As spot tanker rates climbed to a new high during 1970, the Ellesmere Port project began to look like a financial liability before it was even completed. Internal forecasts suggesting an increasing need for the US, as well as Europe and Japan, to import petroleum products and crude implied that there would be a chronic shortage of tankers for some years to come, with an estimated doubling in demand for tankers by 1980. With no tanker fleet of its own, Burmah might have to pay very high rates to charter tankers.

It was therefore proposed that Burmah establish its own tanker fleet 'with the principal object of reducing, as far as possible, the effective cost of crude landed at the Ellesmere Port refinery'. In order to realise economies of scale on its tanker operations, Burmah would operate very large crude carriers (VLCCs) of over 250,000 tonnes, which would give the company substantial surplus carrying capacity. However, since it was possible to charter-in tankers at very favourable long-term rates, and to charter them out again immediately on the spot market, it was argued that the tanker operation would constitute a good source of profit, as well as securing Burmah's own transportation needs.

In accordance with general practice, it was not Burmah's intention to own any vessels: they would be chartered-in on a long-term basis, or leased. Thus there would be no net financing need, and the balance sheet would not be encumbered with any additional debt finance.[1]

By the end of 1973 the company operated 30 vessels. Under the chairmanship of Elias Kulukundis, a former adviser to Aristotle Onassis, Burmah Oil Tankers had been successful at chartering-in on favourable long-term rates and then using the vessels in the single-voyage market. As a result, in 1973 the tankers contributed £18 million profits, about one third of the net operating profits of the whole group.

In 1972 Burmah had arranged to be the sole lessee of a trans-shipment terminal being built for the Bahamas government on Grand Cayman Island. This terminal would take the largest crude carriers from the Middle East and transfer the oil to smaller tankers for shipment to the US East Coast ports, none of which was equipped to handle VLCCs. Burmah intended to use its own vessels to service the Bahamas terminal, and had increased its fleet in anticipation. At the end of 1973 Burmah signed a contract with Shell committing nearly 20 per cent of the terminal's capacity.

In another major development, on the strength of two contracts to transport liquid natural gas (LNG), Burmah arranged for eight LNG vessels to be built in the US by General Dynamics, and financed by a $160 million construction loan from Burmah. On completion the ships were to be owned by a consortium of US leasing companies, and leased to Burmah.

Meanwhile, recognising that it could not hope to be a major force in the oil industry without larger reserves of crude, Burmah had also stepped up exploration in the Gulf of Mexico, Canada, Australia and the North Sea. In 1972 and 1973 alone the company reported the purchase of 31 leases in the Gulf of Mexico area, for a total cost of about $290 million. Numerous wells were drilled with a large measure of success.

---

[1] Though Burmah Oil Tankers had heavy fixed lease commitments not shown on the balance sheet. Note 39(d) to the 1973 accounts read as follows:

'Certain subsidiaries have contractual commitments in respect of tanker in-charters and leased facilities involving hire charges (exclusive of certain operating costs) as follows:

Commitments estimated as payable during 1974: £53 million.

Commitments estimated as payable during 1975: £63 million.

Thereafter extending up to the year 2003 there are similar commitments, the net present value of which discounted at 15 per cent per annum is estimated to amount to £313 million.

It is impossible to predict with certainty circumstances over a period extending beyond the year 2000, but the terms of firm out-charters, contracts of affreightment and other arrangements so far entered into, already provide for income being earned over the period to match a very substantial part of the aggregate amount of the commitments. . . .'

In Canada, limited operations begun in 1959 were widened in 1963 with the acquisition of properties from Colorado Oil and Gas. Burmah's involvement was further increased when it acquired a 67 per cent interest in the Great Plains Development Company, which brought large gas reserves and increased the group's exploration potential. Through Great Plains, Burmah participated in exploration in Western Canada, the Arctic islands and subsequently Alaska.

In Australia, Burmah's interests were represented through a 54 per cent holding in Woodside-Burmah, which owned properties in the Cooper Basin and the North-West shelf. Exploration in the early 1960s yielded gas in commercial quantities; but major success came only in the early 1970s, with the discovery of large gas and condensate deposits in the North-West shelf area.

Burmah's initial experience in the North Sea had not been encouraging. The oil industry had little experience in drilling at depths of over 400 feet, and none of operating in seas where winds touch 130 miles an hour, and occasional 100-foot waves roll by. After several years, the company had located only two small gas fields. But in January 1974 there was a major discovery 100 miles north-east of the Shetlands, on a block that gave Burmah a 30 per cent interest in the Ninian field. With over a billion barrels of estimated recoverable oil, Ninian was the third largest of the British North Sea oil fields. Thus Burmah's crude reserves suddenly expanded enormously; but the company would be faced with the task of finding some £250 million of development funds.

For some years Burmah had been conscious that it had no presence in the world's largest market for oil, the United States, and had been seeking to augment its oil production by acquisitions in the USA. There had been a possibility a few years earlier of Burmah merging with the Continental Oil Company of America, but discussions were terminated partly because it would have been necessary to sell some of the BP shares to finance the deal. Similar discussions with Ladd Petroleum had broken down in 1973. (Burmah's shares in Shell, in contrast, had always been regarded as disposable – see footnote on page 210.)

In January 1974, however, Signal Oil, the US West-Coast conglomerate, agreed to sell its oil interests to Burmah for $420 million in cash (at the start of 1974, £1.00 = $2.32), plus the write-off of $60 million of loans by Signal Oil to the parent company. Signal's domestic US production of some 45,000 barrels a day almost doubled Burmah's crude supplies. At the same time, Signal provided Burmah with a 19 per cent interest in the medium-sized Thistle field in the North Sea. The Chase Manhattan Bank and its international affiliate the Orion Bank arranged a consortium to lend Burmah the entire $420 million needed to finance the Signal deal; and Burmah agreed to ensure that its total debt would never exceed a specified percentage of total capital employed.

In his statement with the 1973 Annual Report and Accounts, Mr Lumsden referred optimistically to these two recent developments (the acquisition of Signal and the exploration successes in the North Sea). He said they 'should bring considerable benefit to the company in future years'.

Questions:

1 Evaluate the commercial reasoning behind the tanker operations and the decision to expand them.
2 What difference would it have made to Burmah's debt ratio at the end of 1973:
   a. If the tanker leases had been capitalised (i.e. the tankers had been shown on the balance sheet as fixed assets and the present value of the tanker lease commitments had been shown as long-term debt)?
   b. Using the market value (rather than the book value) of Burmah's equity?
   c. Both (a) and (b)?
3 Assume that Burmah's tanker leasing commitments averaged £50 million a year from 1974 to 2003 inclusive. What difference would it make to the present value at the end of 1973 if the 15 per cent discount rate had been varied by three percentage points?

The holding of 16.1 million 25p shares in Shell became 19.3 million shares after a 1 for 5 scrip issue in 1963. Then, in 1970, 1.0 million shares were sold; in 1972, 2.0 million shares; and in 1973, 5.0 million shares – leaving 11.3 million Shell shares owned at the end of 1973 (and at the end of 1974).

In the 1971 Annual Report came a suggestion of a major change of attitude with regard to the BP holding. Burmah Oil's new chairman, Mr J. A. Lumsden, said:

> 'The present and potential value of your company's holding in BP is a great financial strength and my predecessors have from time to time referred to it as an integral part of the company's business. As in the parable, however, it is not a talent to be buried and it does have certain disadvantages. Its very size in relation to Burmah's substantial trading operations means that their value often appears to be inadequately reflected in the market valuation of your company's stock. Moreover a portfolio investment of this kind does not provide the cash flow and pre-tax earnings essential to the development and expansion of trading operations and to the achievement of a more satisfactory level of growth. For these reasons it was not considered appropriate to take up the recent BP rights issue.
>
> Your board takes the view that, should an opportunity arise for a major redeployment of the BP holding in a way which would significantly improve the prospective earnings and cash flow of Burmah stock over and above what would be afforded by retention of the BP stock, it would be its duty to recommend to stockholders that Burmah should disinvest itself of a large part or indeed of the whole of the holding.'

4 Why do you suppose Burmah appeared to change its mind in 1971 about its policy towards the investment in BP shares? In what respects, if any, would Mr Lumsden's comments about the BP holding have been inapplicable in 1961?
5 What alternative methods were available to Burmah to finance its $420 million acquisition of Signal Oil in January 1974? What do you see as their advantages and disadvantages?
6 What alternatives were open to Burmah to finance its future share of North Sea development costs, estimated to total some £250 million?

10.4 A Bad Year for Burmah

All things considered, Burmah appeared to be entering 1974 in a fairly satisfactory state – even before the discovery of oil in the Ninian field and the acquisition of Signal Oil (both in January 1974). Since 1965 the company's share price had appreciated by 40 per cent, much the same as the UK market index as a whole (and compared with inflation of about 67 per cent cumulative over the same period). One broker's report forecast a further six-fold growth in trading profits between 1972 and 1976, with the principal growth expected to come from the tanker business.

The *Financial Times* had described 1973 as 'one of the worst Stock Exchange years in memory', with the FT Industrial Ordinary Share Index down 32 per cent. But 1974 was much worse. The Arab oil embargo exacerbated both inflation and recession, and London stock prices experienced their sharpest decline since the great crash of 1929. By the beginning of October 1974, the price of BP shares was only half the December 1973 price. As a result, Burmah's debt ratio exceeded the limits agreed in the Chase loan which financed the Signal acquisition.

The company could either ask its shareholders to put up more equity capital, or it could offer Chase an inducement to relax the agreed borrowing limits. Since its own share price had fallen by well over 50 per cent in less than a year (see Fig. 10.6), Burmah was reluctant to issue equity in October 1974. In exchange for a higher rate of interest, therefore, Chase agreed to value the BP shares at higher than actual market prices for the purpose of satisfying the original loan covenant. At the same time, a new requirement was introduced – that interest charges should be covered at least one-and-a-half times by profits. Burmah felt safe enough in accepting this new requirement, since projections made in May 1974 had indicated that total profits from tankers in 1974 would be similar to 1973's £18 million.

Burmah Oil Tankers' success in 1973 had stemmed largely from its policy of hiring out a large proportion of its fleet on the spot market. 1973 spot tanker rates had risen sharply with the general level of world trade and buoyant American demand for Middle East crude. But the Arab oil embargo at the

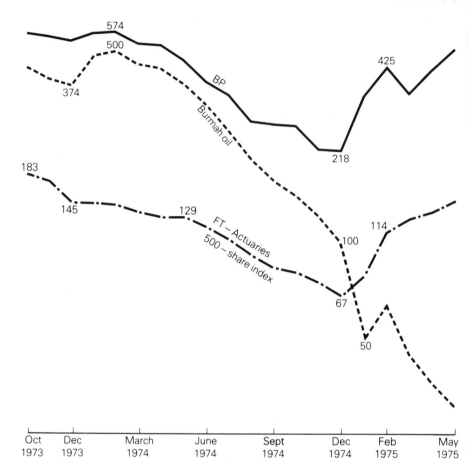

Fig. 10.6: Stock market prices, October 1973 to May 1975. FT-Actuaries 500 Share Index, BP, Burmah Oil.

end of the year dramatically reversed the situation. Within the last three months of 1973, spot tanker rates declined by 75 per cent.

With the company's Bahamas terminal due on stream shortly, Burmah decided not only to keep three of its newly chartered very large crude carriers (VLCCs) in the spot market in 1974, but also to sign long-term charters for three further VLCCs to place them in the spot market too. Unfortunately, not only was the Bahamas terminal behind schedule, but American demand for foreign crude was falling with the five-fold increase in crude oil prices. The only customer for the Bahamas terminal so far contracted accounted for less than 20 per cent of the terminal's capacity.

The first public hint of difficulties came in December 1974, when *Business Week* revealed the renegotiation of the Chase loan and asserted that Burmah had run into 'a serious cash squeeze'. The company was quick to deny the charge, saying that its cash position was 'certainly no worse than anyone else's. We are well aware of our future cash needs, and facilities are available to meet them'.

The statement was not enough to stem the series of rumours that now began to flood the London Stock Exchange. Finally, on a dark and cheerless Christmas Eve, with most of the City having departed to celebrate the season of goodwill, the Chairman of Burmah Oil called on the Bank of England to reveal that the company's tanker operations were now likely to show a

£m.	1973	1974
Ordinary £1 issued share capital	144	144
Reserves	461	149
= Ordinary shareholders' funds	605	293
Preference share capital	19	19
Minority interests	42	35
$ borrowing repayable within one year	—	260
Long-term borrowings	186	227
Deferred liabilities	53	36
	905	870
Fixed assets, net:		
Properties and operating assets	143	158
Exploration and development	161	377
	304	535
Investments:		
Trade and associated companies	71	78
BP and Shell shares (market value)[1]	469[1]	197
Net current assets:		
Current assets	272	406
Less: Current liabilities[2]	(211)[2]	(346)
	61	60
	905	870

[1] Including Shell shares, market value £26m. and £14m.
[2] Including short-term borrowings £84m. and £108m.

Fig. 10.7: Burmah Oil Balance Sheets, 1973 and 1974.

substantial loss for 1974. As a result, the group was forecasting only a small overall profit for the year, and now expected to be in default on its recently renegotiated Chase loan. Furthermore the continued decline in the market value of the company's BP shares had also caused a default on an earlier issue of long-term bonds. Figure 10.7 shows the dramatic change in Burmah balance sheets between the end of 1973 and the end of 1974. At the end of 1974 the board had approved future capital expenditure amounting to £454 million. On New Year's Eve, Burmah's managing director and chief executive, Mr N. J. D. Williams, resigned from the board.

Questions:

1 a. Calculate the debt ratio:
    i. immediately after the Chase $420 million loan early in 1974
    ii. at the end of December 1974.
  b. As above, including short-term borrowing as debt.
  c. As above, including tanker lease commitments as debt.
2 Calculate the interest cover for 1974; allowing for £29m. profits from Signal's operations, and:
  a. assuming tanker and other profits the same as in 1973
  b. assuming tanker losses of £32 million in 1974.
3 a. What proportion of Burmah's holding of BP shares would have had to be sold in January 1974 to finance the Signal Oil deal?
  b. What effect would that have had:
    i. on the profit for 1974?
    ii. on the debt ratio at the end of December 1974?
    iii. on the interest cover for 1974?
4 Assuming that £100 million of new money was needed, should Burmah Oil have made a rights issue of equity shares in October 1974? Why or why not? (Assume a price of 200p per share.)
5 a. Identify what went wrong for Burmah Oil in 1974.
  b. Specifically in what respects, if any, is Burmah's management really open to criticism in respect of what happened in 1974?

10.5 The Bank of England Rescue

One week after the company's first approach to the Bank of England, on New Year's Eve (the last day of Burmah's financial year 1974), Burmah Oil issued the following statement:

> 'Following discussions with H.M. Government and the Bank of England, the following arrangements have been agreed between the Company and the Bank of England to provide interim support to the Company pending realisation of certain major assets in continuation of a programme already in hand.
> 1. It is proposed that certain existing long-term Dollar borrowings

amounting to $650 million will be renegotiated as 12-month borrowings guaranteed by the Bank of England.

2. In addition, the Bank of England has offered certain assistance to enable the Company to deal with its Sterling borrowings.

3. Certain changes will be made in the management of the Company.

4. Messrs Peat, Marwick, Mitchell & Co. will be appointed to assist in the financial management of the Group.

5. A full review of the tanker operations will be undertaken in the light of the independent investigation already commissioned by the Company early in December.

As security for the assistance provided, the Company's unpledged holdings in the shares of the British Petroleum Company and the 'Shell' Transport and Trading Company Limited will be made over to the Bank of England with the right of realisation.

The Bank of England's prompt action in guaranteeing Burmah's dollar obligations was sufficient to solve the company's most pressing problem. But further discussions between Burmah, the Bank and government departments made it increasingly obvious that more was involved than just a technical default.

First, Burmah was under pressure from other lenders who were not covered by the Bank of England's guarantees. Some of these lenders pointed to fine print in their loan agreements which stated that the company would not discriminate against them by providing exclusive security to other lenders. If Burmah's BP and Shell holdings were to be used to provide security, these other lenders wanted to be included.

Second, it became apparent that the tanker operations had lost about £30 million in 1974, with no immediate prospect of any improvement. The company was likely to show an overall loss for the year, rather than the small profit which had been expected only a few weeks earlier.

Third, Burmah had urgent needs for new capital. The company would certainly be unable to issue more debt. With trading in its ordinary shares temporarily suspended, and with unofficial trades occurring at about one-tenth of the price a year earlier, a sale of equity was effectively impossible. Without additional funds, the company would be obliged to cease operations, and would immediately become liable for all future payments on its tanker charters. So the Bank of England's initial help was not enough to save Burmah.

Three weeks after the agreement with the Bank of England, Burmah announced a new support arrangement with the Bank ... and a new chairman. Whereas the company had previously only pledged its BP holdings as security, it now agreed to sell 78 million shares to the Bank at 10 per cent below the then prevailing stock market price of £2.56 each. The sale yielded £179 million cash. The Bank continued to guarantee Burmah's $650 million of American loans, and in addition agreed to provide a standby facility of £75 million to aid the company in its short-term borrowings. As security for this assistance, the Bank was given a mortgage on Burmah's American assets.

It also stipulated that the proceeds from the prospective sale of the Great Plains subsidiary should go towards repayment of the loans, and the company should try to sell its American assets in due course in order to repay the balance.

The link between Burmah Oil and British Petroleum, which had begun in 1908 with the first discovery of oil in the Middle East, effectively ended in January 1975. For the Bank of England, the purchase of 78 million BP shares from Burmah proved to be extremely profitable. Within a year the price of BP shares doubled.

The Shareholders' Action Group

But many Burmah shareholders were less satisfied about what had happened. A number of them formed an Action Group to protest that the purchase price had been unfair. At the 1975 Annual General Meeting of the company, the treasurer of the Action Group declared:

> 'In all their communications, the various government departments have maintained that the price was a fair one for the shareholders. There are over 160,000 of them, and I have neither met nor heard of a single one who agrees ...
>
> 'The method employed for the valuation of BP stock indicates to me, as one who is used to financial negotiations, that those members of the government who seek to support the method employed in the valuation do not know a stock transfer from a poached egg!
>
> 'The average market price over one abnormal month was utterly irrelevant as a measure of the true value of the BP shares.'

Conservative Members of Parliament, then in Opposition, expressed considerable concern about the plight of small investors in Burmah. (The average holding at 31 December 1975 of 141,757 individual shareholders was 464 £1 shares, totalling £66 million nominal. The remaining £78 million nominal share capital outstanding was held by about 12,000 banks, nominees and institutions.) The Burmah Shareholders Action Group became convinced that in the event of a Conservative victory at the next General Election, their claims would be dealt with sympathetically.

Meanwhile, the Action Group's relationship with the Burmah Board of Directors was sometimes a little strained. In the 1975 Annual Report, the new chairman of the company, Alastair Down (a former senior executive of British Petroleum), wrote in his statement to stockholders:

> 'I have thought it right to discuss with the officers of the action group such matters as they have wished to raise with me from time to time. We do not always see eye to eye but I realise that we have similar objectives, although we may sometimes differ as to the best method of achieving them.'

In May 1979, more than four years after the sale of the BP shares to the Bank of England, the Conservatives won a sweeping victory in the General Election, and Mrs Thatcher became Prime Minister. Her husband had been a senior executive (though not a director) of Burmah, following the 1966 acquisition of Castrol. He had been a director of Atlas Preservatives, one of Castrol's subsidiaries. In her Cabinet were several men who had gone on record with comments apparently favourable to the Burmah shareholders. But now that they were in government, some of them seemed to have changed their tune.

After two more years, in May 1981, nothing had happened, except that the Burmah court action against the Bank of England was due to commence in a few weeks. The action was expected to last up to two months. But the *Financial Times* noted that, unless there was an out-of-court settlement, the case might drag on for several years. Both sides were apparently prepared to fight the case, if necessary, through the Appeal Court and the House of Lords. In May 1981 Burmah Oil's 144 million £1 ordinary shares were quoted on the Stock Exchange at 150p each.

The company was claiming the return of 310 million BP shares (after a 4 for 1 split of the £1 stock units into 25p shares), currently worth about £1,200 million – less the original purchase price of £179 million – together with accrued interest. Burmah was claiming that the acquisition was 'unconscionable, inequitable, and unreasonable', and that the Bank took advantage of Burmah 'in breach of its duty of fair dealing'.

According to the London *New Standard* on the first day of the action (2 June 1981):

'Mr Leonard Hoffman, QC for Burmah, compared the multi-million oil giant Burmah Oil with an old illiterate persuaded to sign something he did not understand ... Mr Justice Walton interjected: "You are trying to push back the frontiers of the law in this case."'

Questions:

1 Do you think Burmah shareholders have a legitimate grievance? Against whom? Why or why not?

2 What alternatives were open to Burmah shareholders in January 1975 if they disagreed with the action of the company's directors?

3 Why might the Burmah Shareholders Action Group and the chairman of Burmah Oil 'not always see eye to eye'? Was the chairman correct to say that he and they 'have similar objectives'? If not, in what respects might their objectives differ?

4 Quantify what effect, if any, on Burmah Oil's stock price you would expect from a complete victory for the company in the High Court action against the Bank of England. (Ignore accumulated interest.)

5 'The average market price over one abnormal month was utterly irrelevant as a measure of the true value of the BP shares.' Discuss.

6 In its dealings in BP shares in January 1975, Burmah Oil was 'like an old illiterate persuaded to sign something he did not understand'. Comment.

10.6 The Sell-off

When Mr Alastair Down was appointed to the Board of Directors of Burmah Oil as Chairman and Managing Director, on 27 January 1975, his main tasks were to sell off assets in order to repay $650 million of loans guaranteed by the Bank of England, and to tackle the problems arising from the tanker operations.

The sale of the BP shares gave Burmah the badly needed cash to continue operations; and the guarantees and the additional standby agreement gave the company the time that it needed to sell assets so that it could repay some of the great load of debt. The principal remaining task was to deal with the potential cash drain from the tanker operation. How large this drain might have been is suggested by a confidential Chase Manhattan calculation that under pessimistic assumptions Burmah could lose as much as $760 million from its tanker operations by 1982.

Between the end of 1974 and the end of 1976, borrowings on the balance sheet fell from £487 million to £226 million. The major disposals are shown in Fig. 10.8.

1975			£ m.
January	Great Plains (Canada)	Can. $ 96 m.	41
January	77.8 m. BP £1 stock units	£179 m.[1]	179
July	Edwin Cooper	US $ 46 m.	21
November	6½ m. Woodside-Burmah shares	A $ 5 m.	3
November	4.65 m Shell shares	£ 17 m.	17
December	50% interests in Burmah-Shell (India)	£ 10 m.	10
			271
1976			
January	US Oil and Gas interests	$520 m.[2]	256
March	Interest in Ninian field	£ 90 m.[3]	90
August	Majority interest in other North Sea assets	£103 m.[3]	103
June	3 m. BP £1 stock units	£ 18 m.	18
August	75 m. Woodside-Burmah shares	A $ 68½ m.[4]	48
			515

[1] to the Bank of England
[2] to R. J. Reynolds Inc. (Aminoil)
[3] to British National Oil Corporation
[4] to Broken Hill Proprietary.

Fig. 10.8: Major disposals of Burmah Assets, 1975 and 1976.

The 1979 Annual Report revealed that, as from February 1980, Sir Alastair Down had relinquished his executive duties, though he remained on the board. An ex gratia payment of £100,000 was made to him 'in recognition of his outstanding contribution and achievement in restoring the group's fortunes'. Balance sheets and profit and loss accounts for each year from 1974 to 1980 are summarised in Figs. 10.9, 10.10 and 10.11.

At the end of 1980, the FT-Actuaries 500 Share Index stood at about 50 per cent, in real terms, of its level at the end of 1972. BP shares stood at about 90 per cent of their end-1972 level in real terms at the end of 1980; Burmah Oil shares at 12 per cent.

31 Dec. (£m.)	1974	1975	1976	1977	1978	1979	1980
Shareholders' funds	293	314	345	300	297	325	334
Preference capital	19	19	19	19	19	19	19
Minority interests	35	39	7	5	4	4	5
Short-term loans, BofE	260	274	59	–	–	–	–
Long-term loans, other	227	218	167	244	263	243	252
Deferred liabilities	36	32	32	42	48	40	50
	870	896	629	610	631	631	660
Fixed assets	535	622	180	237	290	297	323
Investment: BP & Shell	197	50	39	18	13	6	5
Other	71	66	57	53	47	44	39
Tanker projects, etc.	14	77	158	72	72	57	39
Long-term receivables	–	–	41	8	5	16	13
Net current assets	53	81	154	222	204	211	241
	870	896	629	610	631	631	660
Market value of Burmah shares (end of year)	147	32	35	40	58	240	268
Employees ('000)	41	36	33	32	32	28	28

Fig. 10.9: Burmah Oil, Balance Sheets, 1974 to 1980.

Year ending 31 Dec. (£m.)	1974	1975	1976	1977	1978	1979	1980
Sales turnover	872	915	846	857	985	1087	1231
Operating profits:							
North America (BOAG)	29	16					
Edwin Cooper	5	2					
India and Pakistan	5	3	4 ⎫	26	32	63	64
Other	18	19	22 ⎭				
	57	40	26				
Oil and Gas							
Automotive:							
Halfords	2	3	4	4	6	8	4
Quinton Hazell	4	3	5	8	10	11	6
Tabbert	–	–	2	2	1	(2)	(2)
	6	6	11	14	17	17	8
Industrial products	4	4	5	6	6	8	7
Engineering	–	2	2	2	1	1	2
	10	12	18	22	24	26	17
Unallocated central exs.	(6)	(10)	(10)	(4)	(4)	(11)	(1)
	61	42	34	44	52	78	80
Burmah Oil Tankers	(32)	(31)	(40)	(37)	(23)	4	4
Net operating profit	29	11	(6)	7	29	83	84
Investment income	26	19	23	18	16	17	19
	55	30	17	25	45	100	103
Interest payable	45	43	25	21	28	33	41
Profit (loss) before tax	10	(13)	(8)	4	17	67	62
Taxation	14	10	1	10	8	22	31
Profit (loss) after tax	(4)	(23)	(9)	(6)	9	45	31
MI, Pref. divs. etc	4	–	1	1	2	2	3
Profit for ordinary	(8)	(23)	(10)	(7)	7	43	28

Fig. 10.10: Burmah Oil, Profit and Loss Accounts, 1974 to 1980.

Year ending 31 Dec. (£m.)	1974	1975	1976	1977	1978	1979	1980
Profit for ordinary	(8)	(23)	(10)	(7)	7	43	28
Extraordinary items:							
Profit on sale assets	4	36	43	–	11	1	4
Tanker cancel fees	–	(38)	(32)	(24)	(15)	4	(3)
Miscellaneous	(3)	(6)	(9)	(2)	–	–	–
	(7)	(31)	(8)	(33)	3	48[1]	29[1]
Ordinary dividends	8	–	–	–	–	9	9
Retained earnings	(15)	(31)	(8)	(33)	3	39	20
Movements in reserves:							
MV investments change	–	32	8	1	(4)	–	–
Currency changes	(9)	20	31	(19)	(2)	(10)	(11)
Other	–	–	–	6	–	(1)	–
Net change to reserves	(24)	21	31	(45)	(3)	28	9

[1] subject to CCA adjustments of − £29m. and − £32m. in 1979 and 1980 respectively.

Fig. 10.11: Burmah Oil, Profit and Loss Appropriation Accounts, 1974 to 1980.

Questions:
1. How much appears to have been lost on Burmah's tanker operations in the five years 1974 to 1978 inclusive? How does this compare with the 'pessimistic' Chase Manhattan estimate of $760 million by 1982?

   What general lessons, if any, can one learn from this series of case studies about:
2. Loan covenants?
3. Stock market values?
4. Financial gearing?
5. Diversification?
6. Conflicts of interest between management and shareholders?

Abbreviations

ACT	Advance Corporation Tax	MMC	Monopolies and Mergers
AGM	Annual General Meeting		Commission
CCA	Current Cost Accounting	MPT	Modern Portfolio Theory
CD	Certificate of Deposit	NPV	Net Present Value
CML	Capital Market Line	P/E	Price/Earnings (ratio)
CPP	Constant Purchasing Power	PAT	Profit After Tax
DCF	Discounted Cash Flow	P&L	Profit & Loss (account)
DPR	Dividend Payout Ratio	plc	public limited company
EBIT	Earnings Before Interest	PSBR	Public Sector Borrowing
	and Tax		Requirement
EOY	End Of Year	ROI	Return on Investment
EPS	Earnings Per Share	RPI	Retail Price Index
FT	Financial Times	USM	Unlisted Securities Market
HC	Historical Cost	WACC	Weighted Average Cost of
HP	Hire Purchase		Capital
IRR	Internal Rate of Return	WIP	Work In Progress

Inflation: Retail Price Index (January 1974 = 100)

Year	Average for year ending December	RPI for December	Annual inflation: year to December %
1950	33	—	—
1960	50	—	—
1970	73	—	—
1971	80	82	9
1972	86	89	$7\frac{1}{2}$
1973	94	98	$10\frac{1}{2}$
1974	109	117	19
1975	135	146	25
1976	157	168	15
1977	182	188	12
1978	197	204	$8\frac{1}{2}$
1979	224	239	17
1980	264	276	15
1981	295	309	12
1982	320	326	$5\frac{1}{2}$
1983	335	343	5

Discounting Factors

The mechanics of discounting are not difficult; and two sets of Tables (A and B) set out on the following pages, contain discounting factors.

Table A shows the present value of £1 receivable at the end of n periods. Thus given an interest rate of 8 per cent a year, £1,000 receivable at the end of four years (EOY 4) has a present value of £735.

Compounding factors (the reciprocals of discounting factors) are not shown here. At an interest rate of 8 per cent a year, £1,000 will compound to £1,361 by the end of year four. We could calculate this by *dividing* £1,000 by 0.735 (the discounting factor we found above).

Normal practice (used in the tables) is to assume that amounts invested will compound once a year at the end of each year (rather than continuously).

Table B shows the present value of £1 *per period* receivable at the end of *each* of the next n periods. Thus given an interest rate of 8 per cent a year, an annuity of £1,000 for the next four years has a total present value of £3,312. (This is the *sum* of the present values of £1,000 receivable EOY 1 *plus* £1,000 receivable EOY 2 *plus* ... Thus: £926 + £857 + £794 + £735 = £3312.)

Where expected cash inflows are the *same* each year (**annuities**), instead of 'capitalising' them and comparing their present value with the initial investment (as in the net present value method), it can sometimes be more convenient to 'annualise' the initial investment, and then compare that **'annualised cost'** with the (equal) annual cash inflows.

Example: A project costing £3,000 is expected to produce equal annual cash inflows of £1,000 for each of the next four years. With an interest rate of 8 per cent a year, we know already that their present value is £3,312. Therefore the project is 'acceptable', with a net present value of + £312. Alternatively the 'annualised cost' is: £3,000/3,312 = £906.

Thus the project is seen to be acceptable, since the (annualised) cost of £906 is less than the annual cash inflow of £1,000.

Where we are not starting from EOY 0, the procedure may require more than a single stage.

Example: To find the present value (at an 8% a year rate of interest) of an annuity receivable at the end of each year from EOY 4 to EOY 7, two simple steps are needed, using Table B:

First:	find the factor for amounts receivable at the end of *each* of years 1 to 7	5.206
Then:	deduct the factor for amounts receivable at the end of *each* of years 1 to 4	3.312
To show:	the factor for amounts receivable at the end of *each* of years 5 to 7	= 1.894

Where the amounts are *different* each year, then separate discount factors, as given in Table A, must be used for each future year.

Table A Present value of £1

Years Hence	1%	2%	4%	6%	8%	10%	12%	14%	15%	16%	18%	20%	22%	24%	25%	26%	28%	30%	35%	40%	45%	50%
1	0.990	0.980	0.962	0.943	0.926	0.909	0.893	0.877	0.870	0.862	0.847	0.833	0.820	0.806	0.800	0.794	0.781	0.769	0.741	0.714	0.690	0.667
2	0.980	0.961	0.925	0.890	0.857	0.826	0.797	0.769	0.756	0.743	0.718	0.694	0.672	0.650	0.640	0.630	0.610	0.592	0.549	0.510	0.476	0.444
3	0.971	0.942	0.889	0.840	0.794	0.751	0.712	0.675	0.658	0.641	0.609	0.579	0.551	0.524	0.512	0.500	0.477	0.455	0.406	0.364	0.328	0.296
4	0.961	0.924	0.855	0.792	0.735	0.683	0.636	0.592	0.572	0.552	0.516	0.482	0.451	0.423	0.410	0.397	0.373	0.350	0.301	0.260	0.226	0.198
5	0.951	0.906	0.822	0.747	0.681	0.621	0.567	0.519	0.497	0.476	0.437	0.402	0.370	0.341	0.328	0.315	0.291	0.269	0.223	0.186	0.156	0.132
6	0.942	0.888	0.790	0.705	0.630	0.564	0.507	0.456	0.432	0.410	0.370	0.335	0.303	0.275	0.262	0.250	0.227	0.207	0.165	0.133	0.108	0.088
7	0.933	0.871	0.760	0.665	0.583	0.513	0.452	0.400	0.376	0.354	0.314	0.279	0.249	0.222	0.210	0.198	0.178	0.159	0.122	0.095	0.074	0.059
8	0.923	0.853	0.731	0.627	0.540	0.467	0.404	0.351	0.327	0.305	0.266	0.233	0.204	0.179	0.168	0.157	0.139	0.123	0.091	0.068	0.051	0.039
9	0.914	0.837	0.703	0.592	0.500	0.424	0.361	0.308	0.284	0.263	0.225	0.194	0.167	0.144	0.134	0.125	0.108	0.094	0.067	0.048	0.035	0.026
10	0.905	0.820	0.676	0.558	0.463	0.386	0.322	0.270	0.247	0.227	0.191	0.162	0.137	0.116	0.107	0.099	0.085	0.073	0.050	0.035	0.024	0.017
11	0.896	0.804	0.650	0.527	0.429	0.350	0.287	0.237	0.215	0.195	0.162	0.135	0.112	0.094	0.086	0.079	0.066	0.056	0.037	0.025	0.017	0.012
12	0.887	0.788	0.625	0.497	0.397	0.319	0.257	0.208	0.187	0.168	0.137	0.112	0.092	0.076	0.069	0.062	0.052	0.043	0.027	0.018	0.012	0.008
13	0.879	0.773	0.601	0.469	0.368	0.290	0.229	0.182	0.163	0.145	0.116	0.093	0.075	0.061	0.055	0.050	0.040	0.033	0.020	0.013	0.008	0.005
14	0.870	0.758	0.577	0.442	0.340	0.263	0.205	0.160	0.141	0.125	0.099	0.078	0.062	0.049	0.044	0.039	0.032	0.025	0.015	0.009	0.006	0.003
15	0.861	0.743	0.555	0.417	0.315	0.239	0.183	0.140	0.123	0.108	0.084	0.065	0.051	0.040	0.035	0.031	0.025	0.020	0.011	0.006	0.004	0.002
16	0.853	0.728	0.534	0.394	0.292	0.218	0.163	0.123	0.107	0.093	0.071	0.054	0.042	0.032	0.028	0.025	0.019	0.015	0.008	0.005	0.003	0.002
17	0.844	0.714	0.513	0.371	0.270	0.198	0.146	0.108	0.093	0.080	0.060	0.045	0.034	0.026	0.023	0.020	0.015	0.012	0.006	0.003	0.002	0.001
18	0.836	0.700	0.494	0.350	0.250	0.180	0.130	0.095	0.081	0.069	0.051	0.038	0.028	0.021	0.018	0.016	0.012	0.009	0.005	0.002	0.001	0.001
19	0.828	0.686	0.475	0.331	0.232	0.164	0.116	0.083	0.070	0.060	0.043	0.031	0.023	0.017	0.014	0.012	0.009	0.007	0.003	0.002	0.001	
20	0.820	0.673	0.456	0.312	0.215	0.149	0.104	0.073	0.061	0.051	0.037	0.026	0.019	0.014	0.012	0.010	0.007	0.005	0.002	0.001	0.001	
21	0.811	0.660	0.439	0.294	0.199	0.135	0.093	0.064	0.053	0.044	0.031	0.022	0.015	0.011	0.009	0.008	0.006	0.004	0.002	0.001		
22	0.803	0.647	0.422	0.278	0.184	0.123	0.083	0.056	0.046	0.038	0.026	0.018	0.013	0.009	0.007	0.006	0.004	0.003	0.001	0.001		
23	0.795	0.634	0.406	0.262	0.170	0.112	0.074	0.049	0.040	0.033	0.022	0.015	0.010	0.007	0.006	0.005	0.003	0.002	0.001			
24	0.788	0.622	0.390	0.247	0.158	0.102	0.066	0.043	0.035	0.028	0.019	0.013	0.008	0.006	0.005	0.004	0.003	0.002	0.001			
25	0.780	0.610	0.375	0.233	0.146	0.092	0.059	0.038	0.030	0.024	0.016	0.010	0.007	0.005	0.004	0.003	0.002	0.001	0.001			
26	0.772	0.598	0.361	0.220	0.135	0.084	0.053	0.033	0.026	0.021	0.014	0.009	0.006	0.004	0.003	0.002	0.002	0.001				
27	0.764	0.586	0.347	0.207	0.125	0.076	0.047	0.029	0.023	0.018	0.011	0.007	0.005	0.003	0.002	0.002	0.001	0.001				
28	0.757	0.574	0.333	0.196	0.116	0.069	0.042	0.026	0.020	0.016	0.010	0.006	0.004	0.002	0.002	0.002	0.001	0.001				
29	0.749	0.563	0.321	0.185	0.107	0.063	0.037	0.022	0.017	0.014	0.008	0.005	0.003	0.002	0.002	0.001	0.001	0.001				
30	0.742	0.552	0.308	0.174	0.099	0.057	0.033	0.020	0.015	0.012	0.007	0.004	0.003	0.002	0.001	0.001	0.001	0.001				
40	0.672	0.453	0.208	0.097	0.046	0.022	0.011	0.005	0.004	0.003	0.001	0.001										
50	0.608	0.372	0.141	0.054	0.021	0.009	0.003	0.001	0.001	0.001												

Table B   Present value of £1 received annually for N years

Years (N)	1%	2%	4%	6%	8%	10%	12%	14%	15%	16%	18%	20%	22%	24%	25%	26%	28%	30%	35%	40%	45%	50%
1	0.990	0.980	0.962	0.943	0.926	0.909	0.893	0.877	0.870	0.862	0.847	0.833	0.820	0.806	0.800	0.794	0.781	0.769	0.741	0.714	0.690	0.667
2	1.970	1.942	1.886	1.833	1.783	1.736	1.690	1.647	1.626	1.605	1.566	1.528	1.492	1.457	1.440	1.424	1.392	1.361	1.289	1.224	1.165	1.111
3	2.941	2.884	2.775	2.673	2.577	2.487	2.402	2.322	2.283	2.246	2.174	2.106	2.042	1.981	1.952	1.923	1.868	1.816	1.696	1.589	1.493	1.407
4	3.902	3.808	3.630	3.465	3.312	3.170	3.037	2.914	2.855	2.798	2.690	2.589	2.494	2.404	2.362	2.320	2.241	2.166	1.997	1.849	1.720	1.605
5	4.853	4.713	4.452	4.212	3.993	3.791	3.605	3.433	3.352	3.274	3.127	2.991	2.864	2.745	2.689	2.635	2.532	2.436	2.220	2.035	1.876	1.737
6	5.795	5.601	5.242	4.917	4.623	4.355	4.111	3.889	3.784	3.685	3.498	3.326	3.167	3.020	2.951	2.885	2.759	2.643	2.385	2.168	1.983	1.824
7	6.728	6.472	6.002	5.582	5.206	4.868	4.564	4.288	4.160	4.039	3.812	3.605	3.416	3.242	3.161	3.083	2.937	2.802	2.508	2.263	2.057	1.883
8	7.652	7.325	6.733	6.210	5.747	5.335	4.968	4.639	4.487	4.344	4.078	3.837	3.619	3.421	3.329	3.241	3.076	2.925	2.598	2.331	2.108	1.922
9	8.566	8.162	7.435	6.802	6.247	5.759	5.328	4.946	4.772	4.607	4.303	4.031	3.786	3.566	3.463	3.366	3.184	3.019	2.665	2.379	2.144	1.948
10	9.471	8.983	8.111	7.360	6.710	6.145	5.650	5.216	5.019	4.833	4.494	4.192	3.923	3.682	3.571	3.465	3.269	3.092	2.715	2.414	2.168	1.965
11	10.368	9.787	8.760	7.887	7.139	6.495	5.937	5.453	5.234	5.029	4.656	4.327	4.035	3.776	3.656	3.544	3.335	3.147	2.752	2.438	2.185	1.977
12	11.255	10.575	9.385	8.384	7.536	6.814	6.194	5.660	5.421	5.197	4.793	4.439	4.127	3.851	3.725	3.606	3.387	3.190	2.779	2.456	2.196	1.985
13	12.134	11.343	9.986	8.853	7.904	7.103	6.424	5.842	5.583	5.342	4.910	4.533	4.203	3.912	3.780	3.656	3.427	3.223	2.799	2.468	2.204	1.990
14	13.004	12.106	10.563	9.295	8.244	7.367	6.628	6.002	5.724	5.468	5.008	4.611	4.265	3.962	3.824	3.695	3.459	3.249	2.814	2.477	2.210	1.993
15	13.865	12.849	11.118	9.712	8.559	7.606	6.811	6.142	5.847	5.575	5.092	4.675	4.315	4.001	3.859	3.726	3.483	3.268	2.825	2.484	2.214	1.995
16	14.718	13.578	11.652	10.106	8.851	7.824	6.974	6.265	5.954	5.669	5.162	4.730	4.357	4.033	3.887	3.751	3.503	3.283	2.834	2.489	2.216	1.997
17	15.562	14.292	12.166	10.477	9.122	8.022	7.120	6.373	6.047	5.749	5.222	4.775	4.391	4.059	3.910	3.771	3.518	3.295	2.840	2.492	2.218	1.998
18	16.398	14.992	12.659	10.828	9.372	8.201	7.250	6.467	6.128	5.818	5.273	4.812	4.419	4.080	3.928	3.786	3.529	3.304	2.844	2.494	2.219	1.999
19	17.226	15.678	13.134	11.158	9.604	8.365	7.366	6.550	6.198	5.877	5.316	4.844	4.442	4.097	3.942	3.799	3.539	3.311	2.848	2.496	2.220	1.999
20	18.046	16.351	13.590	11.470	9.818	8.514	7.469	6.623	6.259	5.929	5.353	4.870	4.460	4.110	3.954	3.808	3.546	3.316	2.850	2.497	2.221	1.999
21	18.857	17.011	14.029	11.764	10.017	8.649	7.562	6.687	6.312	5.973	5.384	4.891	4.476	4.121	3.963	3.816	3.551	3.320	2.852	2.498	2.221	2.000
22	19.660	17.658	14.451	12.042	10.201	8.772	7.645	6.743	6.359	6.011	5.410	4.909	4.488	4.130	3.970	3.822	3.556	3.323	2.853	2.498	2.222	2.000
23	20.456	18.292	14.857	12.303	10.371	8.883	7.718	6.792	6.399	6.044	5.432	4.925	4.499	4.137	3.976	3.827	3.559	3.325	2.854	2.499	2.222	2.000
24	21.243	18.914	15.247	12.550	10.529	8.985	7.784	6.835	6.434	6.073	5.451	4.937	4.507	4.143	3.981	3.831	3.562	3.327	2.855	2.499	2.222	2.000
25	22.023	19.523	15.622	12.783	10.675	9.077	7.843	6.873	6.464	6.097	5.467	4.948	4.514	4.147	3.985	3.834	3.564	3.329	2.856	2.499	2.222	2.000
26	22.795	20.121	15.983	13.003	10.810	9.161	7.896	6.906	6.491	6.118	5.480	4.956	4.520	4.151	3.988	3.837	3.566	3.330	2.856	2.500	2.222	2.000
27	23.560	20.707	16.330	13.211	10.935	9.237	7.943	6.935	6.514	6.136	5.492	4.964	4.524	4.154	3.990	3.839	3.567	3.331	2.856	2.500	2.222	2.000
28	24.316	21.281	16.663	13.406	11.051	9.307	7.984	6.961	6.534	6.152	5.502	4.970	4.528	4.157	3.992	3.840	3.568	3.331	2.857	2.500	2.222	2.000
29	25.066	21.844	16.984	13.591	11.158	9.370	8.022	6.983	6.551	6.166	5.510	4.975	4.531	4.159	3.994	3.841	3.569	3.332	2.857	2.500	2.222	2.000
30	25.808	22.396	17.292	13.765	11.258	9.427	8.055	7.003	6.566	6.177	5.517	4.979	4.534	4.160	3.995	3.842	3.569	3.332	2.857	2.500	2.222	2.000
40	32.835	27.355	19.793	15.046	11.925	9.779	8.244	7.105	6.642	6.234	5.548	4.997	4.544	4.166	3.999	3.846	3.571	3.333	2.857	2.500	2.222	2.000
50	39.196	31.424	21.482	15.762	12.234	9.915	8.304	7.133	6.661	6.246	5.554	4.999	4.545	4.167	4.000	3.846	3.571	3.333	2.857	2.500	2.222	2.000

Glossary

Many of the definitions in this glossary inevitably refer to other words or phrases which may not always be understood. If you come across such a word or phrase, the first thing to do is look for it in its alphabetical position in the glossary; failing that, in the index.

Accepting House: A financial institution, usually a merchant bank, which for a fee will guarantee the payment of a bill of exchange.

Acid Test Ratio: Yardstick of a firm's ability to pay its debts due in the near future. Ratio of liquid assets (cash + debtors) divided by current liabilities. Usually close to 1.0.

Advance Corporation Tax (ACT): Part of corporation tax liability, payable (at basic rate of income tax on *gross* dividends) at same time as net dividends, set off later against 'mainstream' tax.

Annualised Cost: Annuity which, over a known number of years and at a known discount rate, is equivalent to the present value of a particular cash amount.

Annuity: Regular annual amount for a given number of years (in personal affairs, until death). For present values, see Appendix.

Arbitrage: Buying in one market and selling in another to gain from price differences (which this process will reduce but, due to transaction costs, not eliminate).

Asset: Valuable resource owned by a business, acquired at a measurable money cost. Examples: factory, equipment, stocks of materials.

Asset Turnover: Annual sales revenue divided by net assets.

Bad Debt: Debt reckoned to be uncollectable.

Balance Sheet: Statement showing assets and liabilities of a business at a given date.

Bank of England: UK central bank whose main responsibility is integrity of the currency. Also represents official 'authorities' in controlling City institutions and markets.

Bank Overdraft: Facility for borrowing from bank on current account up to agreed limit. Amount borrowed, and interest rate, may fluctuate.

Bankruptcy: Legal process occurring when individual cannot pay liabilities. For companies, called 'liquidation' (or 'winding-up').

Barter: Process of exchanging goods against other goods rather than money.

Bear: Speculator who expects prices to fall, who may sell assets he does not own, hoping to buy back later at a profit.

Beta: Coefficient relating the sensitivity of an investment's return to that of the whole market (according to MPT).

Bill of Exchange: Post-dated cheque which the recipient can 'discount', to receive cash now in return for an interest payment.

Bonus Issue: = 'scrip issue'. Issue of additional shares pro rata to existing shareholders in return for no cash or other assets.

Book Value: Balance sheet amount shown for asset, normally original (HC) cost less any amounts written off.

Break-up Value: Estimated amount realisable for asset on 'break-up' or scrapping, net of disposal costs.

Building Society: Financial institution which receives personal savings and provides loan mortgage funds for people wanting to buy houses, at a variable interest rate.

Bull: Speculator who expects prices to rise, who may buy assets (or options to acquire them) hoping to sell them later at a profit.

Business Risk: The volatility of a business's operating profits (or cash flows), due to the particular assets in which funds are invested, regardless of how those assets are financed.

Capital Allowance: Tax equivalent of depreciation of fixed assets, calculated according to Inland Revenue rules.

Capital Budgeting: Planning use of investment funds, usually including methods of evaluating capital investment projects.

Capital Employed: = Net Assets. Shareholders' funds + long-term debt.

Capital Gain: Part of 'return' on investment in securities, stemming from increase in market value, not from dividends or interest.

Capital Market Line (CML): Straight line, originating at 'risk-free' rate of return, showing relationship of return to market risk.

Capital Rationing: Artificial, often temporary, limitation of amount of funds available for investment, often self-imposed.

Capitalising Factor: Coefficient to translate expected future income into a present 'capital' value, e.g. price/earnings ratio.

Cash: Legal tender banknotes and coins. In accounting usually includes amounts 'owed' to firms by banks on current or deposit account.

Cash Discount: Reduction in price of goods sold, offered in return for prompt settlement by debtor.

Cash Flow: Usually defined as 'retained profits plus depreciation' for a period = 'Internally-generated cash flow'.

Central Bank: Banker to government and to commercial banks, often with a monopoly over issue of banknotes. In UK, the Bank of England.

Certificate of Deposit (CD): Interest-bearing acknowledgement of deposit with a financial institution, usually repayable within months.

Clearing Bank: Major bank (e.g. Barclays, Lloyds, Midland, National Westminster) which exchanges cheques received from other clearing banks at a clearing house daily, settling only the net balance.

Collateral: Asset serving as security for loan.

Conglomerate: Diversified group of companies whose subsidiaries operate in unrelated areas.

Consolidated Accounts: Accounts for a group of companies, 'consolidated' by combining the separate assets and liabilities of all subsidiaries with those of the 'holding' company.

Constant Purchasing Power (CPP) Accounting: Method of inflation accounting which treats money amounts of various dates as 'foreign currencies', using the RPI as the 'exchange rate'.

Convertible Loan: Loan convertible, at holder's option, into ordinary shares on prearranged terms.

Corporation Tax: Tax payable by companies on taxable profits, either at 52 per cent or at reduced 40 per cent rate for smaller companies.

Cost of Capital: The criterion rate of return for capital investment projects, calculated as (risk-adjusted) weighted average of the marginal (after-tax) costs of ordinary, preference and debt capital.

Coupon Rate: Nominal rate of interest payable on fixed-interest securities.

Covenants: Conditions attached to loan agreement restricting borrower's freedom of action (e.g. re dividends, working capital, etc.).

Creditor: Person or company to whom money is due.

Criterion Rate: Required rate of return on capital investment project.

Cumulative: (of preference dividends). Any unpaid preference dividends must be made good before any ordinary dividend may be paid.

Currency Debasement: Process of reducing purchasing power of currency, originally by fraudulently adding base metal to precious metal, now by more sophisticated methods.

Current Asset: Cash or any asset expected to be converted into cash or consumed in normal course of business within 12 months from the balance sheet date. Examples: stocks, debtors.

Current Cost Accounting (CCA): System of current value (not 'inflation') accounting, which a government committee proposed instead of CPP.

Current Liability: Liability due to be paid within 12 months from balance sheet date. Examples: trade creditors, bank overdraft.

Current Ratio: Current assets divided by current liabilities. Measure of liquidity, usually expected to be between 1.5 and 2.0.

Debentures: Long-term liability (from the Latin: 'they are owed').

Debt (as opposed to Equity): Long-term liabilities.

Debt Ratio: Balance sheet measure of gearing. Long-term liabilities divided by total long-term capital employed (= debt plus equity).

Debtor: Person or firm which owes money to a business, usually in respect of goods or services supplied.

Deduction at Source: Process by which payer of wages or dividends deducts income tax (PAYE – Pay As You Earn – and ACT respectively) from amount paid to recipient and transmits it to Inland Revenue on his behalf.

Demand Deposit: Current Account deposit with bank which bears no interest and is withdrawable 'on demand' (i.e. with no notice).

Depreciation: Amount written off cost of fixed asset in accounting period and charged as expense; spreads the total cost over the asset's whole life (usually in equal instalments).

Dilution: Process by which a shareholder's equity interest is reduced by a company issuing additional shares to other shareholders.

Discount Factor: Coefficient reducing future cash amounts to 'present value'.

Discount House: Financial institution which buys bills of exchange at a 'discount' (below face value) and collects in full on maturity.

Discount Rate: Interest rate used in making present value calculations.

Discounted Cash Flow (DCF): Technique (e.g. NPV, IRR) for evaluating capital projects, using interest rate as 'exchange rate over time'.

DCF Yield: DCF technique, also known as internal rate of return.

Disinvestment: Reducing investment by selling or abandoning asset(s).

Diversification: Adding or substituting investments with low or negative co-variance with existing holdings, to reduce total risk of portfolio.

Dividend: Cash paid to shareholder out of profits, if declared by a company's directors.

Dividend Controls: Statutory restrictions on amount of dividends payable by companies, in force in UK for 10 years between 1966 and 1979.

Dividend Cover: Earnings (either HC or CCA) divided by net dividends.

Dividend Payout Ratio (DPR): Reciprocal of dividend cover. Dividends payable as a percentage of profits available for a period.

Dividend Yield: Dividends per share for a year divided by market price. Usually *gross*; but *net* in equity share valuation formula.

Earnings Before Interest and Tax (EBIT): Operating profit for a year, used to calculate interest cover and return on net assets, ignoring complications of tax and gearing.

Earnings Per Share (EPS): Profit after tax divided by number of ordinary shares in issue.

Earnings Yield: EPS divided by market price per share.

EBIT Chart: Graph plotting EPS (on vertical axis) against EBIT level (on horizontal axis); used in making debt versus equity choice.

Equity: Residual financial interest in a firm's assets. Usually means 'owners' equity', referring only to interests of ordinary shareholders (i.e. excluding preference shareholders).

Expected Value: Weighted average of subjective probabilities applied to all possible outcomes anticipated.

External Finance: Funds raised from 'outside' the company; such as issuing new equity shares for cash, borrowing.

Factor: Company which buys trade debts at a discount for cash.

Final Dividend: Second dividend for a year, after interim dividend.

Finance House: Company providing funds to finance HP and leasing.

Financial Lease: Lease giving lessee use of asset over most of its life, providing another way to finance its 'acquisition', in effect.

Financial Objective: (of a company). 'To maximise the wealth of the present ordinary shareholders.'

Financial Risk: Extra volatility of stream of equity earnings due to financial gearing, added to business risk (operational gearing).

Finished Goods: Stocks of completed manufactured products, held for sale.

First-year Tax Allowance: 100 per cent deduction from taxable profits allowed for tax purposes in respect of most purchases of capital assets.

Fixed Asset: Resource, either tangible or intangible, with relatively long life, acquired for use in producing goods or services, not for re-sale in the ordinary course of business.

Fixed Expenses: Expenses which (in the short-term) do not vary with output. Examples: factory rent, administrative salaries.

Flat Yield: Interest yield ignoring capital gain (or loss) on maturity, calculated by dividing annual interest by current market price.

Floating Charge: Charge to creditor which is secured, not against specific assets, but which 'floats' over all (otherwise unsecured) assets, 'crystallising' on occurrence of certain specified events.

Forecasting: Guessing the uncertain future, often in quantified form.

Funds Flow Statement: Accounting statement showing sources and uses (or 'applications') of funds for a period.

Gearing: Proportion of debt in capital structure represents *financial* gearing; proportion of fixed expenses in total operating expenses represents operating (or 'business') gearing.

Gilt-edged Securities: UK government loan stocks.

Going Public: Issuing shares to the public for the first time.

Goodwill: Excess of purchase price paid on acquisition of another firm over net book value of tangible net assets.

Gross Dividend: Amount of dividend before deduction of basic rate income tax. = Net dividends divided by (100 − basic rate income tax) per cent.

Gross Fund: Institutional fund not subject to tax on dividends or capital gains. Example: pension fund.

Group Accounts: Consolidated accounts of all companies belonging to a group of companies with a common holding company.

Guarantee: Personal (or corporate) undertaking to be responsible for the debts of another (person or company) if nominal debtor is unable to pay in full. A personal guarantee by a majority shareholder in a limited company 'undoes' the limited nature of his liability.

Hire Purchase (HP): System of paying for an asset by instalments.

Holding Company: Company owning more than 50 per cent of equity shares in subsidiaries (directly or indirectly), or controlling composition of its board of directors = 'parent' company.

Horizon: Point of time in future beyond which financial calculations are not made explicitly (though including a 'terminal value' in capital project evaluation makes them *implicitly*).

Horizontal Merger: Combination of firms making the same product.

Income Tax: Tax payable on personal incomes (such as dividends or trading profits of sole traders or partnerships). Basic rate is 30 per cent, and graduated rates rise to a maximum 75 per cent on 'unearned' income.

Incremental Cash Flows: Cash flows which will occur as a result of action (e.g. investing in capital project), but not otherwise.

Index-linking: Process of linking payment to the rate of inflation as measured by RPI. Examples: government securities, pensions, tax thresholds, capital gains (from April 1982).

Inflation: Rise in the 'general' level of money prices, measured by the (annual) increase in the Retail Price Index.

Inflation Accounting: Method of adjusting accounts using *money* as the unit of measurement on to a 'constant purchasing power' basis, by index-linking all amounts by reference to the date incurred.

Inflation Premium: Part of the rate of interest, depending on the anticipated future rate of inflation.

Insolvency: Inability to meet financial obligations.

Institutions: Major organisations in the capital and money markets, such as insurance companies and pension funds.

Interest Cover: EBIT divided by annual interest payable.

Interest Rate: Annual rate of compensation for borrowing or lending (money) for a period of time, comprising: (a) pure time-preference, (b) risk premium and (c) inflation premium.

Interim Dividend: First (usually smaller) of two dividends paid in a year by company.

Intermediaries: Financial organisations which separate borrowing from lending and may alter the time-maturity of loans. They profit from economies of scale and specialisation, and reduce risk by diversification.

Internal Finance: Raising funds from 'within' a company, usually referring to retained profits plus depreciation (or perhaps selling off assets owned).

Internal Rate of Return (IRR): Rate of discount which, applied to a capital project, produces a zero NPV.

Introduction: Method of 'going public' without issuing any extra shares, by arranging for a Stock Exchange quotation for existing shares.

Investment (Real): Fixed capital formation; investment in fixed assets.

Investment (Financial): Acquisition of a security, often from existing holder on the secondary market. Hence 'financial' investment does *not* necessarily imply any 'real' investment.

Investment Trust: Company which holds a portfolio of (quoted) investments.

Irredeemable: Loan stock with no maturity date, whose annual interest is a 'perpetuity'.

Issuing House: Financial institution, usually a merchant bank, which arranges new issues of securities (and advises on terms).

Jobber: A person or firm on the Stock Exchange buying and selling shares (owned as principal) by quoting prices to stockbrokers (who act as agents for investors).

Jobber's Turn: Difference between buying price and selling price quoted.

Lease: Commitment (by the 'lessee') to pay rent to the owner ('lessor') in return for the use of an asset.

Lender of Last Resort: The Bank of England lending money to discount houses which otherwise have no cash to pay loans due.

Liability: Amount due to a creditor.

Life Insurance Companies: Financial institutions which insure ('assure') lives and pay annuities, in return for premiums.

Limited Company: Now called 'public limited company' (= plc). A form of business organisation with a separate legal identity, whose owners (shareholders) are not personally liable for the entity's debts.

Liquid Asset: Cash or an asset easily converted into cash (e.g. debtors).

Liquid Resources: Cash or marketable securities. Would *not* normally include debtors.

Liquidation: = 'Winding-up'. The legal process of ending a company's life, by selling all its assets for cash, paying off the liabilities and distributing any residual amount to the shareholders.

Liquidation Value: The amount an asset realises (or would realise) on liquidation, often much less than book value.

Loan Stock: Long-term loan to a company or government body, often negotiable on the Stock Exchange in the secondary market.

Long-term Liability: Liability with a maturity date more than 12 months beyond the balance sheet date.

Loss: Negative profit. Though not the aim, often the result of business.

Mainstream Corporation Tax: Main company liability to corporation tax, payable some months after the end of accounting year; reduced to the extent of ACT paid at the same time as dividends.

Market: May mean the 'capital market' for loans and equity (financial securities). More generally refers to the system of voluntary exchange of goods based on competition and private ownership of property.

Market Risk: The non-diversifiable part of the total risk attaching to an equity investment, measured by 'beta'.

Matching the Maturity: Process of 'matching' the time-period of assets and liabilities, to reduce risk.

Maturity: Time at which a loan falls due for repayment.

Medium of Exchange: The primary function of money, to act as a means by which goods and services can be exchanged indirectly (as opposed to *direct* exchange by barter).

Merchant Bank: Accepting house. Financial institution offering banking and many advisory services to corporate and other customers.

Merger: A combination of two or more formerly independent business units into a single enterprise.

Minority Interest: Part of a group's assets *controlled* by holding company, but *owned* by 'outside' ('minority') shareholders via some of the equity shares in (one or more) subsidiary companies.

Modern Portfolio Theory (MPT): Distinguishes non-diversifiable 'market risk' and 'unique risk' which can be eliminated by holding a properly diversified portfolio. An efficient market will not compensate investors for taking (avoidable) unique risks, so the required rate of return will vary *solely* with market risk (measured by beta).

Negative Interest Rate: 'Real' interest rate, after-tax and net of inflation, which may be negative because while the inflation premium is tax-deductible the 'real' gain from inflation is not taxable.

Net Assets: = Capital employed. Fixed assets + Working capital. (= Total assets − Current liabilities.)

Net Dividend: Amount of cash dividend paid to shareholders, net of basic rate income tax (at 30 per cent of gross dividend) deducted as ACT.

Net Present Value (NPV): Discounted estimated future cash inflows minus (discounted) cash outflow(s). If positive, indicates prima facie acceptability of capital investment project.

Net Realisable Value: Net amount for which asset could be sold.

Net Terminal Value: As for NPV, but with the cash flows *compounded* to future horizon date instead of discounted back to present (value).

New Issue: First-time sale to the public of a company's securities.

Nominal Value: = 'Par value'. Face value of security, unrelated to the market value. Usually refers either to ordinary shares (e.g. with nominal value of 25p each) or to government loan stocks with nominal value of £100.

Non-diversifiable Risk: Market risk.

Offer for Sale: Method of issuing shares on Stock Exchange.

Operating Lease: Lease other than financial lease, usually for short period of time, and cancellable.

Opportunity Cost: The revenue or other benefit that might have been obtained by the 'next best' alternative course of action which has been forgone in favour of the course actually taken.

Ordinary Dividend: Dividend on ordinary shares.

Ordinary Share: Share in a company representing part-ownership, and entitled to dividends if declared by directors, and to share in any residual assets remaining when company is finally wound up.

Partnership: Form of enterprise with two or more owners ('partners'), each of whom has unlimited personal liability to meet the firm's debts.

Payback: Method of evaluating capital projects which calculates how long before initial investment is 'paid back' by later cash inflows. Ignores cash inflows *after* payback, so does *not* measure 'profitability'.

Pension Fund: Financial institution ('gross fund') investing amounts set aside during working life to provide retirement pensions.

'Perfect' Capital Market: Theoretical model of a capital market with 'perfect competition', implying: no transaction costs, no taxes, no economies of scale, no institutional barriers, perfect information.

Perpetuity: Annuity payable for ever.

Placing: Method of issuing new shares on the Stock Exchange.

Portfolio: Group of different securities held by a single owner, which diversifies away some of the 'unique' risk of individual securities.

Post-project Audit: Process of monitoring capital project's outcome.

Preference Share: Form of share capital entitled to fixed rate of dividend (usually cumulative) if declared, and to repayment of a stated amount of money on winding-up, with priority over ordinary shares.

Present Value: Discounted amount of future cash receipts, equivalent to the 'value' of an asset (or security).

Price/Earnings (P/E) **Ratio**: Market price per ordinary share divided by most recent annual earnings per share.

Primary Market: Market for securities which raises new money from public.

Profit: Sales revenue less expenses, for a period.

Profit and Loss (P&L) **Account**: Accounting statement showing result (profit or loss) of operations of a business entity for a period.

Profit Margin: Operating profit as a percentage of sales revenue.

Project Finance: Method of finance whose repayments (and perhaps interest) are tied to a project's operating results.

Prospectus: Advertisement to members of public in respect of an issue of securities, subject to the rules of the Stock Exchange.

Public Sector Borrowing Requirement (PSBR): Annual amount borrowed by government to cover excess of 'public sector' spending over tax and other revenues.

Purchasing Power: Value of money. What money will buy in 'real' terms, often measured by the 'basket of goods and services' comprising the constituent items in the Retail Price Index.

Quantity Theory of Money: Theory which (oversimplified) holds that the value of money (and the rate of inflation) will in the long run be related to the amount of money issued (the 'money supply').

Quoted Security: Security traded on the Stock Exchange, with price 'quoted' daily.

Raw Materials: Input to manufacturing process, often held for a time as stock.

Receiver: Official managing company's affairs on behalf of debenture-holders or others, often as a preliminary to winding-up.

Redemption: Repayment of loan or preference capital.

Re-investment Rate: Assumption (explicit or implicit) about the rate of return able to be earned on cash inflows 're-invested' in a business during a capital project's life.

Required Rate of Return: The rate of return needed for a capital project to be profitable. Used as discount rate for NPV, as criterion for IRR.

Reserves: Shareholders' funds other than issued share capital, e.g. share premium, retained profits. May not be represented by cash, so 'reserves' are *not* available for 'spending'.

Retail Price Index (RPI): Monthly statistic measuring (against base date January 1974 = 100.0) money prices of representative 'basket of goods'. The year-on-year rate of increase in the RPI is commonly regarded as 'the' annual rate of (general) inflation. See Appendix for details of RPI since 1970 (page 230).

Retained Profits: Amount of profits made by a company (either for the latest year or cumulatively), and not paid out in dividends.

Return on Equity: Profit after tax divided by shareholders' funds.

Return on Investment (ROI): Usually means return on net assets.

Return on Net Assets: Operating profit before interest and tax (= EBIT) divided by net assets (= by capital employed). = 'Primary Efficiency Ratio'.

Rights Issue: Issue usually of ordinary shares, to existing shareholders, to raise cash.

Risk: Volatility about a mean (average) 'expected value'. More loosely, possibility of loss (either likelihood or extent). Sometimes treated as synonymous with 'uncertainty'.

Risk Premium: Part of interest rate relating to perceived risk of investment.

Risk-free Rate of Return: Rate of return available in market on securities regarded as having *no* risk (usually only if government-guaranteed). An inflation premium is added separately.

Risk-free Securities: Government securities regarded as virtually certain to pay interest and capital amount on due dates.

Sale and Leaseback: Method of raising finance by selling capital asset for lump sum, while continuing to use it in return for lease payments. In effect, a capital disinvestment.

Secondary Market: Market for securities in which existing holders can buy and sell securities without directly involving the original issuer.

Security (collateral): Legal charge on asset(s) by lender. In the event of default, secured creditor is entitled to priority of repayment out of proceeds of disposal of the charged asset(s).

Security (share): Any stocks or shares, usually 'quoted'.

Selling Short: Selling assets not owned, in the hope of buying back later, after the market price has fallen.

Share: Partial ownership of ordinary capital of company.

Share Premium: Excess of issue price over nominal price of share.

Share Split: Process of dividing share capital into more shares of smaller nominal amount each. Reduces market price per share pro rata without affecting the total market value.

Shareholders' Funds: Amount shown in company balance sheet as attributable to ordinary (and sometimes preference) shareholders.

Specific Risk: Unique risk of security, which can be diversified away by holding a suitable portfolio.

Speculator: Anyone who acts on view about the uncertain future.

Stag: Bull of new issues, hoping for an immediate rise in market price when dealings start, giving a quick profit on any shares allotted.

Stock (inventory): Holding of goods, either as raw materials, work in progress, or finished goods, with a view to sale (perhaps after further processing) in the ordinary course of business.

Stock (share): Similar to ordinary share in company, but may be divisible into smaller money amounts for dealing purposes.

Stock Appreciation: Part of apparent HC accounting profit on stocks (inventories) due solely to an increase in their price.

Stock Exchange: Market for buying and selling securities.

Stock Relief: Tax allowance intended to prevent tax being charged on stock appreciation.

Stock Turnover: Accounting ratio dividing sales turnover for a year by amount of stock held. Reciprocal of 'days' sales in stock'.

Stockbroker: Agent for investor, on whose behalf he buys or sells shares on the Stock Exchange, dealing with jobbers (acting as principals).

Store of Wealth: Traditional function of money, impaired by inflation.

Subsidiary: Company most of whose equity shares are owned by another (its 'holding' or 'parent' company).

Synergy: What is hoped on merger to make $2 + 2 = 5$. Often elusive.

Tender Method: Method of issuing shares to public, leaving price to be settled by demand for shares, thus discouraging stags (who can hardly expect much further appreciation when dealing starts).

Term Loan: Loan (probably from a bank) for a fixed period of time (often between one and seven years).

Term Structure of Interest Rates: The pattern of interest rates over different periods of time, e.g. from three months to 25 years.

Time Deposit: Deposit (account) with bank, withdrawable by giving a definite period of notice (often seven days), and bearing interest.

Time Preference: Ratio between someone's valuation of a good now and his valuation of an otherwise identical good at some future date.

Trade Credit: Normal business arrangement to buy and sell goods 'on credit', i.e. not settling in cash until some time later.

Transaction Cost: The cost of undertaking a transaction, e.g. taxes, commissions, administrative costs.

Treasury Bill: Three-month government bills of exchange.

Turn: The difference between the prices at which jobbers buy and sell securities.

Uncertainty: Lack of knowledge about the future. Differs from 'risk', which usually assumes known probabilities of possible outcomes.

Underwriter: Person or firm agreeing, for a fee, to meet the financial consequences of a risk, e.g. on new share issues.

Unique Risk: Specific risk of company or project, which can be diversified away by holding a suitable portfolio (unlike market risk).

Unit of Account: Numeraire in accounting. Traditionally the monetary unit, but in times of inflation an alternative – the 'constant purchasing power unit' – has been suggested.

Unit of Constant Purchasing Power: Money amount adjusted (by reference to date of transaction) by Retail Price Index, to improve usefulness of accounting, especially in comparisons over time.

Unit Trust: Financial enterprise holding range of securities; suitable vehicle for small unit-holder to spread his risk.

Unlisted Securities Market (USM): Recently-started market for securities of companies too small for full 'listing' ('quotation'); subject to less stringent rules.

Unquoted Company: Company whose shares are not quoted on the Stock Exchange. Hence shareholders may find it hard to sell their shares.

Unrecovered ACT: ACT unable to be (fully) set off against 'mainstream' UK tax liability, e.g. due to losses or profits earned abroad, which has to be written off as an extra expense.

Unsecured Creditor: Creditor without security.

Value Added: Difference between sales revenue and cost of bought-in materials and services. Roughly = profit plus wages.

Variable Expense: Expense which varies directly with level of output.

Venture Capital: Equity finance for high-risk new or small business.

Vertical Merger: Combination of two (or more) businesses engaged in different stages of production process in same industry, e.g. brewery buying pubs, or tyre manufacturer buying rubber plantations.

Wealth: Well-offness, expressed in terms of money, normally related to (ultimately) marketable assets.

Weighted Average Cost of Capital (WACC): Average of the after-tax marginal costs of various kinds of long-term capital (debt, equity, etc.), 'weighted' by their market value.

Wholesale Banking: Banking in large sums of money, with financial institutions or large companies, as opposed to 'retail' banking with members of the public.

Winding-up: = Liquidation. Process of ending a company's life, by selling all the assets, paying off creditors and distributing anything left over to ordinary shareholders.

Work-in-progress (WIP): Partly-completed stocks in manufacturing process.

Working Capital: Excess of current assets over current liabilities.

Yield: Rate of return on investment (usually security). Interest or dividend divided by current market price.

Yield to Redemption: Yield on loan stock including element of capital gain anticipated when principal (nominal amount) is repaid (at 'par') on maturity, in addition to the 'flat' yield of annual interest.

Index

See also list of Abbreviations on page 222.
G indicates an entry in the Glossary (pages 226–237).